PHARMACOLOGY -1

FOR PHARMACY GRADUATES

DR. J. DINESH BABU

Made with ♥ on the Notion Press Platform
www.notionpress.com

Contents

Preface

Pharmacology is a foundational subject in the field of pharmacy and medicine. It deals with the study of drugs, their sources, properties, and effects on living organisms. This book, "Pharmacology -1," has been crafted to serve as a comprehensive guide for students who are embarking on their journey to understand the intricate world of pharmacology.

The contents of this book are structured to align with the syllabus prescribed by the Pharmacy Council of India (PCI) for undergraduate pharmacy students. Each chapter is designed to provide a clear and concise explanation of key pharmacological concepts, ensuring that students can grasp the material with ease.

Chapter 1 introduces the **basics of pharmacology**, including definitions, scope, and key concepts. **Chapter 2** delves into **drug-receptor interactions**, exploring how drugs interact with biological systems. **Chapter 3** covers the **pharmacokinetics** of drugs, explaining how drugs are absorbed, distributed, metabolized, and excreted by the body. **Chapter 4** focuses on **pharmacodynamics**, detailing the mechanisms of drug action and the relationship between drug concentration and effect.

In **Chapter 5**, the book examines **adverse drug reactions and drug interactions**, highlighting the importance of understanding these aspects to ensure safe and effective drug therapy. **Chapter 6** explores the **process of drug discovery and clinical evaluation**, providing insights into how new drugs are developed and tested. **Chapter 7** and **Chapter 8** focus on the **pharmacology of the peripheral and central nervous systems**, respectively, covering drugs that affect these critical systems.

To support the learning process, the book includes numerous examples and illustrations that clarify complex concepts. The glossary at the end of the book provides definitions of key terms, which students can refer to as they progress through the chapters.

I hope that this book will serve as a valuable resource for students and educators alike, helping to build a strong foundation in pharmacology. I also believe that it will foster a deeper appreciation of the role that drugs play in the treatment of diseases and the maintenance of health.

Dr. J. Dinesh Babu

August 2024

Pharmacology -1

Dr. J. Dinesh Babu
Associate Professor
Vijaya College of Pharmacy
Hayatnagar, Munagnoor
India
Published by Notion Press
Notion Press, Inc.
800, West El Camino Real #180,
California USA 94040
Notion Press Media Pvt Ltd
#7, Red Cross Road,
Egmore, Chennai, Tamil Nadu 600008
Email ID: publish@notionpress.com
Phone Number: +91 44 46315631

About Author

Dr. J. Dinesh Babu

Dr. J. Dinesh Babu, an Associate Professor at Vijaya College of Pharmacy, Hayath Nagar, has over 10 years of dedicated experience in pharmaceutical education and leadership. He earned his Ph.D. in Pharmacology from VELS University, Pallavaram, Tamil Nadu, Chennai. With over 25 articles published in esteemed national and international journals, his research focuses on various phytochemical constituents and their studies in animal subjects. Dr. Dinesh Babu has received several awards recognizing his excellence in teaching. He is a member of SPER and APTI and has guided many UG and PG students, helping shape their careers in pharmaceutical sciences.

• • •

• • •

• • •

Other Books authored By **Dr. J. Dinesh Babu**

CHAPTER I

Introduction to Pharmacology

1.1 Definition and Scope of Pharmacology

Definition of Pharmacology

Pharmacology is the branch of science that deals with the study of drugs, their nature, properties, and effects on living organisms. The term 'pharmacology' is derived from the Greek words 'pharmakon,' meaning drug, and 'logos,' meaning study. The field encompasses the discovery, chemistry, composition, identification, biological and physiological effects, uses, and manufacturing of drugs. The origins of pharmacology can be traced back to ancient civilizations where early humans used natural substances to treat illnesses. However, it was not until the 19th century that pharmacology began to develop as a distinct scientific discipline. The understanding of pharmacology requires a multidisciplinary approach, integrating knowledge from chemistry, biology, and medicine to understand how drugs interact with the body to produce therapeutic effects. The primary goal of pharmacology is to develop drugs that are safe and effective in treating various diseases and conditions.

Historical Landmarks

The history of pharmacology is rich with significant milestones and key historical figures who have contributed to the field's evolution. Hippocrates, known as the father of medicine, laid the foundation for the use of medicinal substances in ancient Greece. Galen, a prominent physician in Roman times, advanced the understanding of drug formulations and their therapeutic uses. During the medieval period, the Arab world, particularly Avicenna, made substantial contributions to the knowledge of medicinal plants and their applications. The Renaissance brought renewed interest in scientific exploration, leading to significant progress in the study of drugs. The 19th century marked the birth of modern pharmacology with the work of scientists like Friedrich Sertürner, who isolated morphine from opium, and Rudolf Buchheim, who established the first pharmacology department. Advances in the 20th century, such as the discovery of antibiotics by Alexander Fleming and the development of vaccines, revolutionized medicine and public health. These milestones have paved the way for the contemporary understanding and application of pharmacology in medicine.

Scope of Pharmacology

The scope of pharmacology is vast and includes several sub-disciplines that focus on different aspects of drugs and their effects. Clinical pharmacology involves the study of drugs in humans, focusing on the efficacy, safety, and therapeutic use of medications. Molecular pharmacology examines drug interactions at the molecular level, exploring the mechanisms by which drugs exert their effects on cellular processes. Systemic pharmacology looks at the effects of drugs on different organ systems within the body, providing insight into how drugs can be used to treat specific diseases. Pharmacokinetics and pharmacodynamics are critical areas that study the absorption, distribution, metabolism, and excretion of drugs, as well as the relationship between drug concentrations and their effects. Pharmacology also plays a crucial role in healthcare and drug development. In healthcare, pharmacologists work closely with other medical professionals to ensure that patients receive the most appropriate and effective treatments. In drug development, pharmacologists are involved in the entire process, from the initial discovery of new drug compounds to their development and testing in clinical trials. This interdisciplinary field requires collaboration with chemists, biologists, and clinicians to create drugs that can improve health outcomes and save lives. As such, pharmacology is an essential and dynamic field that continually evolves with advances in science and technology, driving innovation in medicine and improving patient care.

1.2 Nature and Source of Drugs

Natural Sources

Drugs have been derived from natural sources for centuries, and these sources continue to play a crucial role in modern medicine. **Plants** have been a primary source of medicinal compounds since ancient times. Historically, various cultures utilized plants for their healing properties. For example, the use of willow bark to alleviate pain dates back to ancient civilizations; it was later discovered that willow bark contains salicin, a precursor to aspirin. Numerous plant-derived drugs have been identified and isolated, such as morphine from the opium poppy, quinine from the cinchona tree, and digitalis from the foxglove plant. The extraction of these compounds involves processes like maceration, percolation, and solvent extraction, which help isolate the active ingredients for therapeutic use. **Animals** have also contributed significantly to drug development. Animal products and by-products have been used in traditional remedies and modern pharmaceuticals. For instance, insulin, initially extracted from the pancreas of cattle and pigs, revolutionized the treatment of diabetes. Another example is the anticoagulant drug heparin, which is derived from animal tissues. These drugs illustrate the diverse contributions of animal sources to pharmacology. **Minerals** have provided a range of therapeutic agents used in medicine. Mineral-based drugs include various salts and elements that have specific medical applications. For example, lithium salts are used in the treatment of bipolar disorder, and iron supplements are crucial for treating anemia. The use of minerals in drug formulations underscores their importance in addressing a wide array of health conditions.

Table 1.1: **Historical Landmarks in Pharmacology**

Year	Event	Key Figure
1805	Isolation of morphine from opium	Friedrich Sertürner
1870	Introduction of the hypodermic needle	Alexander Wood
1897	Synthesis of aspirin	Felix Hoffmann
1928	Discovery of penicillin	Alexander Fleming

Table 1.2: **Natural Sources of Drugs**

Source	Example Drug	Use
Plants	Morphine	Pain relief
Animals	Insulin	Diabetes management
Minerals	Lithium carbonate	Bipolar disorder treatment

Synthetic and Semi-synthetic Drugs

The development of synthetic and semi-synthetic drugs has greatly expanded the pharmacological arsenal available to healthcare professionals. **Synthetic drugs** are artificially created in laboratories through chemical processes, offering several advantages over naturally derived drugs. The development of synthetic drugs allows for greater control over the purity, potency, and consistency of the medication. This control reduces the variability that can occur with natural sources. Additionally, synthetic drugs can be designed to target specific biological pathways, enhancing their efficacy and minimizing side effects. An example of a significant synthetic drug is sulfanilamide, one of the first antibiotics, which led to the development of many other antibacterial agents. **Semi-synthetic drugs** are chemically modified derivatives of naturally occurring substances. These modifications often enhance the therapeutic properties of the original compounds, making them more effective or safer. For example, semi-synthetic penicillins, such as amoxicillin and methicillin, were developed to overcome limitations of natural penicillin, such as bacterial resistance and acid sensitivity. The importance of semi-synthetic drugs lies in their ability to combine the benefits of natural products with the advantages of chemical modifications, resulting in more versatile and effective treatments.

1.3 Essential Drugs Concept

Definition and Importance

The concept of essential drugs is a critical aspect of global health policy, aiming to ensure that necessary medications are available to all individuals. According to the **World Health Organization (WHO)**, essential drugs are those that "satisfy the priority health care needs of the population." These drugs are selected based on their efficacy, safety, quality, and cost-effectiveness, and they are intended to be accessible at all times in adequate amounts and in appropriate dosage forms. The **criteria for a drug to be considered essential** include its relevance to public health needs, evidence of its efficacy and safety, and comparative cost-effectiveness. The selection process also considers the prevalence of diseases, the availability of alternative therapies, and the potential for misuse or resistance.

The **impact of essential drugs on global health** is profound and far-reaching. By providing a core list of medications that address the most pressing health concerns, the essential drugs concept helps to optimize the allocation of limited healthcare resources, particularly in low- and middle-income countries. This approach ensures that the most effective and necessary treatments are prioritized, thereby improving health outcomes and reducing mortality and morbidity. Essential drugs play a vital role in combating major health challenges such as infectious diseases, chronic conditions, and maternal and child health issues. For example, the availability of essential antibiotics can significantly reduce deaths from bacterial infections, while access to antiretroviral drugs is crucial in managing HIV/AIDS.

Furthermore, the implementation of essential drug lists by countries worldwide supports the development of national health policies and formulary management. It also guides the procurement and distribution of medicines, ensuring that healthcare systems are better equipped to meet the needs of their populations. The WHO's Model List of Essential Medicines serves as a benchmark for countries to develop their own national lists, tailored to their specific health priorities and resources. This harmonized approach promotes equity in healthcare access and fosters a more efficient and sustainable use of medicines globally.

1.4 Routes of Drug Administration

Oral Administration

Oral administration is one of the most common and convenient routes for drug delivery. This method involves swallowing a drug in the form of tablets, capsules, liquids, or powders, allowing it to be absorbed through the gastrointestinal tract.

Advantages of oral administration are numerous, making it a preferred choice for both patients and healthcare providers. The primary advantage is **convenience**; oral medications are easy to administer without the need for specialized equipment or professional assistance, making them suitable for self-administration. This route also offers a wide **variety of dosage forms**, such as tablets, capsules, and syrups, catering to different patient needs and preferences. Additionally, oral medications are generally more **cost-effective** compared to other routes, both in terms of production and administration. The absorption of drugs through the gastrointestinal tract provides a **prolonged duration of action**, which is beneficial for chronic conditions that require steady drug levels over time. Furthermore, oral administration allows for **systemic effects**, making it effective for treating a wide range of diseases and conditions.

However, there are several **disadvantages** associated with oral administration that must be considered. One significant drawback is the **variable absorption** of drugs due to differences in gastrointestinal pH, motility, and the presence of food, which can affect the drug's bioavailability. Certain drugs may also be **inactivated by digestive enzymes or acidic pH** in the stomach, reducing their effectiveness. For example, insulin cannot be taken orally because it is broken down in the gastrointestinal tract before it can exert its therapeutic effect. Another limitation is the **slow onset of action** compared to other routes like intravenous administration, which may not be suitable for emergencies requiring rapid drug effects. Additionally, some patients, such as those who are unconscious, vomiting, or have difficulty swallowing, may be unable to take medications orally. The **first-pass metabolism** in the liver can also reduce the amount of active drug reaching systemic circulation, necessitating higher doses or alternative routes.

Examples of drugs commonly administered orally include **analgesics** like ibuprofen and acetaminophen, which are used to relieve pain and reduce fever. **Antibiotics** such as amoxicillin and ciprofloxacin are often prescribed in oral forms to treat bacterial infections. **Antihypertensive drugs** like enalapril and metoprolol are used to manage high blood pressure, while **oral hypoglycemics** like metformin and glipizide are critical in the management of diabetes. **Vitamin and mineral supplements**, such as vitamin D and iron, are also typically taken orally to correct deficiencies and maintain health.

Table 1.3: **Routes of Drug Administration**

Route	Advantages	Disadvantages
Oral	Easy administration	First-pass metabolism
Intravenous (IV)	Rapid effect	Risk of infection
Intramuscular (IM)	Prolonged release	Pain at injection site

Table 1.4: **Synthetic and Semi-Synthetic Drugs**

Type	Description	Example
Synthetic Drugs	Created in laboratories	Sulfanilamide
Semi-Synthetic Drugs	Modified natural substances	Amoxicillin, Methicillin

Intravenous Administration

Intravenous Administration

Intravenous (IV) administration involves delivering a drug directly into the bloodstream through a vein. This route is commonly used in clinical settings for its ability to provide rapid and controlled drug delivery.

Advantages of intravenous administration are significant and make this route essential for various medical scenarios. The primary advantage is the **rapid onset of action**, as the drug is immediately introduced into the circulation, making it ideal for emergency situations where quick therapeutic effects are necessary, such as in the administration of **epinephrine during anaphylactic shock** or **thrombolytic agents during a heart attack**. Another advantage is the **precise control over drug levels** in the bloodstream, allowing for accurate dosing and consistent therapeutic effects. This control is particularly important in critical care settings and for drugs with a narrow therapeutic index, where maintaining specific blood concentrations is crucial to avoid toxicity or ineffectiveness. Intravenous administration also bypasses the **gastrointestinal tract and first-pass metabolism**, ensuring 100% bioavailability of the drug. This is beneficial for drugs that are poorly absorbed orally or are extensively metabolized in the liver. Additionally, IV administration allows for the **administration of large volumes of fluids and electrolytes**, which is essential in patients requiring rehydration or parenteral nutrition.

Despite these advantages, there are several **disadvantages** associated with intravenous administration. One major drawback is the **requirement for trained healthcare professionals** to perform the procedure, as improper technique can lead to complications such as phlebitis, infection, or infiltration of the drug into surrounding tissues. This requirement makes IV administration less convenient and more costly compared to oral administration. There is also the risk of **immediate adverse reactions**, as the drug is rapidly delivered into the bloodstream. If an allergic reaction or drug toxicity occurs, it can be severe and require prompt medical intervention. Additionally, the **invasiveness of the procedure** can cause discomfort and anxiety for patients, particularly those who require frequent or prolonged IV therapy. The need for **sterile equipment and aseptic technique** increases the complexity and cost of IV administration, and there is a higher risk of systemic infections if proper procedures are not followed.

Examples of drugs commonly administered intravenously include **antibiotics** such as vancomycin and piperacillin-tazobactam, which are used to treat severe infections and ensure high plasma concentrations. **Chemotherapeutic agents** like cisplatin and doxorubicin are delivered intravenously to achieve effective drug levels while minimizing the impact on the gastrointestinal tract. **Analgesics and anesthetics** such as morphine and propofol are often administered IV for rapid pain relief and sedation. **Intravenous fluids** and electrolytes, including saline and lactated Ringer's solution, are essential for rehydration and maintaining electrolyte balance in critically ill patients. Additionally, **emergency medications** like epinephrine, atropine, and naloxone are delivered intravenously to provide immediate therapeutic effects in life-threatening situations.

Intramuscular Administration

Intramuscular Administration

Intramuscular (IM) administration involves injecting a drug directly into the muscle tissue. This route is commonly used for medications that require slow, sustained absorption or when other routes are not suitable.

Advantages of intramuscular administration include several key benefits that make it a preferred choice in certain clinical situations. One significant advantage is the **relatively fast absorption** of drugs compared to oral administration, yet slower than intravenous, providing a balance between immediate and prolonged effects. This makes it suitable for medications that need to act quickly but do not require the rapid onset associated with IV administration. IM injections can deliver **larger volumes of medication** compared to subcutaneous injections, allowing for the administration of depot formulations, which release the drug slowly over time, ensuring **sustained therapeutic levels**. This is particularly useful for long-term treatments such as depot antipsychotics or hormone therapies. The **muscle tissue has a good blood supply**, which aids in the absorption of the drug into the bloodstream, ensuring more predictable pharmacokinetics compared to the subcutaneous route. Additionally, IM administration bypasses the gastrointestinal tract, avoiding issues related to **oral bioavailability** and **first-pass metabolism**, which can inactivate certain drugs. This route is also advantageous for patients who are unable to take medications orally due to vomiting, unconsciousness, or digestive disorders.

However, there are several **disadvantages** associated with intramuscular administration that need to be considered. One of the main drawbacks is the **potential for pain and discomfort** at the injection site, which can be a barrier for patient compliance, especially with frequent or long-term treatments. There is also a risk of **local adverse reactions** such as swelling, redness, and infection at the injection site, which requires careful technique and monitoring. Another disadvantage is the **possibility of injury to nerves or blood vessels** during the injection, which necessitates proper training and anatomical knowledge to minimize these risks. IM injections can also be associated with **delayed onset** compared to intravenous administration, which may not be suitable for emergency situations requiring immediate drug action. Additionally, certain medications can cause **muscle tissue irritation or necrosis** if not administered correctly, leading to complications and reduced effectiveness.

Examples of drugs commonly administered intramuscularly include **vaccines** such as the influenza vaccine and the tetanus toxoid, which are given IM to ensure adequate immune response and absorption. **Antibiotics** like penicillin G and ceftriaxone are often administered IM for the treatment of severe infections, particularly when IV access is not available or necessary. **Hormonal therapies** such as testosterone and progesterone are frequently delivered via IM injections for sustained release and stable blood levels. **Antipsychotic medications** like haloperidol decanoate and risperidone long-acting injection are administered intramuscularly to provide long-term control of psychiatric symptoms in patients with schizophrenia or bipolar disorder. Additionally, **emergency medications** such as epinephrine for anaphylaxis can be given IM when immediate IV access is not feasible, providing a rapid and effective response to life-threatening allergic reactions.

Subcutaneous Administration

Subcutaneous Administration

Subcutaneous (SC) administration involves injecting a drug into the tissue layer between the skin and muscle. This route is used for medications that require slow, sustained absorption and is commonly employed for vaccines, insulin, and other treatments that need consistent drug levels over time.

Advantages of subcutaneous administration include several benefits that make it an effective and convenient route for many medications. One of the main advantages is the **ease of administration**; SC injections can often be self-administered by patients after proper training, enhancing patient independence and reducing the need for frequent clinic visits. This is particularly beneficial for chronic conditions that require regular dosing, such as diabetes. The **slow and steady absorption** of drugs through the subcutaneous tissue allows for prolonged therapeutic effects, which is useful for medications that need to maintain stable blood levels. SC administration is also less invasive and generally less painful compared to intramuscular injections, making it more acceptable to patients who require frequent injections. Additionally, the risk of serious complications, such as nerve or blood vessel damage, is lower with SC injections due to the relatively superficial nature of the injection site.

However, there are several **disadvantages** associated with subcutaneous administration. One notable drawback is the **limited volume** that can be injected subcutaneously, typically up to 2 mL, which restricts its use for drugs that require larger doses. This limitation can necessitate multiple injections for a single dose, potentially leading to patient discomfort and reduced adherence. Another disadvantage is the **variable absorption rate** influenced by factors such as blood flow, site of injection, and local tissue characteristics, which can affect the consistency of drug levels. This variability can be problematic for medications that require precise dosing. Additionally, SC injections can cause **local adverse reactions** such as pain, redness, swelling, and irritation at the injection site, which can be bothersome to patients. For certain drugs, there is also a risk of **tissue necrosis** or lipodystrophy with repeated injections, which can lead to localized fat tissue changes and affect drug absorption.

Examples of drugs commonly administered subcutaneously include **insulin**, which is used to manage blood glucose levels in patients with diabetes. Insulin is typically injected into the subcutaneous tissue of the abdomen, thigh, or upper arm, providing a consistent and controlled release of the hormone. **Anticoagulants** such as enoxaparin (a low-molecular-weight heparin) are also administered subcutaneously to prevent blood clots in patients at risk for thromboembolic events. **Hormonal therapies** like human growth hormone and certain contraceptives are given via SC injections to ensure sustained release and stable blood levels. **Vaccines** such as the MMR (measles, mumps, and rubella) vaccine and certain immunotherapy treatments for allergies are delivered subcutaneously to stimulate an immune response. Additionally, **biologic drugs** like monoclonal antibodies for autoimmune diseases and cancer treatments are often administered SC to provide long-term therapeutic effects.

Topical Administration

Topical Administration

Topical administration involves applying a drug directly to the skin or mucous membranes. This route is commonly used for localized treatment of dermatological conditions, pain management, and infections, as well as for delivering systemic medications through transdermal patches.

Advantages of topical administration are numerous, making it a preferred method for both local and systemic therapies. One significant advantage is the ability to **target specific areas** directly, providing high local drug concentrations at the site of application while minimizing systemic exposure and potential side effects. This targeted approach is particularly beneficial for treating skin conditions such as eczema, psoriasis, and localized infections. Topical administration also **bypasses the gastrointestinal tract** and first-pass metabolism in the liver, enhancing bioavailability for certain medications and avoiding gastrointestinal side effects. This route is generally **non-invasive** and easy to use, improving patient compliance, especially in those who are averse to injections or oral medications. The **controlled release** of drugs through formulations like creams, ointments, gels, and patches allows for sustained therapeutic effects over time. For systemic treatments, transdermal patches offer a steady absorption rate, maintaining stable blood levels and improving the effectiveness of medications for conditions such as chronic pain and hormone replacement therapy.

However, there are several **disadvantages** associated with topical administration that must be considered. One notable drawback is the **limited absorption** through the skin, which can be affected by factors such as skin integrity, hydration, and thickness. This limitation can reduce the effectiveness of certain drugs, particularly for systemic treatments. Additionally, **skin irritation or allergic reactions** can occur at the site of application, causing discomfort and potentially leading to discontinuation of the therapy. The **variability in drug absorption** due to individual differences in skin condition and environmental factors can result in inconsistent therapeutic outcomes. For transdermal patches, there is a risk of **adhesion problems**, where the patch may not stick properly to the skin, reducing drug delivery efficiency. Another disadvantage is the potential for **systemic absorption** in unintended areas, particularly if large amounts are applied or if the drug is used on damaged skin, leading to unintended systemic effects.

Examples of drugs commonly administered topically include **corticosteroids** like hydrocortisone and betamethasone, which are used to reduce inflammation and treat conditions such as eczema and psoriasis. **Antifungal creams** and ointments containing clotrimazole or miconazole are applied to treat localized fungal infections like athlete's foot and ringworm. **Analgesic creams** and gels containing lidocaine or capsaicin are used to relieve localized pain and discomfort. **Antibiotic ointments** such as those containing neomycin and bacitracin are applied to prevent infection in minor cuts, scrapes, and burns. **Transdermal patches** delivering systemic medications include nicotine patches for smoking cessation, fentanyl patches for chronic pain management, and hormone replacement therapy patches containing estrogen or testosterone. Additionally, **topical treatments for acne** containing benzoyl peroxide or retinoids are widely used to manage acne vulgaris.

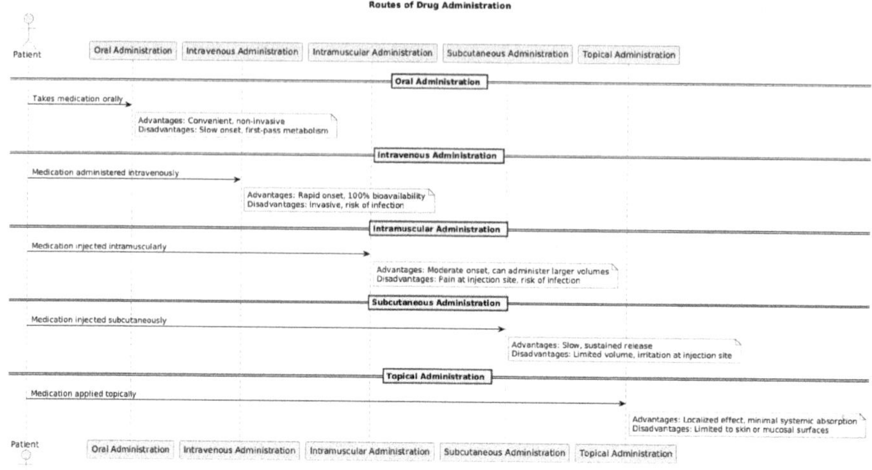

Table 1.5: **Essential Drugs Concept**

Criterion	Description
Relevance to Public Health Needs	Drug addresses major health issues
Evidence of Efficacy and Safety	Proven effectiveness and safety through studies
Comparative Cost-Effectiveness	Affordable and provides good value for money

Table 1.6: **Drug Administration Examples**

Route	Example Drug	Condition Treated
Oral	Ibuprofen	Pain and inflammation
Intravenous	Vancomycin	Severe bacterial infections
Intramuscular	Vaccines	Preventative immunization

CHAPTER II

Basic Concepts in Pharmacology

2.1 Drug-Receptor Interactions

Agonists and Antagonists

Definitions, Mechanisms, and Examples

Drug-receptor interactions are fundamental to the action of many drugs. The concept involves the binding of drugs to specific cellular receptors to produce a therapeutic effect. These interactions can be categorized primarily into **agonists** and **antagonists**, each with distinct mechanisms of action and implications for drug therapy.

Agonists are drugs that bind to and activate receptors, mimicking the action of endogenous substances. They have both **affinity** (the ability to bind to a receptor) and **intrinsic activity** (the ability to activate the receptor and produce a physiological response). When an agonist binds to a receptor, it stabilizes the receptor in its active form, leading to a series of intracellular events that result in the drug's therapeutic effects. For example, **morphine** is an opioid agonist that binds to opioid receptors in the brain and spinal cord, mimicking the action of endogenous endorphins to produce pain relief. Another example is **albuterol**, a beta-2 adrenergic agonist used in the treatment of asthma. Albuterol binds to beta-2 receptors in the lungs, causing bronchodilation and relief of asthma symptoms.

Antagonists, on the other hand, are drugs that bind to receptors but do not activate them. Instead, they block or dampen the action of agonists, either endogenous or exogenous. Antagonists have **affinity** but lack **intrinsic activity**. By occupying the receptor sites, antagonists prevent agonists from binding and activating the receptor, thereby inhibiting the biological response. There are different types of antagonists, including competitive and non-competitive antagonists. **Competitive antagonists** bind reversibly to the same site on the receptor as the agonist. Their inhibitory effect can be overcome by increasing the concentration of the agonist. For example, **propranolol** is a competitive antagonist of beta-adrenergic receptors. It competes with epinephrine and norepinephrine for binding to beta receptors, thereby reducing heart rate and blood pressure. **Non-competitive antagonists**, however, bind irreversibly or to a different site on the receptor, and their effects cannot be reversed by increasing the concentration of the agonist. An example of a non-competitive antagonist is **phenoxybenzamine**, which irreversibly binds to alpha-adrenergic receptors and is used to manage pheochromocytoma by reducing vasoconstriction and blood pressure.

Agonists and antagonists can also exhibit **partial agonism** or **inverse agonism**. **Partial agonists** bind to and activate receptors but produce a weaker, or partial, response compared to full agonists. They have affinity and intrinsic activity but less than that of full agonists. **Buprenorphine**, a partial agonist at opioid receptors, is used in the treatment of opioid addiction because it produces sufficient agonistic effects to alleviate withdrawal symptoms without causing the full euphoria of stronger opioids. **Inverse agonists** bind to the same receptors as agonists but induce the opposite pharmacological response. They stabilize the receptor in its inactive form, reducing the baseline activity of the receptor. An example is **naloxone**, which not only acts as an antagonist to opioid receptors but can also produce inverse agonist effects in the presence of certain opioid agonists, reversing opioid overdose symptoms.

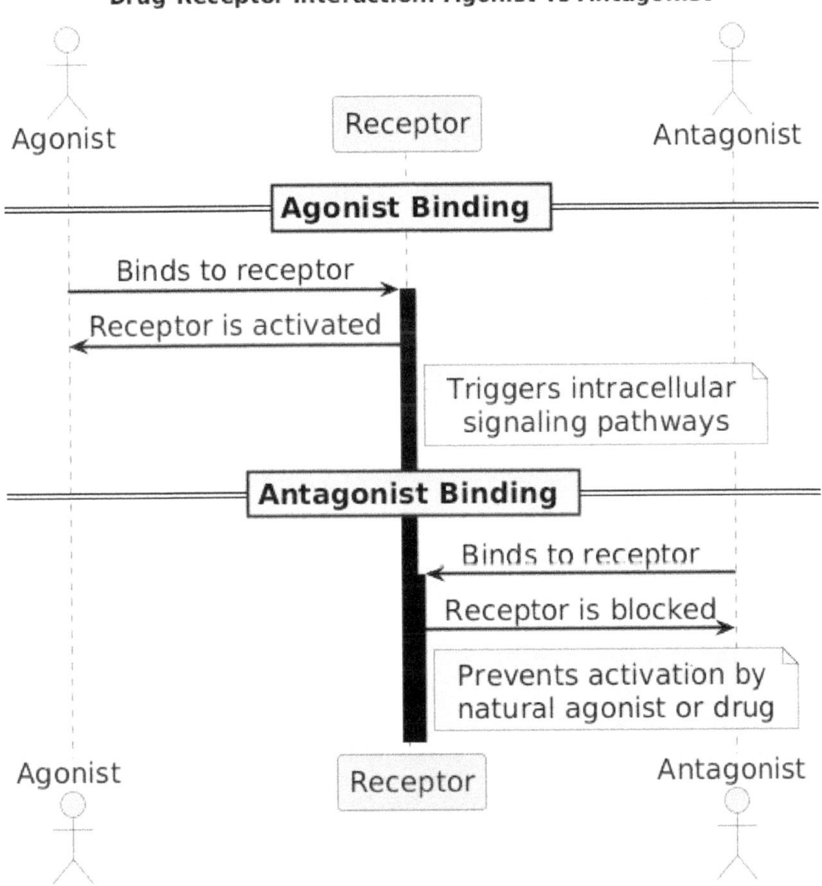

Differences Between Agonists and Antagonists

Understanding the differences between **agonists** and **antagonists** is fundamental to pharmacology, as these two types of drugs interact with receptors in distinct ways to produce their effects.

Agonists and **antagonists** differ primarily in their mechanisms of action, effects on receptors, and resulting physiological responses:

Mechanisms of Action:

- **Agonists**: These drugs bind to receptors and mimic the action of endogenous (natural) substances. They have both **affinity** (ability to bind to a receptor) and **intrinsic activity** (ability to activate the receptor). When an agonist binds to a receptor, it stabilizes the receptor in its active form, leading to a biological response.

  - **Example**: **Morphine** is an opioid agonist that binds to opioid receptors, mimicking endorphins to produce pain relief.

- **Antagonists**: These drugs also bind to receptors but do not activate them. Instead, they block or dampen the action of agonists. Antagonists have **affinity** but lack **intrinsic activity**. By occupying the receptor sites, they prevent agonists from binding and activating the receptor, thus inhibiting the biological response.

  - **Example**: **Propranolol** is a beta-adrenergic antagonist that blocks the effects of epinephrine and norepinephrine, reducing heart rate and blood pressure.

Effects on Receptors:

- **Agonists**: Activate receptors to produce a physiological response. The response can be full, partial, or inverse, depending on the type of agonist.

  - **Full Agonists**: Fully activate the receptor, producing a maximum response.
  - **Partial Agonists**: Partially activate the receptor, producing a sub-maximal response even at full receptor occupancy.
  - **Inverse Agonists**: Bind to the same receptors as agonists but induce the opposite pharmacological response, stabilizing the receptor in its inactive form.

- **Antagonists**: Do not activate receptors. They prevent agonists from activating the receptors, thereby inhibiting any physiological response that would have been produced by the agonist.

  - **Competitive Antagonists**: Reversibly bind to the same site as the agonist, and their inhibitory effect can be overcome by increasing the concentration of the agonist.

- **Non-competitive Antagonists**: Bind irreversibly or to a different site on the receptor, and their effects cannot be reversed by increasing the concentration of the agonist.

Physiological Responses:

- **Agonists**: Produce a physiological effect by activating receptors. The nature of the response depends on the type of receptor and the biological system involved.
    - **Example: Albuterol**, a beta-2 adrenergic agonist, causes bronchodilation by activating beta-2 receptors in the lungs, which is beneficial in treating asthma.
- **Antagonists**: Inhibit physiological responses by blocking receptor activation. They are often used to prevent or reduce undesired effects caused by endogenous substances or other drugs.
    - **Example: Naloxone** is an opioid antagonist that binds to opioid receptors without activating them, effectively reversing opioid overdose symptoms by displacing the opioid agonists from the receptors.

Table 2.1: **Types of Drug-Receptor Interactions**

Type	Description	Example
Agonist	Binds to receptor, activates it	Morphine
Antagonist	Binds to receptor, blocks it	Naloxone

Table 2.2: **Mechanisms of Drug Tolerance**

Mechanism	Description	Example
Pharmacokinetic	Increased drug metabolism	Phenobarbital
Pharmacodynamic	Decreased receptor sensitivity	Opioids

Table 2.3: **Types of Drug Dependence**

Type	Description	Example
Physical Dependence	Withdrawal symptoms upon discontinuation	Benzodiazepines
Psychological Dependence	Compulsive drug-seeking behavior	Cocaine

Spare Receptors

Concept and Significance

The concept of **spare receptors** is an important principle in pharmacology that helps explain how certain drugs can achieve maximal effects even when not all receptors are occupied. Spare receptors refer to the phenomenon where a maximal cellular response can be achieved with only a fraction of the total receptor population being occupied by an agonist. This implies that there are more receptors available than are necessary to produce a full biological response.

The presence of spare receptors can be understood through the following points:

- **Receptor Reserve**: The idea is that the cell has a "reserve" of extra receptors that are not required for eliciting a maximum response. This reserve allows for a significant amplification of the signal initiated by the agonist.
- **Efficiency of Signal Transduction**: Spare receptors indicate that the coupling efficiency between the receptor activation and the intracellular response mechanisms is very high. This means that once a certain threshold of receptor occupancy is reached, the intracellular signaling pathways are sufficiently activated to produce a maximal response.

- **Examples**: In the heart, β-adrenergic receptors demonstrate spare receptor characteristics. Even when only a small proportion of these receptors are occupied by an agonist like epinephrine, a full increase in heart rate and contractility can be achieved.

Implications for Drug Efficacy and Potency

The presence of spare receptors has significant implications for the **efficacy** and **potency** of drugs:

- **Drug Efficacy**: Efficacy refers to the maximum effect a drug can produce. Spare receptors mean that drugs can achieve their maximum effect without occupying all available receptors. This allows for a full therapeutic response even at lower concentrations of the drug, as only a subset of receptors needs to be activated to achieve the desired effect.
  - **Example**: A drug that acts on spare receptors will appear to have a high efficacy because it can produce a maximal effect at lower receptor occupancy. This is seen with drugs like isoproterenol, a β-adrenergic agonist, which can produce full cardiac stimulation without fully occupying all β-adrenergic receptors.
- **Drug Potency**: Potency is a measure of the concentration of a drug required to produce a given effect. Drugs acting on systems with spare receptors tend to have higher potency because lower doses are needed to activate the necessary number of receptors to elicit a full response.
  - **Example**: If a drug requires only 10% receptor occupancy to achieve a full effect, it will have a high potency as even small amounts of the drug can produce significant therapeutic effects.
- **Competitive Antagonism**: The concept of spare receptors also affects the interpretation of competitive antagonism. In the presence of spare receptors, an antagonist must block a larger proportion of the receptor population to reduce the agonist's effect significantly. This means that the apparent potency of a competitive antagonist can be lower in systems with spare receptors, as more antagonist is required to occupy enough receptors to diminish the response.

◦ **Example:** In a system with a high number of spare receptors, a competitive antagonist like propranolol would need to occupy a significant number of β-adrenergic receptors to reduce the effect of an agonist like isoproterenol, making the antagonist appear less potent.

2.2 Drug Tolerance and Dependence

Addiction, Tolerance, Dependence

Definitions and Differences

Understanding the concepts of addiction, tolerance, and dependence is crucial in pharmacology, as these phenomena affect how drugs are used, their efficacy, and their potential for abuse.

Addiction

Addiction is a complex condition characterized by compulsive drug use despite harmful consequences. It is a chronic disorder involving psychological and physical aspects. Addiction often includes a craving for the drug, an inability to control use, continued use despite negative consequences, and a loss of interest in other activities. The defining features of addiction include the overwhelming desire to obtain and use the drug, and an inability to stop using it. Addiction involves changes in brain function, particularly in the areas related to reward, motivation, and memory, making it a mental health disorder as well.

- **Example:** Opioid addiction involves compulsive use of drugs like heroin or prescription painkillers, leading to significant health, social, and economic problems.

Tolerance

Tolerance refers to a state where a person's response to a drug decreases with repeated use, requiring higher doses to achieve the same effect. Tolerance can develop to various drug effects, not just the primary therapeutic effect, and can lead to an increased risk of overdose as users take larger amounts to achieve the desired effect. It can be due to pharmacokinetic changes (e.g., increased drug metabolism) or pharmacodynamic changes (e.g., changes in receptor sensitivity or number).

- **Example**: With chronic use of morphine, a person may need progressively higher doses to achieve the same level of pain relief, indicating the development of tolerance.

Dependence

Dependence is a condition where the body adapts to the presence of a drug, leading to withdrawal symptoms if the drug use is abruptly stopped or reduced. Dependence can be physical or psychological. **Physical dependence** involves physiological adaptation to the drug, while **psychological dependence** involves emotional or mental preoccupation with the drug's effects. Dependence does not necessarily imply addiction, but it often accompanies it. When someone is dependent, they may not exhibit the compulsive behaviors seen in addiction, but they will experience withdrawal symptoms without the drug.

- **Example**: A person who takes benzodiazepines for an extended period may experience anxiety, tremors, and seizures if the medication is suddenly discontinued, indicating physical dependence.

Differences

The key differences between addiction, tolerance, and dependence lie in their characteristics and implications for drug use:

- **Addiction** is characterized by compulsive drug-seeking behavior and use despite negative consequences. It is a chronic brain disorder that involves both psychological and physical elements. Addiction is driven by changes in brain function related to reward and motivation, leading to uncontrollable cravings and continued use.
- **Tolerance** involves a reduced response to a drug over time, necessitating higher doses to achieve the same effect. Tolerance is primarily a pharmacological phenomenon, resulting from the body's adaptation to the drug. It does not necessarily involve compulsive drug use or dependence.
- **Dependence** refers to the body's adaptation to a drug, resulting in withdrawal symptoms when the drug is not taken. Dependence can be physical, psychological, or both, and it often develops with regular use of certain medications. Unlike addiction, dependence does not necessarily involve compulsive behavior or continued use despite harm.

Mechanisms and Clinical Implications

Mechanisms of Drug Tolerance and Dependence

Tolerance

Mechanisms: Tolerance develops through several mechanisms, which can be broadly classified into pharmacokinetic and pharmacodynamic tolerance.

- **Pharmacokinetic Tolerance:** Also known as dispositional tolerance, this occurs when the body becomes more efficient at metabolizing or excreting the drug. For example, repeated use of certain drugs can induce liver enzymes that metabolize the drug, leading to decreased drug levels in the blood and reduced efficacy. An example of this is the induction of the cytochrome P450 enzyme system by barbiturates.
- **Pharmacodynamic Tolerance:** This type involves changes at the cellular level in response to prolonged drug exposure. These changes can include downregulation (decrease in the number of receptors) or desensitization (reduced receptor sensitivity) of receptors. For instance, chronic exposure to opioids can lead to a decrease in opioid receptor sensitivity, necessitating higher doses to achieve the same effect.

Clinical Implications: The development of tolerance has significant clinical implications. It can lead to the need for increased dosages to maintain therapeutic effects, which can increase the risk of side effects and toxicity. For example, opioid tolerance can result in patients requiring higher doses for pain relief, which increases the risk of respiratory depression and overdose. Tolerance can also contribute to the phenomenon of dose escalation, where patients continually increase their dosage to achieve the desired effect, potentially leading to addiction and other complications.

Dependence

Mechanisms: Dependence results from the body's adaptation to the presence of a drug, leading to homeostatic changes that offset the drug's effects. When drug use is stopped, these adaptations manifest as withdrawal symptoms. The mechanisms underlying dependence can be physiological, involving neurotransmitter systems, or psychological, involving behavioral reinforcement.

- **Physiological Dependence**: Chronic drug use can lead to changes in neurotransmitter levels and receptor activity. For example, long-term use of benzodiazepines can cause downregulation of GABA receptors, leading to increased excitability of neurons. Upon discontinuation, this results in withdrawal symptoms such as anxiety, insomnia, and seizures.
- **Psychological Dependence**: This involves the reinforcement of drug use behavior through the brain's reward system. Drugs that stimulate the release of dopamine in the brain's reward pathways can create a psychological craving for the drug, contributing to continued use and difficulty in cessation.

Clinical Implications: Dependence has important clinical implications, particularly regarding withdrawal management and the risk of relapse. Patients who are physically dependent on a drug may require a carefully managed tapering schedule to reduce withdrawal symptoms safely. For example, patients dependent on opioids may need to be gradually weaned off the drug to minimize withdrawal symptoms such as nausea, vomiting, and pain. Psychological dependence requires addressing the behavioral aspects of addiction, often through counseling, support groups, and other psychosocial interventions. Dependence also complicates the treatment of chronic conditions, as stopping the drug can lead to a resurgence of the original symptoms along with withdrawal effects.

Addiction

Mechanisms: Addiction involves complex interactions between genetic, environmental, and neurobiological factors. It primarily affects the brain's reward system, particularly involving the neurotransmitter dopamine.

- **Neurobiological Changes**: Chronic drug use leads to alterations in the brain's reward circuitry, including changes in the mesolimbic dopamine system. This results in increased cravings and compulsive drug-seeking behavior. For instance, repeated use of addictive substances can enhance dopamine release in the nucleus accumbens, reinforcing the desire to continue using the drug.
- **Behavioral and Environmental Factors**: Environmental cues and stressors can trigger cravings and relapse. Behavioral reinforcement, such as the pleasurable effects of the drug, further perpetuates the cycle of addiction.

Clinical Implications: Addiction has profound clinical implications, as it often leads to severe health, social, and economic consequences. Treatment of addiction requires a comprehensive approach, including medical, psychological, and social interventions. Medications such as methadone or buprenorphine can be used to manage opioid addiction by reducing cravings and withdrawal symptoms. Behavioral therapies, including cognitive-behavioral therapy (CBT) and contingency management, are essential for addressing the psychological aspects of addiction. Additionally, support groups and rehabilitation programs play a crucial role in helping individuals maintain long-term sobriety and prevent relapse.

Tachyphylaxis, Idiosyncrasy, Allergy

Definitions and Examples

Tachyphylaxis

Definition: Tachyphylaxis is a phenomenon where there is a rapid decrease in the response to a drug after repeated administration over a short period of time. This occurs even when the doses are administered at intervals that would normally be effective. Unlike tolerance, which develops more gradually, tachyphylaxis can happen within minutes to hours of drug use.

Examples:

- **Nasal Decongestants**: Drugs like oxymetazoline and phenylephrine used as nasal decongestants can cause tachyphylaxis. Initially, these drugs constrict blood vessels in the nasal passages, reducing congestion. However, with repeated use over a short period, their effectiveness diminishes, leading to rebound congestion.
- **Nitroglycerin**: Used for angina, nitroglycerin can exhibit tachyphylaxis. Continuous use of nitroglycerin patches can lead to reduced efficacy, necessitating a nitrate-free interval to restore drug sensitivity.

Idiosyncrasy

Definition: Idiosyncrasy refers to an unusual or abnormal reaction to a drug that is different from the typical effect observed in most patients. These reactions are often unpredictable and not related to the pharmacological action of the drug. Idiosyncratic reactions are usually due to genetic differences in metabolism or immune responses.

Examples:

- **Primaquine**: An antimalarial drug, primaquine can cause hemolytic anemia in individuals with glucose-6-phosphate dehydrogenase (G6PD) deficiency. This idiosyncratic reaction occurs because these patients lack the enzyme needed to protect red blood cells from oxidative damage.
- **Phenytoin**: Some patients may develop severe skin reactions such as Stevens-Johnson syndrome or toxic epidermal necrolysis when taking phenytoin, an anticonvulsant drug. These idiosyncratic reactions are not dose-dependent and are believed to involve genetic predispositions.

Allergy

Definition: Drug allergy is an immune-mediated response to a medication that occurs after previous sensitization to the same or a structurally similar drug. Allergic reactions to drugs are unpredictable and can range from mild to life-threatening. They involve the immune system's recognition of the drug as a foreign substance, leading to an allergic response.

Examples:

- **Penicillin**: One of the most common drug allergies involves penicillin. Patients allergic to penicillin may experience symptoms ranging from mild skin rashes to severe anaphylaxis, which can include difficulty breathing, swelling, and a drop in blood pressure.
- **Sulfonamides**: Allergic reactions to sulfonamide antibiotics can present as rashes, fever, and even more severe reactions like Stevens-Johnson syndrome or anaphylaxis. The allergy is due to the immune system's reaction to the sulfonamide molecule or its metabolites.

Summary:

- **Tachyphylaxis** involves a rapid decrease in drug effectiveness with repeated use over a short period, as seen with nasal decongestants and nitroglycerin.
- **Idiosyncrasy** refers to abnormal and unpredictable drug reactions due to genetic differences, like hemolytic anemia with primaquine in G6PD-deficient patients or severe skin reactions with phenytoin.
- **Allergy** is an immune-mediated response to a drug following sensitization, with common examples including penicillin and sulfonamide allergies.

Mechanisms and Clinical Significance

Tachyphylaxis

Mechanisms: The exact mechanisms of tachyphylaxis can vary depending on the drug and context but generally involve the following:

- **Receptor Desensitization:** Repeated stimulation of receptors can lead to their desensitization, where the receptors become less responsive to the drug. This can happen through phosphorylation of the receptor, changes in receptor conformation, or receptor internalization.
- **Depletion of Mediators:** Some drugs work by releasing endogenous mediators from storage sites. With repeated drug administration, these mediators can be depleted faster than they are replenished, reducing the drug's effectiveness.
- **Feedback Inhibition:** The body may activate feedback mechanisms that counteract the drug's effects. For example, continuous use of nasal decongestants can lead to rebound vasodilation due to the body's attempt to maintain homeostasis.

Clinical Significance: Tachyphylaxis has important clinical implications, particularly in the management of chronic conditions.

- **Reduced Efficacy:** The rapid development of tachyphylaxis can lead to a decreased therapeutic effect, necessitating higher doses or alternative medications. For example, patients using nitroglycerin for angina may require a nitrate-free interval to restore drug sensitivity.
- **Risk of Overuse:** In an attempt to overcome reduced efficacy, patients might increase the dose or frequency of use, potentially leading to adverse effects or toxicity. For instance, overuse of nasal decongestants can worsen nasal congestion due to rebound effects.

Idiosyncrasy

Mechanisms: Idiosyncratic drug reactions are often due to genetic differences that affect drug metabolism, immune responses, or cellular targets.

- **Genetic Polymorphisms:** Variations in genes encoding drug-metabolizing enzymes (e.g., CYP450 enzymes) or drug targets (e.g., receptors) can lead to unexpected reactions. For example, individuals with G6PD deficiency lack the enzyme needed to protect red blood cells from oxidative stress, leading to hemolytic anemia with certain drugs.

- **Immune-mediated Responses**: Some idiosyncratic reactions involve immune system activation, even though they are not typical allergic responses. For example, hypersensitivity reactions to anticonvulsants like phenytoin can involve complex immune mechanisms leading to severe skin reactions.

Clinical Significance: Idiosyncratic reactions are significant because they are unpredictable and can be severe.

- **Patient Safety**: Identifying individuals at risk for idiosyncratic reactions through genetic testing or careful history-taking can help prevent adverse events. For example, screening for G6PD deficiency before prescribing certain drugs can prevent hemolytic anemia.
- **Drug Development and Regulation**: Understanding idiosyncratic reactions is crucial for drug development and post-marketing surveillance. Regulatory agencies may require warnings or contraindications for populations at risk.

Allergy

Mechanisms: Drug allergies involve immune system sensitization and subsequent reactions upon re-exposure to the drug.

- **Type I Hypersensitivity**: This involves IgE antibodies and can lead to anaphylaxis. Upon re-exposure, the drug binds to IgE on mast cells and basophils, causing the release of histamine and other mediators, leading to symptoms like hives, swelling, and anaphylaxis.
- **Type II-IV Hypersensitivity**: These reactions involve different immune mechanisms, including antibody-mediated cytotoxicity (Type II), immune complex formation (Type III), and T-cell mediated responses (Type IV). Examples include drug-induced hemolytic anemia (Type II) and contact dermatitis (Type IV).

Clinical Significance: Drug allergies are significant for their potential severity and impact on patient care.

- **Immediate Management**: Recognizing and promptly treating severe allergic reactions, such as anaphylaxis with epinephrine, is crucial for patient safety.
- **Drug Avoidance and Alternatives**: Identifying drug allergies through patient history and, if necessary, skin testing, helps avoid repeat exposure. Alternative medications must be considered to provide safe and effective treatment.
- **Patient Education**: Educating patients about their drug allergies, including symptoms of reactions and the importance of avoiding the offending drug, is essential for preventing future incidents.

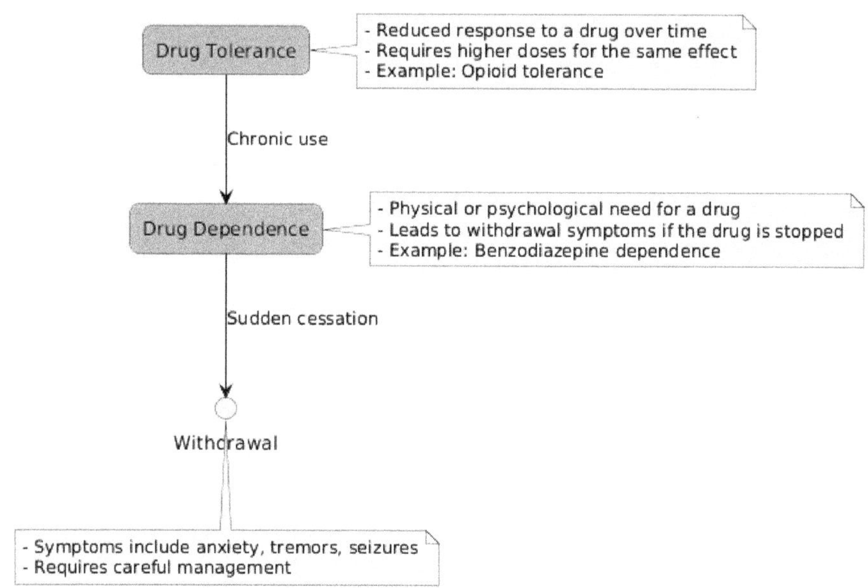

CHAPTER III

Pharmacokinetics

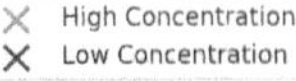

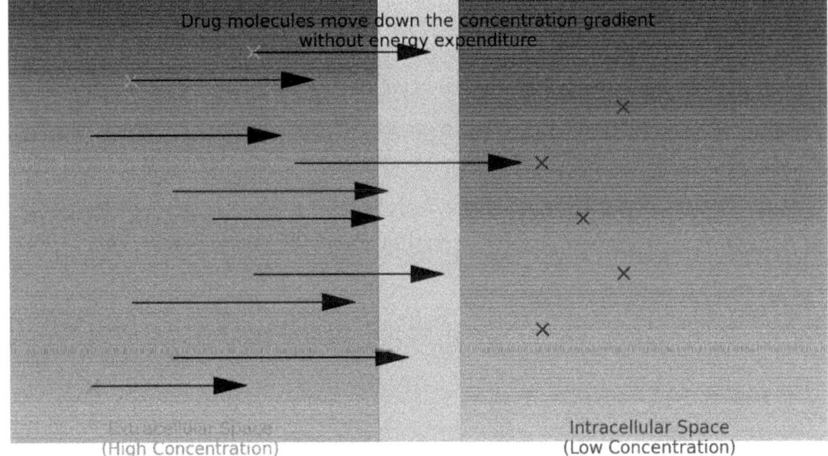

3.1 Membrane Transport Mechanisms

Passive Diffusion

Definition, Characteristics, and Examples

Definition

Passive diffusion is a fundamental process in pharmacokinetics, referring to the movement of drug molecules across cell membranes from an area of higher concentration to an area of lower concentration, without the need for energy expenditure. This type of transport relies on the concentration gradient of the drug and the inherent kinetic energy of the molecules.

Characteristics

- **Concentration Gradient:** Passive diffusion occurs down a concentration gradient, meaning that drug molecules move from a region of higher concentration to one of lower concentration until equilibrium is reached.

- **No Energy Requirement**: This process does not require cellular energy (ATP), as it relies on the natural kinetic movement of molecules.
- **Molecular Properties**: For a drug to passively diffuse across cell membranes, it typically needs to be small, nonpolar, and lipophilic (fat-soluble). Hydrophilic (water-soluble) drugs generally do not passively diffuse as easily across lipid bilayers.
- **Membrane Permeability**: The rate of passive diffusion is influenced by the permeability of the cell membrane, which depends on the lipid solubility of the drug, the membrane surface area, and the thickness of the membrane.
- **Fick's Law of Diffusion**: This law describes the rate of diffusion, stating that the rate is proportional to the concentration gradient, the surface area of the membrane, and the permeability coefficient of the drug, and inversely proportional to the thickness of the membrane.

Examples

- **Oxygen and Carbon Dioxide**: These small, nonpolar molecules readily diffuse across cell membranes through passive diffusion, allowing for efficient gas exchange in the lungs and tissues.
- **Lipophilic Drugs**: Drugs such as diazepam (a benzodiazepine) and other lipid-soluble medications can easily diffuse through the lipid bilayer of cell membranes. Diazepam, for instance, rapidly crosses the blood-brain barrier to exert its effects on the central nervous system.
- **Steroid Hormones**: Natural hormones like cortisol and synthetic ones like prednisone are lipophilic and diffuse passively through cell membranes to bind to intracellular receptors and exert their effects.
- **Alcohol**: Ethanol is another example of a substance that diffuses passively across cell membranes due to its small size and moderate lipophilicity, allowing it to be absorbed quickly from the gastrointestinal tract into the bloodstream.

Active Transport

Definition, Characteristics, and Examples

Definition

Active transport is a mechanism by which drug molecules move across cell membranes from an area of lower concentration to an area of higher concentration, against the concentration gradient. This process requires energy expenditure, typically in the form of adenosine triphosphate (ATP), and involves specific transporter proteins embedded in the cell membrane.

Characteristics

- **Energy Requirement**: Unlike passive diffusion, active transport requires cellular energy (usually ATP) to move molecules against their concentration gradient.
- **Specificity**: Active transport involves specific transporter proteins that recognize and bind to particular molecules. These transporters have binding sites that are selective for the molecules they transport.
- **Saturation**: The transport process can become saturated when all transporter proteins are occupied. This means that there is a maximum rate at which molecules can be transported, known as the transport maximum (Tm).
- **Competition**: Molecules that are structurally similar can compete for the same transporter. This can affect the rate at which each molecule is transported.
- **Types of Active Transport**: Active transport can be divided into primary active transport, where ATP is directly used to transport molecules, and secondary active transport, which uses the energy from an electrochemical gradient established by primary active transport.

Examples

- **Sodium-Potassium Pump (Na+/K+ ATPase)**: This is a classic example of primary active transport. The pump moves sodium ions out of the cell and potassium ions into the cell against their concentration gradients, maintaining essential electrochemical gradients across the cell membrane. This process is crucial for various cellular functions, including nerve impulse transmission and muscle contraction.
- **Glucose Transport in the Intestine (SGLT1)**: The sodium-glucose linked transporter 1 (SGLT1) in the intestinal epithelium is an example of secondary active transport. It uses the sodium gradient established by the Na+/K+ ATPase to transport glucose into the cells against its concentration gradient. This is important for the absorption of glucose from the gut.

- **Proton Pump (H^+/K^+ ATPase)**: Found in the stomach lining, this pump is responsible for secreting hydrochloric acid into the stomach lumen. The pump moves hydrogen ions (protons) into the stomach in exchange for potassium ions, which is essential for digestion.
- **Multidrug Resistance Proteins (MDRs)**: These are transporter proteins involved in the efflux of various drugs and toxins out of cells, particularly in cancer cells. By actively transporting chemotherapeutic agents out of the cells, these proteins contribute to the phenomenon of multidrug resistance in cancer treatment.

Clinical Significance

- **Drug Absorption and Distribution**: Active transport mechanisms are crucial for the absorption and distribution of certain drugs. For example, the transport of levodopa, used in Parkinson's disease, into the brain involves active transport across the blood-brain barrier.
- **Drug Interactions**: Understanding active transport can help predict drug interactions. Drugs that compete for the same transporter can affect each other's absorption and efficacy. For example, probenecid can inhibit the renal tubular secretion of penicillin, prolonging its half-life.
- **Overcoming Resistance**: In cancer treatment, targeting MDR proteins can help overcome resistance to chemotherapeutic agents, making treatments more effective.

Endocytosis

Definition, Characteristics, and Examples

Definition

Endocytosis is a cellular process in which substances are brought into the cell by engulfing them with the cell membrane. This mechanism allows cells to internalize macromolecules, particles, and even other cells. Endocytosis can be classified into different types based on the size and nature of the material being internalized and the specific cellular pathways involved.

Characteristics

- **Energy Requirement**: Endocytosis is an active process that requires energy, usually in the form of adenosine triphosphate (ATP).

- **Vesicle Formation**: During endocytosis, the cell membrane invaginates around the material to be internalized, forming a vesicle that pinches off and moves into the cell's interior.
- **Specificity**: Endocytosis can be selective, with cells using receptor-mediated endocytosis to target specific molecules. This involves receptors on the cell surface that recognize and bind to specific ligands.
- **Types of Endocytosis**: There are several forms of endocytosis, including phagocytosis, pinocytosis, and receptor-mediated endocytosis.

  - **Phagocytosis**: Often referred to as "cell eating," this type involves the engulfment of large particles such as debris, pathogens, or other cells. It is common in immune cells like macrophages and neutrophils.
  - **Pinocytosis**: Known as "cell drinking," this type involves the non-specific uptake of extracellular fluid and small solutes into vesicles. It is a continuous process in many cell types.
  - **Receptor-Mediated Endocytosis**: This highly specific process involves the binding of ligands to cell surface receptors, triggering vesicle formation and internalization. It allows for the selective uptake of specific molecules like hormones, nutrients, and antibodies.

Examples

- **Phagocytosis of Pathogens**: Macrophages and neutrophils, which are types of immune cells, use phagocytosis to engulf and destroy bacteria and other pathogens. For instance, when a macrophage encounters a bacterium, it engulfs the bacterium in a phagosome, which then fuses with a lysosome to degrade the pathogen.
- **Receptor-Mediated Endocytosis of LDL**: Low-density lipoprotein (LDL), which carries cholesterol in the blood, binds to LDL receptors on the surface of cells. This complex is then internalized via receptor-mediated endocytosis, allowing the cell to obtain cholesterol for membrane synthesis and other functions.
- **Pinocytosis in Kidney Cells**: Cells in the proximal tubules of the kidneys use pinocytosis to reabsorb solutes and fluids from the filtrate, helping to maintain fluid and electrolyte balance in the body.
- **Endocytosis of Insulin**: Insulin binds to its receptor on the surface of target cells, such as liver and muscle cells, triggering receptor-mediated endocytosis. This allows the cells to internalize insulin and initiate

downstream signaling pathways that regulate glucose uptake and metabolism.

Clinical Significance

- **Drug Delivery**: Understanding endocytosis mechanisms can aid in the design of drug delivery systems. For example, nanoparticle-based drugs can be engineered to exploit receptor-mediated endocytosis to enhance targeted delivery to specific cells or tissues.
- **Disease Mechanisms**: Disruptions in endocytosis pathways can contribute to disease. For example, defective receptor-mediated endocytosis of LDL due to mutations in the LDL receptor leads to familial hypercholesterolemia, a condition characterized by high cholesterol levels and an increased risk of cardiovascular disease.
- **Viral Entry**: Many viruses, including the influenza virus and SARS-CoV-2, exploit endocytosis to enter host cells. Understanding these mechanisms can inform the development of antiviral therapies that block viral entry.
- **Therapeutic Antibodies**: Monoclonal antibodies used in cancer therapy often rely on receptor-mediated endocytosis for their efficacy. For instance, trastuzumab (Herceptin) targets the HER2 receptor on breast cancer cells, leading to receptor internalization and downregulation, which inhibits tumor growth.

3.2 Absorption of Drugs

Factors Affecting Drug Absorption

Physiological Factors

Drug absorption is a critical aspect of pharmacokinetics, as it determines the onset, intensity, and duration of a drug's action. Several physiological factors can influence the absorption of drugs, affecting their bioavailability and therapeutic efficacy.

pH and Drug Ionization

- **pH and Ionization**: The pH of the absorption site significantly affects drug absorption, particularly for weak acids and bases. Drugs exist in either ionized or non-ionized forms depending on the pH of their environment. The non-ionized form of a drug is typically more lipid-soluble and can diffuse across cell membranes more readily than the ionized form. For instance, weak acids like aspirin are better absorbed in the acidic environment of the stomach, while weak bases like codeine are better absorbed in the more alkaline environment of the small intestine.

- **Example**: The pH partition hypothesis explains why the stomach's acidic pH facilitates the absorption of weak acids but impedes the absorption of weak bases.

Blood Flow to Absorption Site

- **Blood Flow**: Adequate blood flow to the absorption site is essential for efficient drug absorption. Enhanced blood flow ensures that the drug is rapidly removed from the absorption site and distributed throughout the body. Regions with high blood flow, such as the small intestine, are generally more efficient at drug absorption than areas with lower blood flow, like the stomach.
- **Example**: Subcutaneous and intramuscular injections rely on adequate blood flow for absorption. For instance, the absorption of insulin can vary depending on the blood flow to the injection site.

Surface Area

- **Surface Area**: The surface area available for drug absorption plays a crucial role in determining the extent of absorption. Larger surface areas allow for more drug molecules to be absorbed simultaneously. The small intestine, with its extensive surface area due to villi and microvilli, is the primary site for the absorption of most orally administered drugs.
- **Example**: Drugs like oral antibiotics are primarily absorbed in the small intestine due to its large surface area, which facilitates efficient absorption.

Gastrointestinal Motility

- **Gastrointestinal Motility**: The rate of gastric emptying and intestinal transit time can influence drug absorption. Delayed gastric emptying can slow the delivery of drugs to the small intestine, where absorption is typically more efficient. Conversely, rapid transit through the intestines can reduce the contact time between the drug and the absorptive surface, potentially decreasing absorption.

- **Example:** Conditions like gastroparesis (delayed gastric emptying) can impair the absorption of drugs that are primarily absorbed in the small intestine.

Presence of Food

- **Presence of Food:** Food can have varying effects on drug absorption. It can either enhance, delay, or reduce absorption depending on the drug's properties and the nature of the food. Food can alter gastric pH, delay gastric emptying, and interact with the drug, forming complexes that are less readily absorbed.
- **Example:** The absorption of some drugs, such as certain antibiotics like tetracyclines, can be reduced when taken with food, particularly dairy products, due to the formation of insoluble complexes with calcium.

Gastrointestinal pH

- **Gastrointestinal pH:** The pH of different segments of the gastrointestinal tract affects the solubility and ionization of drugs. The stomach's acidic pH and the small intestine's alkaline pH create different environments that can favor or hinder the absorption of specific drugs.
- **Example:** Enteric-coated formulations are designed to resist the acidic environment of the stomach and dissolve in the more alkaline pH of the small intestine to ensure proper drug release and absorption.

Enzymatic Activity

- **Enzymatic Activity:** The presence of digestive enzymes in the gastrointestinal tract can impact drug absorption, particularly for drugs that are susceptible to enzymatic degradation. Enzymes can break down drug molecules before they are absorbed, reducing bioavailability.
- **Example:** Peptide drugs like insulin are degraded by proteolytic enzymes in the gastrointestinal tract, which is why they cannot be administered orally.

Gut Microbiota

- **Gut Microbiota**: The intestinal flora can metabolize certain drugs, affecting their absorption and bioavailability. The metabolic activity of gut bacteria can either activate prodrugs or inactivate active drugs before they are absorbed.
- **Example**: The gut microbiota can metabolize the cardiac glycoside digoxin, reducing its bioavailability and therapeutic effect.

Drug-Specific Factors

Solubility

Definition: Solubility is the ability of a drug to dissolve in a given solvent, typically gastrointestinal fluids for oral drugs. Drugs must be in solution form to be absorbed across cell membranes.

Characteristics:

- **Water Solubility**: Drugs that are highly water-soluble can dissolve easily in the aqueous environment of the gastrointestinal tract, facilitating absorption.
- **Lipid Solubility**: Lipid-soluble drugs can easily cross cell membranes by passive diffusion, making them well-absorbed through biological membranes.
- **Example**: Highly water-soluble drugs like paracetamol are rapidly absorbed in the gastrointestinal tract, while lipid-soluble drugs like diazepam are efficiently absorbed due to their ability to cross cell membranes.

Formulation

Definition: The formulation of a drug refers to the way the drug is prepared and presented for administration, which can influence its absorption characteristics.

Characteristics:

- **Immediate-Release Formulations**: Designed to dissolve quickly and release the active drug immediately after administration. This can lead to rapid onset of action.
- **Controlled-Release Formulations**: Designed to release the active drug slowly over time, providing a prolonged therapeutic effect and reducing the frequency of dosing.

- **Example**: Immediate-release tablets of ibuprofen provide quick pain relief, while controlled-release formulations of metformin help maintain steady blood glucose levels over an extended period.

Particle Size

Definition: The size of drug particles in a formulation can affect the rate and extent of drug dissolution and absorption.

Characteristics:

- **Smaller Particle Size**: Increases the surface area for dissolution, enhancing the rate of absorption.
- **Micronization**: A process that reduces the particle size of a drug to the micron level, improving its solubility and absorption.
- **Example**: Micronized fenofibrate has improved absorption compared to non-micronized formulations due to its increased surface area.

Chemical Stability

Definition: The chemical stability of a drug refers to its ability to maintain its chemical integrity and potency over time under various environmental conditions.

Characteristics:

- **Degradation in Gastrointestinal Tract**: Some drugs may be unstable in the acidic environment of the stomach or may be degraded by enzymes in the gastrointestinal tract.
- **Protection Mechanisms**: Enteric coatings and protective excipients can be used to enhance the stability of such drugs.
- **Example**: Omeprazole is sensitive to stomach acid and is formulated with an enteric coating to protect it from degradation until it reaches the more alkaline environment of the small intestine.

Permeability

Definition: Permeability refers to the ability of a drug to cross cell membranes to reach systemic circulation.

Characteristics:

- **High Permeability**: Drugs with high permeability can easily cross cell membranes and are generally well-absorbed.

- **Low Permeability**: Drugs with low permeability may require special formulation techniques or delivery systems to enhance their absorption.
- **Example**: Highly permeable drugs like propranolol are absorbed efficiently across the gastrointestinal tract, while low-permeability drugs like furosemide may have variable absorption.

Prodrug Design

Definition: A prodrug is an inactive or less active derivative of a drug that is metabolized in the body to release the active drug.

Characteristics:

- **Improved Absorption**: Prodrugs can be designed to enhance solubility, permeability, or stability, improving the absorption and bioavailability of the active drug.
- **Targeted Release**: Prodrugs can be designed to release the active drug at specific sites in the body, improving therapeutic outcomes.
- **Example**: Enalapril is a prodrug that is converted to its active form, enalaprilat, in the body. This conversion enhances its oral bioavailability compared to directly administering enalaprilat.

Drug Polymorphism

Definition: Polymorphism refers to the occurrence of different crystalline forms of a drug, which can affect its physical and chemical properties, including solubility and stability.

Characteristics:

- **Different Polymorphs**: Can have varying solubilities and dissolution rates, influencing the drug's absorption and bioavailability.
- **Selection of Polymorphs**: The most stable and bioavailable polymorph is typically selected during drug formulation.
- **Example**: The anti-inflammatory drug indomethacin exists in multiple polymorphic forms, with Form I being more soluble and better absorbed than Form II.

pKa and Ionization

Definition: The pKa of a drug is the pH at which the drug exists in equal proportions of its ionized and non-ionized forms.

Characteristics:

- **Ionization State**: Affects the drug's solubility and ability to cross cell membranes. Non-ionized forms are generally more lipid-soluble and better absorbed.
- **pH-Dependent Absorption**: Drugs are absorbed differently at various pH levels depending on their pKa values.
- **Example**: Aspirin (acetylsalicylic acid) has a pKa of 3.5, meaning it is mostly non-ionized in the acidic environment of the stomach, facilitating its absorption.

Bioavailability

Definition and Calculation

Definition

Bioavailability is a pharmacokinetic parameter that measures the extent and rate at which an administered drug reaches the systemic circulation, thereby becoming available at the site of action. It is a critical factor in determining the correct dosage for non-intravenous routes of administration. Bioavailability is often expressed as a percentage of the administered dose that reaches the systemic circulation in an unchanged form.

- **Absolute Bioavailability**: This compares the bioavailability of the active drug in systemic circulation following non-intravenous administration (e.g., oral, intramuscular) with the bioavailability of the same drug following intravenous administration.

Relative Bioavailability: This compares the bioavailability of two different formulations or dosage forms of the same drug when administered by the same route.

The bioavailability of a drug is calculated using the area under the curve (AUC) from the plasma concentration-time graph. The AUC represents the total drug exposure over time. For absolute bioavailability, the formula is:

$$F = \left(\frac{AUC_{\text{oral}}}{AUC_{\text{IV}}}\right) \times \left(\frac{Dose_{\text{IV}}}{Dose_{\text{oral}}}\right) \times 100$$

Where:

- F is the bioavailability expressed as a percentage.

- AUC_{oral} is the area under the plasma concentration-time curve after oral administration.
- AUC_{IV} is the area under the plasma concentration-time curve after intravenous administration.
- $Dose_{IV}$ is the dose administered intravenously.
- $Dose_{oral}$ is the dose administered orally.

For relative bioavailability, the formula is:

$$F = \left(\frac{AUC_{test}}{AUC_{reference}}\right) \times \left(\frac{Dose_{reference}}{Dose_{test}}\right) \times 100$$

Where:

- F is the relative bioavailability expressed as a percentage.
- AUC_{test} is the area under the plasma concentration-time curve for the test formulation.
- $AUC_{reference}$ is the area under the plasma concentration-time curve for the reference formulation.
- $Dose_{test}$ is the dose of the test formulation.
- $Dose_{reference}$ is the dose of the reference formulation.

Clinical Significance

- **Drug Efficacy and Safety**: Understanding the bioavailability of a drug helps in determining the correct dosage required to achieve therapeutic levels without causing toxicity. A drug with low bioavailability might need a higher dose or an alternative route of administration to be effective.
- **Formulation Development**: Bioavailability studies guide the development of drug formulations to enhance absorption. Techniques such as the use of prodrugs, nanoparticles, or lipid-based formulations can improve bioavailability.

Regulatory Approval: Regulatory agencies require bioavailability data to ensure the consistency and effectiveness of new drug formulations. Bioequivalence studies, comparing generic drugs to their brand-name counterparts, rely on bioavailability data to ensure therapeutic equivalence.

Table 3.1: **Factors Affecting Drug Absorption**

Factor	Description	Example
pH	Drug ionization	Aspirin absorption i
Blood flow	Increased absorption with increased blood flow	Injection sites
Surface area	Larger surface area enhances absorption	Small intestine

Table 3.2: **Volume of Distribution (Vd)**

Drug	Volume of Distribution (L/kg)	Classificatio
Warfarin	0.1	Low Vd
Digoxin	7	High Vd

3.3 Distribution of Drugs

Volume of Distribution

Definition, Significance, and Calculation

Definition

Volume of distribution (Vd) is a pharmacokinetic parameter that describes the distribution of a drug throughout the body relative to the concentration of the drug in the plasma. It is an apparent volume that represents the degree to which a drug is distributed in body tissues as opposed to the plasma. Vd is not a real physiological volume but a theoretical one that helps in understanding how extensively a drug spreads into various body compartments.

Significance

- **Drug Distribution**: Vd provides insight into the extent of a drug's distribution in body tissues. A large Vd indicates extensive distribution into tissues, whereas a small Vd suggests the drug remains largely in the plasma.
- **Dosing**: Understanding Vd is crucial for determining the appropriate loading dose of a drug to achieve the desired plasma concentration.
- **Drug Clearance and Half-Life**: Vd, in combination with clearance (Cl), influences the drug's half-life (t1/2). A drug with a large Vd and low clearance will have a longer half-life.

Calculation

The volume of distribution can be calculated using the following formula:

Where: Vd= Dose/ C_0

Where:

- Vd is the volume of distribution.
- Dose is the amount of drug administered.
- C_0 is the initial plasma concentration of the drug immediately after administration (extrapolated from the plasma concentration-time curve).

Protein Binding

Mechanism, Importance, and Examples

Mechanism

Protein binding refers to the reversible interaction between a drug and plasma proteins such as albumin, alpha-1-acid glycoprotein, and lipoproteins. When a drug binds to these proteins, it forms a complex that is usually too large to cross cell membranes, effectively limiting its distribution to tissues.

- **Free and Bound Drug**: Drugs in the bloodstream exist in two forms: bound to plasma proteins and free (unbound). Only the free drug is pharmacologically active and able to diffuse across cell membranes to exert its therapeutic effects.
- **Equilibrium**: The binding process is dynamic, with a constant equilibrium between bound and unbound drug. As the free drug is metabolized or excreted, more of the bound drug is released to maintain the equilibrium.

Importance

- **Drug Activity**: The extent of protein binding affects the drug's bioavailability and activity. Highly protein-bound drugs have a lower concentration of free drug available to interact with target sites.
- **Drug Interactions**: Drugs can compete for binding sites on plasma proteins, leading to potential drug-drug interactions. Displacement of one drug by another can increase the free concentration of the displaced drug, potentially leading to toxicity.

- **Pharmacokinetics**: Protein binding influences the volume of distribution, clearance, and half-life of a drug. Drugs that are highly protein-bound tend to have a lower volume of distribution and longer half-life.

Examples

- **Warfarin**: Warfarin is an anticoagulant that is highly bound to plasma albumin (approximately 99%). The small percentage of free warfarin is responsible for its anticoagulant effect. Displacement of warfarin by other drugs (e.g., aspirin) can lead to increased free warfarin levels and a higher risk of bleeding.
- **Phenytoin**: Phenytoin, an anticonvulsant, is also highly protein-bound (about 90%). Changes in plasma protein levels (e.g., due to liver disease) or displacement by other drugs can significantly affect phenytoin's free concentration and therapeutic effect.
- **Diazepam**: Diazepam, a benzodiazepine used for anxiety and seizures, binds extensively to plasma proteins (95-99%). The high degree of protein binding influences its long half-life and duration of action.

3.4 Metabolism of Drugs

Phases of Drug Metabolism

Drug metabolism is a vital process that transforms lipophilic drug molecules into more hydrophilic compounds that can be easily excreted from the body. This process occurs primarily in the liver and involves two main phases: Phase I and Phase II reactions.

Phase I Reactions

Definition

Phase I reactions, also known as functionalization reactions, involve chemical modifications of the drug molecule, introducing or unmasking functional groups (-OH, -NH2, -SH, -COOH). These reactions usually result in a modest increase in the drug's polarity, preparing it for further Phase II conjugation reactions.

Types of Phase I Reactions

1. **Oxidation**
2. **Reduction**
3. **Hydrolysis**

Oxidation

Definition: Oxidation is the most common type of Phase I reaction. It involves the addition of oxygen or the removal of hydrogen from the drug molecule, catalyzed primarily by the cytochrome P450 enzyme system (CYP450) in the liver.

Mechanism:

- **Cytochrome P450 Enzymes**: The CYP450 enzymes play a key role in drug oxidation. These enzymes introduce an oxygen atom into the drug molecule, often resulting in the formation of an alcohol, aldehyde, or carboxylic acid.
- **Mixed-Function Oxidases**: These enzymes utilize molecular oxygen, incorporating one oxygen atom into the substrate (the drug) and reducing the other oxygen atom to water.

Examples:

- **Codeine to Morphine**: The oxidation of codeine by CYP2D6 to form morphine, which is the active analgesic.
- **Ethanol to Acetaldehyde**: The conversion of ethanol to acetaldehyde by alcohol dehydrogenase (ADH) and further to acetic acid by aldehyde dehydrogenase (ALDH).

Reduction

Definition: Reduction reactions involve the gain of electrons or the addition of hydrogen to the drug molecule. These reactions are less common than oxidation and typically occur under anaerobic conditions in the liver.

Mechanism:

- **Reduction Enzymes**: Reductive enzymes, such as reductases, catalyze these reactions, often acting on nitro groups (-NO2), azo groups (-N=N-), and carbonyl groups (C=O) in drug molecules.

Examples:

- **Chloramphenicol**: The reduction of the nitro group in chloramphenicol to form its active amine derivative.

- **Warfarin**: The conversion of the ketone form of warfarin to its alcohol form under reductive conditions.

Hydrolysis

Definition: Hydrolysis involves the cleavage of chemical bonds by the addition of water. This reaction typically targets ester and amide bonds in drug molecules.

Mechanism:

- **Esterases and Amidases**: Enzymes like esterases and amidases catalyze hydrolysis reactions, breaking down ester and amide bonds to form more polar metabolites.

Examples:

- **Aspirin (Acetylsalicylic Acid)**: Hydrolysis of aspirin by esterases to produce salicylic acid and acetic acid.
- **Procainamide**: The hydrolysis of procainamide, an antiarrhythmic drug, to produce procaine and related metabolites.

Significance

- **Detoxification**: Phase I reactions are crucial for detoxifying potentially harmful xenobiotics and endogenous compounds.
- **Activation of Prodrugs**: Some drugs are administered in an inactive form (prodrugs) and require Phase I metabolism to convert them into their active forms.
- **Drug-Drug Interactions**: The activity of CYP450 enzymes can be affected by various drugs, leading to significant drug-drug interactions. For instance, drugs that inhibit CYP450 can increase the plasma levels of drugs metabolized by the same enzymes, potentially leading to toxicity.

Phase II Reactions

Phase II Reactions: Conjugation

Definition

Phase II reactions, also known as conjugation reactions, involve the coupling (conjugation) of the drug or its Phase I metabolite with an endogenous substrate, such as glucuronic acid, sulfate, acetate, amino acids, or glutathione. These reactions result in the formation of highly polar, water-soluble compounds that are more easily excreted from the body, primarily via the kidneys or bile.

Types of Phase II Reactions

1. **Glucuronidation**
2. **Sulfation**
3. **Acetylation**
4. **Amino Acid Conjugation**
5. **Glutathione Conjugation**
6. **Methylation**

Glucuronidation

Definition: Glucuronidation is the most common Phase II reaction. It involves the transfer of glucuronic acid from uridine diphosphate-glucuronic acid (UDP-GA) to the drug or its metabolite.

Mechanism:

- **Enzyme:** UDP-glucuronosyltransferase (UGT) catalyzes this reaction.
- **Substrates:** Drugs with hydroxyl, carboxyl, amine, or sulfhydryl groups are common substrates for glucuronidation.

Examples:

- **Morphine:** Morphine is glucuronidated to morphine-6-glucuronide and morphine-3-glucuronide, which are more water-soluble.
- **Acetaminophen:** Acetaminophen undergoes glucuronidation to form acetaminophen glucuronide, enhancing its excretion.

Sulfation

Definition: Sulfation involves the transfer of a sulfate group from 3'-phosphoadenosine-5'-phosphosulfate (PAPS) to the drug or its metabolite.

Mechanism:

- **Enzyme:** Sulfotransferases (SULTs) catalyze this reaction.
- **Substrates:** Phenols, alcohols, and aromatic amines are common substrates for sulfation.

Examples:

- **Epinephrine:** Epinephrine is sulfated to epinephrine sulfate, which is more easily excreted.
- **Estrone:** Estrone undergoes sulfation to form estrone sulfate.

Acetylation

Definition: Acetylation involves the transfer of an acetyl group from acetyl coenzyme A (acetyl-CoA) to the drug or its metabolite.

Mechanism:

- **Enzyme:** N-acetyltransferases (NATs) catalyze this reaction.
- **Substrates:** Drugs containing aromatic amines or hydrazines are commonly acetylated.

Examples:

- **Isoniazid:** Isoniazid, used in tuberculosis treatment, is acetylated to acetylisoniazid.
- **Sulfamethoxazole:** Sulfamethoxazole is acetylated to N4-acetylsulfamethoxazole.

Amino Acid Conjugation

Definition: Amino acid conjugation involves the conjugation of drugs with amino acids like glycine, glutamine, or taurine.

Mechanism:

- **Enzyme:** Various transferases catalyze these reactions.
- **Substrates:** Drugs containing carboxylic acid groups are common substrates.

Examples:

- **Salicylic Acid:** Salicylic acid is conjugated with glycine to form salicyluric acid.
- **Bile Acids:** Bile acids are conjugated with glycine or taurine to form bile salts.

Glutathione Conjugation

Definition: Glutathione conjugation involves the transfer of glutathione (GSH) to the drug or its metabolite.

Mechanism:

- **Enzyme**: Glutathione S-transferases (GSTs) catalyze this reaction.
- **Substrates**: Electrophilic compounds, including reactive intermediates, are common substrates.

Examples:

- **Acetaminophen**: A toxic metabolite of acetaminophen, N-acetyl-p-benzoquinone imine (NAPQI), is detoxified by conjugation with glutathione.
- **Bromobenzene**: Bromobenzene is conjugated with glutathione to form non-toxic products.

Methylation

Definition: Methylation involves the transfer of a methyl group from S-adenosylmethionine (SAM) to the drug or its metabolite.

Mechanism:

- **Enzyme**: Methyltransferases catalyze this reaction.
- **Substrates**: Drugs with hydroxyl, amine, or thiol groups can be methylated.

Examples:

- **Epinephrine**: Epinephrine is methylated by catechol-O-methyltransferase (COMT) to form metanephrine.
- **Histamine**: Histamine is methylated by histamine N-methyltransferase to form N-methylhistamine.

Significance

- **Detoxification**: Phase II reactions generally produce metabolites that are more water-soluble and less pharmacologically active, facilitating their excretion via urine or bile.

- **Drug Safety**: Conjugation reactions often detoxify reactive intermediates produced during Phase I metabolism, reducing the risk of adverse effects.
- **Genetic Variability**: Genetic polymorphisms in Phase II enzymes can affect drug metabolism rates, influencing drug efficacy and the risk of side effects. For example, slow acetylators of isoniazid are at higher risk for drug-induced hepatotoxicity.

Enzyme Induction and Inhibition

Mechanisms, Examples, and Clinical Relevance

Enzyme Induction

Mechanisms

Enzyme induction refers to the process by which certain substances increase the activity or expression of drug-metabolizing enzymes, primarily in the liver. This results in an accelerated rate of drug metabolism.

- **Transcriptional Activation**: Inducers often increase the transcription of genes encoding drug-metabolizing enzymes. This is typically mediated by nuclear receptors such as the pregnane X receptor (PXR), constitutive androstane receptor (CAR), and aryl hydrocarbon receptor (AhR).
- **Increased Enzyme Synthesis**: Enhanced transcription leads to increased synthesis of enzyme proteins, which boosts the metabolic capacity of the liver.
- **Protein Stabilization**: Some inducers may also stabilize enzyme proteins, reducing their degradation and increasing their functional lifespan.

Examples

- **Rifampin**: This antibiotic is a potent inducer of CYP3A4, leading to increased metabolism of drugs like oral contraceptives, reducing their effectiveness.
- **Phenytoin**: An anticonvulsant that induces CYP3A4 and CYP2C9, accelerating the metabolism of drugs such as warfarin and corticosteroids.
- **St. John's Wort**: A herbal supplement that induces CYP3A4 and P-glycoprotein, affecting drugs like cyclosporine and oral contraceptives.

Clinical Relevance

- **Reduced Drug Efficacy**: Enzyme induction can lead to decreased plasma concentrations of co-administered drugs, reducing their efficacy. For example, rifampin-induced CYP3A4 can decrease the effectiveness of oral contraceptives, leading to contraceptive failure.
- **Altered Dosage Requirements**: Drugs metabolized by induced enzymes may require dosage adjustments to maintain therapeutic levels. For example, patients on phenytoin may need higher doses of warfarin to achieve anticoagulant effects.
- **Drug-Drug Interactions**: Understanding enzyme induction is critical to managing potential drug-drug interactions. Clinicians must be aware of which drugs can induce enzymes and adjust therapy accordingly to prevent therapeutic failure or toxicity.

Enzyme Inhibition

Mechanisms

Enzyme inhibition involves the reduction of enzyme activity by certain substances, leading to decreased drug metabolism and increased plasma levels of the drug.

- **Competitive Inhibition**: Inhibitors compete with the substrate for binding to the active site of the enzyme. This type of inhibition is usually reversible.
- **Non-Competitive Inhibition**: Inhibitors bind to a site other than the active site, causing a change in enzyme conformation and reducing its activity. This can be reversible or irreversible.
- **Mechanism-Based Inhibition**: Also known as suicide inhibition, this involves the inhibitor binding to the enzyme and causing its permanent inactivation through the formation of a stable complex.

Examples

- **Cimetidine**: This H2-receptor antagonist inhibits multiple CYP enzymes, including CYP1A2, CYP2C9, CYP2D6, and CYP3A4, leading to increased levels of drugs like warfarin and theophylline.
- **Ketoconazole**: An antifungal that is a potent inhibitor of CYP3A4, resulting in increased plasma concentrations of drugs like midazolam

and statins.

- **Grapefruit Juice**: Contains furanocoumarins that inhibit CYP3A4 in the intestinal wall, leading to increased bioavailability of drugs like simvastatin and felodipine.

Clinical Relevance

- **Increased Drug Toxicity**: Enzyme inhibition can lead to elevated plasma levels of drugs, increasing the risk of toxicity. For example, concurrent use of ketoconazole and midazolam can result in excessive sedation and respiratory depression due to elevated midazolam levels.
- **Prolonged Drug Effects**: Inhibition of drug-metabolizing enzymes can extend the duration of action of drugs. For example, cimetidine can prolong the effects of warfarin, increasing the risk of bleeding.
- **Drug-Drug Interactions**: Awareness of enzyme inhibition is essential for preventing adverse drug interactions. Clinicians should monitor patients closely and adjust dosages when inhibitors are co-administered with drugs metabolized by the same enzymes.

3.5 Excretion of Drugs

Renal Excretion

Mechanism, Factors Affecting Renal Excretion, and Examples

Mechanism

Renal excretion is the primary route for the elimination of many drugs and their metabolites from the body. It involves several processes that take place in the kidneys:

1. **Glomerular Filtration**:
    - **Process**: Blood is filtered through the glomerulus, allowing free (unbound) drugs and small molecules to pass into the renal tubule. Large molecules and drugs bound to plasma proteins are generally not filtered.
    - **Filtration Rate**: The glomerular filtration rate (GFR) is a key determinant of how much drug is filtered. Normal GFR is about 120 mL/min in healthy adults.
2. **Tubular Secretion**:

- **Process:** Active transport mechanisms in the proximal tubules secrete drugs from the blood into the renal tubule. This process can involve specific transport proteins for organic acids (e.g., penicillin) and organic bases (e.g., histamine).
- **Energy Dependence:** Tubular secretion requires energy and can be a site of competition between drugs for the same transport proteins.

3. **Tubular Reabsorption:**

- **Process:** As the filtrate moves through the renal tubule, water is reabsorbed, concentrating the drug within the tubule. Depending on the drug's properties, it may passively diffuse back into the blood.
- **Influence of pH:** The reabsorption of weak acids and bases is influenced by the pH of the urine. Weak acids are more likely to be reabsorbed in acidic urine, whereas weak bases are more likely to be reabsorbed in alkaline urine.

Factors Affecting Renal Excretion
Several factors influence the efficiency of renal drug excretion:

1. **GFR:** Higher GFR increases the rate of drug filtration and excretion. Conditions that reduce GFR, such as renal impairment, decrease drug excretion.

- **Example:** Drugs like digoxin, which are primarily excreted by glomerular filtration, require dose adjustment in patients with reduced GFR.

2. **Plasma Protein Binding:** Drugs that are highly bound to plasma proteins are not readily filtered at the glomerulus. Only the free fraction of the drug is subject to excretion.

- **Example:** Warfarin, which is highly protein-bound, has a low rate of glomerular filtration.

3. **Active Tubular Secretion:** The efficiency of active secretion mechanisms can affect drug excretion rates. Competition for transport proteins can also alter the excretion of certain drugs.

- **Example**: Probenecid inhibits the tubular secretion of penicillin, prolonging its plasma half-life.

4. **Urine pH**: The pH of the urine can alter the ionization state of drugs, affecting their reabsorption in the renal tubules. Alkalinization or acidification of urine can be used therapeutically to enhance the excretion of certain drugs.

   - **Example**: Alkalinizing the urine (e.g., with sodium bicarbonate) can enhance the excretion of aspirin (a weak acid) in cases of overdose.

5. **Renal Blood Flow**: Increased renal blood flow enhances drug delivery to the kidneys, increasing filtration and excretion rates.

   - **Example**: Conditions that reduce renal blood flow, such as heart failure, can decrease the excretion of drugs like lithium.

Examples

1. **Penicillin**: Penicillin is actively secreted by the renal tubules and is excreted rapidly. Probenecid can be co-administered to inhibit its secretion and prolong its action.
2. **Methotrexate**: This chemotherapeutic agent is excreted both by glomerular filtration and active tubular secretion. Its excretion is affected by urine pH, with alkalinization increasing its elimination.
3. **Digoxin**: Primarily excreted by glomerular filtration, digoxin's clearance is significantly affected by renal function. Dose adjustments are necessary in patients with renal impairment to avoid toxicity.
4. **Aspirin**: Aspirin and its metabolites are excreted by the kidneys. Urine alkalinization can increase the renal excretion of salicylates, which is useful in the management of aspirin overdose.

Non-Renal Routes of Drug Excretion

Biliary, Pulmonary, and Other Routes

Biliary Excretion

Mechanism: Drugs and their metabolites are secreted into the bile by liver cells. This process often involves active transport mechanisms that move drugs from the hepatocytes into the bile canaliculi. Once in the bile, these substances are transported to the intestine and can be excreted in the feces.

- **Enterohepatic Recirculation**: Some drugs excreted in the bile can be reabsorbed in the intestine and returned to the liver via the portal circulation. This recycling can prolong the drug's presence in the body and its effects.
- **Molecular Characteristics**: Drugs with a high molecular weight, polar characteristics, and those that are conjugated (e.g., glucuronides) are more likely to be excreted via the bile.

Examples:

- **Morphine**: Morphine and its glucuronide metabolites are excreted in the bile and can undergo enterohepatic recirculation.
- **Erythromycin**: This antibiotic is partly excreted in the bile, which can be an important elimination pathway, especially in cases of renal impairment.

Clinical Relevance: Biliary excretion can be significant for drug interactions and toxicity. Drugs that undergo enterohepatic recirculation may require dose adjustments to avoid prolonged effects or toxicity.

Pulmonary Excretion

Mechanism: Volatile substances and gases are eliminated through the lungs via exhalation. This process is mainly governed by passive diffusion and the concentration gradient between the blood and the alveolar air.

- **Volatility**: Drugs that are gases or volatile liquids are excreted through the pulmonary route.
- **Solubility**: The rate of pulmonary excretion depends on the solubility of the substance in blood and its vapor pressure.

Examples:

- **Anesthetic Gases**: Drugs like nitrous oxide and halothane are administered as inhalation anesthetics and are primarily excreted unchanged through the lungs.

- **Alcohol**: Ethanol is partly excreted through the lungs, which is the basis for breathalyzer tests used to estimate blood alcohol concentration.

Clinical Relevance: Pulmonary excretion is important for the elimination of anesthetic gases and other volatile compounds. It also provides a non-invasive method for monitoring substances like alcohol.

Other Routes of Excretion

1. **Sweat and Saliva**:
   - **Mechanism**: Drugs can diffuse into sweat and saliva from the bloodstream. These routes are generally minor compared to renal and biliary excretion but can contribute to drug elimination.
   - **Examples**:
     - **Caffeine**: Excreted in small amounts in sweat and saliva.
     - **Heavy Metals**: Some heavy metals, like arsenic and mercury, can be excreted through sweat.
2. **Mammary Excretion**:
   - **Mechanism**: Drugs can be secreted into breast milk, which can be significant for nursing infants.
   - **Examples**:
     - **Lithium**: Excreted in breast milk and can affect the nursing infant.
     - **Tetracycline**: An antibiotic that can be present in breast milk and potentially harm a nursing infant.
3. **Gastrointestinal Excretion**:
   - **Mechanism**: Some drugs are directly excreted into the gastrointestinal tract through the intestinal mucosa. This can occur via passive diffusion or active transport.
   - **Examples**:
     - **Metformin**: Part of its elimination is through the gastrointestinal tract.

- **Chloramphenicol:** An antibiotic that can be excreted into the intestinal lumen.

4. **Tears and Hair:**

    - **Mechanism:** Although minor, drugs can be excreted in tears and incorporated into hair shafts.
    - **Examples:**

        - **Tears:** Certain medications like rifampin can discolor tears.
        - **Hair:** Drugs like methamphetamine can be detected in hair and used for forensic or compliance testing

3.6 Kinetics of Elimination

First-Order Kinetics

Definition, Characteristics, and Examples

Definition

First-order kinetics refers to a type of drug elimination where the rate of elimination is directly proportional to the drug concentration in the plasma. This means that a constant fraction or percentage of the drug is eliminated per unit time. Most drugs are eliminated from the body via first-order kinetics, particularly at therapeutic doses.

Characteristics

- **Proportional Elimination:** The amount of drug eliminated per unit time decreases as the drug concentration decreases, but the fraction of the drug eliminated remains constant.

    - For example, if 10% of the drug is eliminated per hour, the actual amount eliminated will decrease as the drug concentration decreases, but the percentage will remain 10%.

- **Exponential Decline:** Plasma drug concentration decreases exponentially over time. The plot of plasma concentration versus time on a linear scale yields a curved line, whereas the same plot on a logarithmic scale yields a straight line.
- **Half-Life ($t_{1/2}$):** The half-life is constant and does not change with different concentrations of the drug. It is the time required for the

plasma concentration of the drug to reduce by half.

- For example, if a drug has a half-life of 4 hours, the plasma concentration will decrease to half its initial value every 4 hours.

- **Rate of Elimination**: The rate of elimination can be described by the elimination rate constant (k), which is related to the half-life by the formula: $k=0.693/t_{1/2}$
- **Steady-State Concentration**: For drugs administered continuously or repeatedly, a steady-state concentration is reached when the rate of drug administration equals the rate of elimination. In first-order kinetics, steady-state concentration is achieved after about 4-5 half-lives.
- **Examples**
- **Paracetamol (Acetaminophen)**: At therapeutic doses, paracetamol is eliminated by first-order kinetics. If the concentration of paracetamol in the plasma is high, the rate of elimination is higher, but the proportion of the drug eliminated per unit time remains constant.
- **Phenytoin**: At low therapeutic doses, phenytoin follows first-order kinetics. However, at higher doses, phenytoin elimination switches to zero-order kinetics due to saturation of metabolic enzymes.
- **Ibuprofen**: This non-steroidal anti-inflammatory drug (NSAID) is eliminated from the body via first-order kinetics, with a half-life of approximately 2 hours. This means that the concentration of ibuprofen in the plasma will decrease by half every 2 hours.
- **Clinical Relevance**
- **Dosing Regimens**: Understanding first-order kinetics helps in designing appropriate dosing regimens. Since a constant fraction of the drug is eliminated, maintaining therapeutic levels can be achieved by consistent dosing intervals.
- **Toxicity Management**: For drugs that follow first-order kinetics, predicting the time required to reach non-toxic levels after an overdose is possible by knowing the half-life.
- **Drug Monitoring**: Regular monitoring of plasma drug levels can help ensure that a drug remains within its therapeutic range, avoiding subtherapeutic or toxic levels.
- **Mathematical Representation**

The relationship between plasma concentration and time in first-order kinetics can be described by the equation: $Ct=C_0 \times e^{-kt}$

Where:

- Ct is the plasma concentration at time ttt.
- C_0 is the initial plasma concentration.
- k is the elimination rate constant.
- t is the time.

Zero-Order Kinetics

Definition, Characteristics, and Examples

Definition

Zero-order kinetics refers to a type of drug elimination where the rate of elimination is constant and independent of the drug concentration in the plasma. This means that a fixed amount of the drug is eliminated per unit time, regardless of the concentration.

Characteristics

- **Constant Rate of Elimination**: Unlike first-order kinetics, where a constant fraction of the drug is eliminated, zero-order kinetics involves the elimination of a constant amount of the drug per unit time.
    - For example, if 10 mg of a drug is eliminated per hour, this rate remains constant irrespective of the plasma concentration.
- **Linear Decline**: The plasma drug concentration decreases linearly over time. The plot of plasma concentration versus time on a linear scale yields a straight line.
- **Saturation of Elimination Pathways**: Zero-order kinetics typically occurs when the drug's elimination pathways (such as metabolic enzymes or transporters) are saturated. Once saturation occurs, the system cannot increase the rate of elimination in response to increasing drug concentrations.
- **Variable Half-Life**: Unlike first-order kinetics, the half-life in zero-order kinetics is not constant and depends on the initial drug concentration. As the concentration decreases, the time required to reduce the concentration by half increases.
- **Risk of Accumulation**: Because the rate of elimination is constant, higher doses can lead to disproportionate increases in plasma drug levels, increasing the risk of toxicity.

Examples

- **Ethanol (Alcohol)**: Ethanol is one of the most common examples of a drug that follows zero-order kinetics. The liver's capacity to metabolize ethanol is limited by the enzyme alcohol dehydrogenase. Typically, the body metabolizes ethanol at a rate of about 10-15 mg/dL per hour, regardless of the concentration in the blood.
- **Phenytoin**: At therapeutic or higher doses, phenytoin exhibits zero-order kinetics due to the saturation of hepatic enzymes responsible for its metabolism. This non-linear pharmacokinetics means that small increases in dose can lead to large increases in plasma concentration, making dose adjustment challenging.
- **Aspirin**: At high doses, aspirin can follow zero-order kinetics. The metabolic pathways for aspirin become saturated, resulting in a constant rate of elimination.

Clinical Relevance

- **Dosing Regimens**: Drugs that exhibit zero-order kinetics require careful dosing to avoid accumulation and toxicity. Because the rate of elimination is constant, small increases in dose can lead to significant increases in drug concentration.
- **Toxicity Management**: Understanding zero-order kinetics is crucial in managing overdoses. Since the elimination rate is constant, predicting the time required for the drug concentration to decrease to non-toxic levels is more straightforward but slower compared to first-order kinetics.
- **Therapeutic Monitoring**: Drugs following zero-order kinetics often require therapeutic drug monitoring to maintain plasma concentrations within the therapeutic range and avoid toxicity. For example, phenytoin levels need to be regularly checked to ensure they stay within the safe range.

Mathematical Representation

In zero-order kinetics, the rate of change in drug concentration over time is constant and can be represented by the equation: $dC/dt=-k_0$ Where:

- dC/dt is the rate of change of drug concentration over time.

- k_0 is the zero-order rate constant (amount of drug eliminated per unit time).
- The concentration at any time t can be described by:
  $Ct = C_0 - k_0 \times t$ Where:
- Ct is the plasma concentration at time ttt.
- C_0 is the initial plasma concentration.
- k_0 is the zero-order elimination rate constant.
- t is the time.

CHAPTER IV

Pharmacodynamics

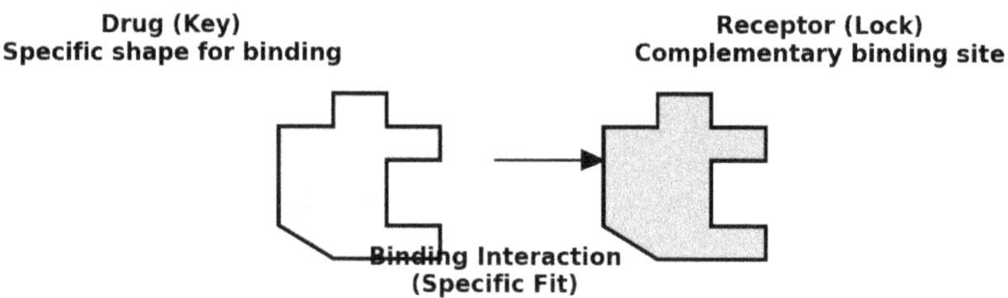

Lock and Key Model for Interaction between Drug and Receptor

4.1 Principles and Mechanisms of Drug Action

Receptor Theories

Lock and Key Model

Definition: The lock and key model is one of the earliest and most straightforward theories to explain the interaction between drugs and their specific receptors. It was proposed by Emil Fischer in 1894 and describes how the drug (the key) fits precisely into the receptor (the lock) to produce a biological effect.

Characteristics:

- **Specificity**: The model emphasizes the specificity of drug-receptor interactions, suggesting that only drugs with the correct shape and chemical properties can bind to a particular receptor.

- **Complementarity**: The receptor has a specific three-dimensional structure that matches the drug, similar to how a key fits into a lock.
- **Static Interaction**: The lock and key model assumes a static interaction where the receptor and drug do not undergo significant conformational changes upon binding.

Examples:

- **Acetylcholine and Nicotinic Receptors**: Acetylcholine, a neurotransmitter, binds specifically to nicotinic receptors on muscle cells to induce muscle contraction, much like a key fitting into a lock.
- **Enzyme Inhibitors**: Many enzyme inhibitors, such as methotrexate inhibiting dihydrofolate reductase, follow the lock and key model, where the inhibitor fits precisely into the active site of the enzyme.

Induced Fit Model

Definition: The induced fit model, proposed by Daniel Koshland in 1958, refines the lock and key model by suggesting that the binding of a drug to its receptor induces a conformational change in the receptor. This change enhances the fit between the drug and the receptor, optimizing the interaction and the subsequent biological response.

Characteristics:

- **Conformational Flexibility**: The receptor is not rigid but flexible, allowing it to adjust its shape to fit the drug more precisely upon binding.
- **Dynamic Interaction**: The binding of the drug induces a change in the receptor's structure, enhancing the interaction and the drug's efficacy.
- **Broader Specificity**: This model explains how receptors can bind to a broader range of structurally similar drugs, as the receptor can adapt to different molecules.

Examples:

- **Hexokinase and Glucose**: When glucose binds to hexokinase, the enzyme undergoes a conformational change that facilitates the phosphorylation of glucose, illustrating the induced fit model.
- **G-Protein Coupled Receptors (GPCRs)**: Many GPCRs exhibit induced fit behavior, where binding of an agonist induces a conformational

change in the receptor, leading to activation of intracellular signaling pathways.

Clinical Relevance

Understanding receptor theories is crucial for drug development and therapeutic application. These models help in predicting how drugs will interact with their targets and guide the design of new drugs with better efficacy and fewer side effects.

- **Drug Design**: The lock and key model and the induced fit model are fundamental in rational drug design, enabling the creation of drugs that specifically target receptors with high affinity.
- **Therapeutic Efficacy**: Drugs that fit well into their receptors (either through lock and key or induced fit mechanisms) are more likely to be effective at lower doses, reducing the risk of side effects.
- **Side Effect Management**: Understanding these models helps in predicting off-target effects, where drugs might interact with unintended receptors, leading to side effects.

Classification of Receptors

Ionotropic, Metabotropic, Enzyme-Linked, and Intracellular Receptors

Receptors are specialized proteins that bind to specific molecules (ligands) such as hormones, neurotransmitters, or drugs, and initiate a cellular response. They are classified based on their structure and mechanism of action into four main types: ionotropic, metabotropic, enzyme-linked, and intracellular receptors.

Ionotropic Receptors

Definition: Ionotropic receptors, also known as ligand-gated ion channels, are receptors that directly control the opening of an ion channel upon ligand binding. These receptors are integral membrane proteins that change conformation to form a pore through which ions can pass.

Characteristics:

- **Rapid Response**: The opening of ion channels leads to immediate changes in ion flux across the membrane, resulting in rapid cellular responses.

- **Direct Coupling**: The receptor and ion channel are part of the same protein complex, providing direct coupling between ligand binding and channel opening.
- **Selectivity**: These channels are selective for specific ions such as Na+, K+, Ca2+, or Cl-.

Examples:

- **Nicotinic Acetylcholine Receptor**: This receptor is activated by acetylcholine and allows the influx of Na+ ions, leading to depolarization and muscle contraction.
- **GABA_A Receptor**: Activated by gamma-aminobutyric acid (GABA), this receptor allows Cl- ions to enter the cell, resulting in hyperpolarization and inhibition of neuronal activity.

Metabotropic Receptors

Definition: Metabotropic receptors, also known as G-protein-coupled receptors (GPCRs), are receptors that activate intracellular signaling cascades through the interaction with G-proteins upon ligand binding. They do not form an ion channel themselves but modulate other cellular processes.

Characteristics:

- **Slower Response**: The activation of intracellular signaling pathways takes longer than the direct ion flow in ionotropic receptors, resulting in slower responses.
- **Amplification**: One ligand-receptor interaction can activate multiple G-proteins, leading to an amplified cellular response.
- **Diverse Effects**: GPCRs can activate various intracellular signaling pathways, leading to a wide range of cellular responses.

Examples:

- **Beta-Adrenergic Receptors**: Activated by epinephrine and norepinephrine, these receptors stimulate adenylate cyclase through Gs proteins, increasing cAMP levels and leading to increased heart rate and force of contraction.

- **Muscarinic Acetylcholine Receptors**: These receptors, when activated by acetylcholine, can activate phospholipase C through Gq proteins, resulting in the production of IP3 and DAG, and subsequent intracellular Ca2+ release.

Enzyme-Linked Receptors

Definition: Enzyme-linked receptors, also known as receptor tyrosine kinases (RTKs), are receptors that possess intrinsic enzymatic activity or are associated with enzymes. Ligand binding induces receptor dimerization and activation of their intrinsic kinase activity, leading to phosphorylation of tyrosine residues on the receptor and downstream signaling proteins.

Characteristics:

- **Intrinsic Enzymatic Activity**: These receptors often have an intrinsic tyrosine kinase activity that is activated upon ligand binding.
- **Dimerization**: Ligand binding typically induces receptor dimerization or oligomerization, which is necessary for activation.
- **Signal Transduction**: Phosphorylated tyrosine residues serve as docking sites for intracellular signaling proteins, initiating a cascade of downstream signaling events.

Examples:

- **Epidermal Growth Factor Receptor (EGFR)**: Binding of epidermal growth factor (EGF) to EGFR induces receptor dimerization and activation of its kinase activity, leading to cell proliferation and differentiation.
- **Insulin Receptor**: Insulin binding induces dimerization and autophosphorylation of the receptor, activating pathways that regulate glucose uptake and metabolism.

Intracellular Receptors

Definition: Intracellular receptors, also known as nuclear receptors, are located within the cell (either in the cytoplasm or nucleus) and typically bind to lipophilic ligands that can cross the cell membrane. Upon ligand binding, these receptors often act as transcription factors, directly influencing gene expression.

Characteristics:

- **Ligand Accessibility**: These receptors bind to lipophilic molecules that can diffuse through the cell membrane.
- **Gene Regulation**: Ligand-bound receptors translocate to the nucleus (if not already there) and bind to specific DNA sequences, regulating the transcription of target genes.
- **Long-Term Effects**: The effects mediated by intracellular receptors are generally slower in onset but longer-lasting due to changes in gene expression.

Examples:

- **Glucocorticoid Receptor**: Binds to glucocorticoids like cortisol, translocates to the nucleus, and regulates genes involved in metabolism, immune response, and stress responses.
- **Estrogen Receptor**: Activated by estrogen, it regulates the transcription of genes involved in reproductive function and secondary sexual characteristics.

Conclusion

The classification of receptors into ionotropic, metabotropic, enzyme-linked, and intracellular types provides a framework for understanding how drugs and endogenous ligands interact with cells to produce specific physiological responses. Each type of receptor has unique characteristics and mechanisms of action that influence drug design, therapeutic strategies, and our understanding of cellular signaling processes.

4.2 Signal Transduction Mechanisms

G-Protein–Coupled Receptors

Structure, Mechanism, and Examples

Structure

G-Protein–Coupled Receptors (GPCRs) are a large and diverse group of membrane receptors that play a crucial role in cell signaling. They share a common structural framework characterized by:

- **Seven Transmembrane Domains**: GPCRs span the cell membrane seven times, forming a serpentine structure with extracellular, transmembrane, and intracellular regions.
- **Extracellular N-Terminus**: This part of the receptor interacts with ligands such as hormones, neurotransmitters, and sensory stimuli.

- **Intracellular C-Terminus**: This region interacts with intracellular G-proteins to transmit the signal inside the cell.
- **G-Protein Binding Sites**: Located on the intracellular loops and the C-terminal tail, these sites are critical for coupling with G-proteins.

Mechanism

The activation of GPCRs involves a multi-step process:

1. **Ligand Binding**: The extracellular ligand binds to the GPCR, inducing a conformational change in the receptor.
2. **G-Protein Activation**: The conformational change in the GPCR allows it to interact with a nearby G-protein. G-proteins are heterotrimeric proteins composed of α, β, and γ subunits. In its inactive state, the G-protein is bound to GDP.
3. **GDP-GTP Exchange**: Upon interaction with the activated GPCR, the α subunit of the G-protein releases GDP and binds GTP, leading to the dissociation of the α subunit from the βγ dimer.
4. **Effector Interaction**: The GTP-bound α subunit and the βγ dimer can interact with various downstream effectors such as enzymes (e.g., adenylate cyclase, phospholipase C) and ion channels, triggering different signaling pathways.
5. **Signal Termination**: The intrinsic GTPase activity of the α subunit hydrolyzes GTP to GDP, inactivating the G-protein and allowing it to reassociate with the βγ dimer, ready for another cycle of activation.

Examples

Beta-Adrenergic Receptors:

- **Ligand**: Epinephrine and norepinephrine.
- **Pathway**: Activation of β1-adrenergic receptors in the heart increases cyclic AMP (cAMP) levels via activation of adenylate cyclase, leading to increased heart rate and force of contraction.
- **Clinical Relevance**: Beta-blockers like propranolol inhibit β-adrenergic receptors to manage hypertension and arrhythmias.

Muscarinic Acetylcholine Receptors (M2 subtype):

- **Ligand**: Acetylcholine.
- **Pathway**: Activation of M2 receptors in the heart leads to the inhibition of adenylate cyclase, reducing cAMP levels, and opening of K+ channels, resulting in decreased heart rate.
- **Clinical Relevance**: Drugs like atropine block muscarinic receptors to treat bradycardia and reduce secretions during surgery.

Rhodopsin:

- **Ligand**: Light (photon).
- **Pathway**: Rhodopsin, a GPCR in the retina, activates transducin (a G-protein), which activates phosphodiesterase, reducing cGMP levels and leading to the closure of cGMP-gated ion channels, ultimately resulting in hyperpolarization of photoreceptor cells.
- **Clinical Relevance**: Understanding rhodopsin signaling is crucial for developing treatments for visual disorders.

Opioid Receptors:

- **Ligand**: Endogenous opioids (e.g., endorphins) and exogenous opioids (e.g., morphine).
- **Pathway**: Activation of opioid receptors inhibits adenylate cyclase, reducing cAMP levels, and opens K+ channels while closing Ca2+ channels, leading to decreased neuronal excitability and pain perception.
- **Clinical Relevance**: Opioid analgesics like morphine are used for pain management, but they also have potential for addiction and abuse.

Clinical Relevance

Understanding GPCR structure and function is essential for drug development and therapeutic applications:

- **Drug Design**: Many drugs target GPCRs due to their pivotal role in numerous physiological processes. Agonists can mimic the action of natural ligands, while antagonists can block receptor activity.
- **Therapeutic Targets**: GPCRs are involved in various diseases, including cardiovascular diseases, respiratory disorders, and mental health conditions. Targeting GPCRs can modulate disease pathways and provide therapeutic benefits.

- **Side Effects:** Drugs targeting GPCRs can have off-target effects, leading to side effects. Knowledge of GPCR signaling pathways helps in designing more selective drugs with fewer adverse effects.

4.2 Signal Transduction Mechanisms

Ion Channel Receptors

Structure, Mechanism, and Examples

Structure

Ion Channel Receptors are a type of membrane protein that forms channels or pores in the cell membrane, allowing specific ions to flow in and out of the cell. They are integral to various physiological processes, including nerve signal transmission and muscle contraction. The key structural features of ion channel receptors include:

- **Transmembrane Domains:** These channels span the cell membrane and are composed of multiple subunits that come together to form a central pore. Each subunit has multiple transmembrane segments that create the channel.
- **Pore Region:** The central pore is the functional part of the ion channel that allows ions to pass through. The selectivity of the channel for specific ions is determined by the structure of this pore.
- **Extracellular and Intracellular Regions:** Ion channel receptors have extracellular and intracellular regions that are involved in channel gating and interaction with signaling molecules or ligands.
- **Gating Mechanisms:** The opening and closing of ion channels are regulated by various mechanisms, including ligand binding, voltage changes, or mechanical stress.

Mechanism

The mechanism of ion channel receptors involves several steps:

1. **Ligand Binding or Voltage Change:** Ion channels can be activated by various stimuli. For ligand-gated channels, a specific neurotransmitter or other signaling molecule binds to the extracellular domain of the receptor. For voltage-gated channels, a change in the membrane potential triggers the channel's opening.
2. **Channel Opening:** Upon activation, the channel undergoes a conformational change that opens the central pore, allowing specific

ions to flow through the membrane. The selectivity of the channel ensures that only certain types of ions can pass.

3. **Ion Flow**: The ions move across the membrane following their electrochemical gradient. This movement generates electrical signals or contributes to cellular responses, such as muscle contraction or neurotransmitter release.
4. **Channel Closure**: After a brief period of ion flow, the channel closes either through a conformational change or through inactivation mechanisms, stopping the flow of ions. This closure resets the channel to its inactive state, ready for the next activation cycle.

Examples

Nicotinic Acetylcholine Receptors (nAChRs):

- **Structure**: Composed of five subunits that form a central ion channel. The binding of acetylcholine to the receptor causes a conformational change, opening the channel.
- **Mechanism**: When acetylcholine binds to the receptor, it opens the channel, allowing Na+ ions to enter the cell, leading to depolarization of the postsynaptic membrane.
- **Clinical Relevance**: Agonists like nicotine activate nAChRs, while antagonists like curare block them. These receptors are crucial in neuromuscular junctions and are targets for treatments of conditions like myasthenia gravis.

Voltage-Gated Sodium Channels:

- **Structure**: Composed of a large α subunit that forms the pore and auxiliary β subunits that modulate channel activity. The α subunit contains multiple transmembrane domains that respond to changes in membrane potential.
- **Mechanism**: These channels open in response to depolarization of the cell membrane, allowing Na+ ions to enter the cell and propagate action potentials along nerves.
- **Clinical Relevance**: Sodium channel blockers like lidocaine are used as local anesthetics, while certain antiarrhythmic drugs target these channels to treat cardiac arrhythmias.

GABA_A Receptors:

- **Structure**: Comprised of five subunits forming a chloride ion channel. The binding of γ-aminobutyric acid (GABA) to the receptor opens the channel.
- **Mechanism**: GABA binding causes the channel to open, allowing Cl- ions to enter the neuron, leading to hyperpolarization and inhibition of neuronal firing.
- **Clinical Relevance**: Benzodiazepines and barbiturates act as positive allosteric modulators of GABA_A receptors, enhancing their inhibitory effect and are used to treat anxiety and epilepsy.

NMDA Receptors:

- **Structure**: A subtype of glutamate receptor with a channel that is permeable to Ca2+, Na+, and K+ ions. It is composed of multiple subunits (NR1, NR2, and sometimes NR3).
- **Mechanism**: Activation by glutamate and glycine leads to the opening of the channel, allowing Ca2+ and Na+ to enter the cell, which is crucial for synaptic plasticity and memory formation.
- **Clinical Relevance**: NMDA receptor antagonists like ketamine are used as anesthetics and have been explored for treating depression due to their effects on synaptic plasticity.

Clinical Relevance

Understanding the structure and mechanism of ion channel receptors is vital for drug development and therapeutic applications:

- **Drug Design**: Targeting ion channels can modulate cellular excitability and neurotransmission. For example, channel blockers or activators can be used to treat neurological disorders, cardiac arrhythmias, and muscle diseases.
- **Therapeutic Targets**: Ion channels are involved in a wide range of diseases, making them important targets for drug interventions. Specific drugs can be designed to selectively interact with these channels to provide therapeutic benefits with minimal side effects.
- **Side Effects**: The non-selective action of some ion channel drugs can lead to unwanted side effects. Detailed knowledge of channel structure

and function helps in developing more selective and safer therapies.

4.2 Signal Transduction Mechanisms

Transmembrane Enzyme-Linked Receptors

Structure, Mechanism, and Examples

Structure

Transmembrane Enzyme-Linked Receptors are a type of cell surface receptor that functions as both a receptor and an enzyme. These receptors span the cell membrane and are characterized by their ability to catalyze biochemical reactions within the cell upon activation. The key structural features include:

- **Extracellular Domain**: This domain is located outside the cell and is responsible for binding to specific ligands, such as hormones or growth factors. It often contains ligand-binding sites that are crucial for receptor activation.
- **Transmembrane Domain**: This segment spans the cell membrane and anchors the receptor in place. It typically consists of one or more hydrophobic regions that traverse the lipid bilayer.
- **Intracellular Domain**: Located inside the cell, this domain has intrinsic enzymatic activity or is linked to intracellular signaling cascades. It is responsible for initiating downstream signaling pathways upon receptor activation.

Mechanism

The mechanism of action for transmembrane enzyme-linked receptors involves several key steps:

1. **Ligand Binding**: The process begins when a ligand, such as a growth factor or hormone, binds to the extracellular domain of the receptor. This binding induces a conformational change in the receptor.
2. **Receptor Dimerization or Oligomerization**: In many cases, ligand binding causes two or more receptor molecules to come together (dimerize or oligomerize), which is often necessary for receptor activation.
3. **Autophosphorylation or Activation**: Upon dimerization, the intracellular domain of the receptor becomes activated. Many transmembrane enzyme-linked receptors have intrinsic kinase activity,

meaning they can add phosphate groups to themselves or to other proteins. This process is called autophosphorylation.

4. **Downstream Signaling**: The phosphorylation events activate various intracellular signaling pathways by recruiting and activating other signaling proteins. These pathways can lead to changes in gene expression, enzyme activity, or cellular metabolism.
5. **Cellular Response**: The ultimate outcome of receptor activation includes alterations in cellular processes such as growth, differentiation, or metabolism.

Examples

1. Receptor Tyrosine Kinases (RTKs):

- **Structure**: RTKs have an extracellular ligand-binding domain, a single transmembrane helix, and an intracellular kinase domain that adds phosphate groups to tyrosine residues on proteins.
- **Mechanism**: Ligand binding leads to receptor dimerization and autophosphorylation of tyrosine residues. This activates downstream signaling pathways involving proteins like Ras, MAPK, and PI3K.
- **Examples**:
  - **Epidermal Growth Factor Receptor (EGFR)**: Involved in cell growth and differentiation. Mutations or overexpression are associated with cancers.
  - **Insulin Receptor**: Regulates glucose uptake and metabolism. Its dysfunction is linked to diabetes.

2. Receptor Serine/Threonine Kinases:

- **Structure**: These receptors have an extracellular ligand-binding domain and an intracellular kinase domain that phosphorylates serine and threonine residues.
- **Mechanism**: Ligand binding induces receptor dimerization and activation of the serine/threonine kinase domain, leading to phosphorylation of downstream signaling proteins.
- **Examples**:

- **Transforming Growth Factor-beta (TGF-β) Receptors**: Involved in regulating cell growth and differentiation. Abnormalities are associated with fibrosis and cancer.
- **Bone Morphogenetic Protein (BMP) Receptors**: Important for bone development and repair.

3. Receptor Guanylate Cyclases:

- **Structure**: These receptors have an extracellular domain for ligand binding and an intracellular guanylate cyclase domain that synthesizes cyclic GMP (cGMP).
- **Mechanism**: Ligand binding activates the guanylate cyclase activity, increasing intracellular cGMP levels, which then modulates various signaling pathways.
- **Examples**:
    - **Atrial Natriuretic Peptide (ANP) Receptor**: Regulates blood pressure and fluid balance. Dysfunction is linked to cardiovascular diseases.

Clinical Relevance

Understanding the structure and mechanism of transmembrane enzyme-linked receptors is crucial for several reasons:

- **Drug Development**: These receptors are key targets for drug development due to their roles in numerous physiological and pathological processes. Drugs can be designed to either activate or inhibit these receptors to treat various conditions.
- **Therapeutic Targets**: Many diseases, including cancers, cardiovascular disorders, and metabolic diseases, involve aberrant signaling through these receptors. Targeted therapies can specifically address these issues by modulating receptor activity.
- **Side Effects**: Since these receptors are involved in fundamental cellular processes, drugs affecting them can have significant side effects. Detailed knowledge helps in designing selective drugs with minimized adverse effects.

4.2 Signal Transduction Mechanisms

JAK-STAT Binding Receptors
Structure, Mechanism, and Examples
Structure

JAK-STAT Binding Receptors are a class of cell surface receptors that play a crucial role in mediating cellular responses to a variety of extracellular signals, including cytokines and growth factors. They are characterized by the following structural features:

- **Extracellular Domain**: This part of the receptor is exposed to the extracellular environment and is responsible for binding specific ligands, such as cytokines. The extracellular domain often consists of multiple domains or motifs that recognize and interact with ligands.
- **Transmembrane Domain**: The transmembrane domain anchors the receptor in the cell membrane and connects the extracellular domain with the intracellular signaling machinery. It typically consists of a hydrophobic region that spans the lipid bilayer.
- **Intracellular Domain**: This region is crucial for signal transduction and interacts with Janus Kinases (JAKs). The intracellular domain lacks intrinsic enzymatic activity but recruits JAKs to initiate signaling pathways.

Mechanism

The **JAK-STAT** signaling pathway is a critical mechanism for transmitting signals from extracellular ligands to the cell's interior. The process involves several steps:

1. **Ligand Binding**: The pathway begins when a ligand, such as a cytokine, binds to the extracellular domain of the JAK-STAT receptor. This binding induces a conformational change in the receptor and brings together two or more receptor molecules.
2. **Receptor Dimerization**: Ligand binding often results in the dimerization or oligomerization of the receptor. This structural change is essential for the activation of associated JAKs.
3. **Activation of JAKs**: Janus Kinases (JAKs) are intracellular tyrosine kinases that are non-covalently associated with the cytoplasmic domain of the receptor. Upon receptor dimerization, JAKs are activated through autophosphorylation, which means they add phosphate groups to themselves.

4. **Phosphorylation of Receptor Tyrosines**: Activated JAKs phosphorylate tyrosine residues on the intracellular domain of the receptor. This phosphorylation creates docking sites for Signal Transducers and Activators of Transcription (STAT) proteins.
5. **Recruitment and Phosphorylation of STATs**: STAT proteins bind to the phosphorylated tyrosines on the receptor. JAKs then phosphorylate the STAT proteins on specific tyrosine residues, which causes them to dissociate from the receptor.
6. **Translocation to the Nucleus**: Phosphorylated STATs form dimers or higher-order oligomers and translocate to the nucleus. Once inside the nucleus, they act as transcription factors to regulate the expression of target genes.
7. **Gene Expression**: The nuclear STAT dimers bind to specific DNA sequences in the promoter regions of target genes, leading to the transcription of genes involved in various cellular processes such as growth, differentiation, and immune responses.
8. **Signal Termination**: The signaling pathway is terminated by dephosphorylation of STATs and JAKs, and by the action of protein inhibitors.

Examples

1. Interferon Receptors:

- **Structure**: These receptors bind to interferons, which are signaling proteins released by cells in response to viral infections.
- **Mechanism**: Upon interferon binding, the JAK-STAT pathway is activated, leading to the expression of antiviral genes. STAT1 and STAT2 are often involved in this process.
- **Clinical Relevance**: Defects in this pathway can lead to immune deficiencies or increased susceptibility to infections.

2. Erythropoietin Receptor:

- **Structure**: This receptor binds erythropoietin, a hormone that stimulates red blood cell production.
- **Mechanism**: Binding of erythropoietin leads to activation of JAK2, which phosphorylates and activates STAT5. Activated STAT5 then promotes the expression of genes involved in erythrocyte production.

- **Clinical Relevance**: Mutations in the erythropoietin receptor or JAK2 can cause disorders like polycythemia vera.

3. Growth Hormone Receptor:

- **Structure**: The receptor binds growth hormone and is involved in growth regulation.
- **Mechanism**: Growth hormone binding activates JAK2, which phosphorylates STAT5. Phosphorylated STAT5 then regulates genes associated with growth and metabolism.
- **Clinical Relevance**: Disruptions in this pathway can lead to growth disorders such as dwarfism or gigantism.

4. Prolactin Receptor:

- **Structure**: Binds prolactin, a hormone involved in lactation and reproductive health.
- **Mechanism**: Prolactin binding activates JAK2, leading to the phosphorylation of STAT5. Activated STAT5 regulates genes involved in lactation and reproductive functions.
- **Clinical Relevance**: Abnormalities can lead to hyperprolactinemia, affecting reproductive health and lactation.

Clinical Relevance

Understanding the JAK-STAT pathway is essential for several reasons:

- **Target for Therapies**: The JAK-STAT pathway is targeted by various therapeutic agents, including JAK inhibitors, which are used to treat autoimmune diseases and certain cancers.
- **Disease Associations**: Dysregulation of this pathway is associated with numerous diseases, including cancers, autoimmune disorders, and inflammatory conditions.
- **Biomarkers**: Components of the JAK-STAT pathway can serve as biomarkers for disease diagnosis and prognosis, as well as for monitoring the effectiveness of treatments.

4.2 Signal Transduction Mechanisms

Transcription Factor-Regulating Receptors

Structure, Mechanism, and Examples

Structure

Transcription Factor-Regulating Receptors are a distinct class of cell surface receptors involved in mediating cellular responses by directly influencing gene expression. These receptors are characterized by their ability to regulate transcription factors, which are proteins that control the transcription of specific genes. Key structural features include:

- **Extracellular Domain**: This region of the receptor is responsible for binding to specific ligands such as hormones or growth factors. It often consists of ligand-binding domains that recognize and bind to the extracellular signaling molecules.
- **Transmembrane Domain**: The transmembrane domain spans the lipid bilayer of the cell membrane, anchoring the receptor in place and facilitating communication between the extracellular and intracellular environments.
- **Intracellular Domain**: This region interacts with intracellular signaling pathways and transcription factors. It typically contains domains that can be phosphorylated or otherwise modified to activate or inhibit transcription factors.

Mechanism

The mechanism of action for transcription factor-regulating receptors involves several key steps:

1. **Ligand Binding**: The process begins when a ligand (e.g., a hormone or growth factor) binds to the extracellular domain of the receptor. This interaction causes a conformational change in the receptor.
2. **Receptor Activation**: The conformational change in the receptor is transmitted through the transmembrane domain to the intracellular domain. This activation often involves phosphorylation or other post-translational modifications.
3. **Recruitment of Transcription Factors**: The activated intracellular domain recruits specific transcription factors to the receptor. These transcription factors may be present in the cytoplasm or become activated as a result of receptor binding.
4. **Transcription Factor Activation**: Upon recruitment, transcription factors are often phosphorylated or otherwise modified, which activates

their DNA-binding ability.

5. **Nuclear Translocation**: Activated transcription factors translocate to the nucleus, where they bind to specific DNA sequences in the promoter regions of target genes.
6. **Gene Transcription**: The binding of transcription factors to DNA promotes or inhibits the transcription of target genes, leading to changes in gene expression and subsequent cellular responses.
7. **Signal Termination**: The signaling pathway is terminated by deactivation or degradation of the transcription factors, or by the removal of the ligand from the receptor.

Examples

1. Steroid Hormone Receptors

- **Structure**: These receptors are intracellular and include the steroid hormone receptor domains: ligand-binding, DNA-binding, and transactivation domains.
- **Mechanism**: Steroid hormones (e.g., cortisol, estrogen) diffuse through the cell membrane and bind to intracellular receptors. The receptor-ligand complex then translocates to the nucleus, binds to specific DNA sequences (hormone response elements), and regulates the transcription of target genes.
- **Examples**: Estrogen receptors (ERs), glucocorticoid receptors (GRs).
- **Clinical Relevance**: Dysregulation of steroid hormone receptors is associated with diseases such as hormone-dependent cancers (e.g., breast cancer, prostate cancer) and inflammatory conditions.

2. Thyroid Hormone Receptors

- **Structure**: These receptors are located in the nucleus and consist of DNA-binding domains and ligand-binding domains.
- **Mechanism**: Thyroid hormones (e.g., thyroxine, triiodothyronine) bind to thyroid hormone receptors in the nucleus. The receptor-ligand complex then interacts with specific thyroid hormone response elements on DNA, modulating gene expression.
- **Examples**: Thyroid hormone receptor alpha (TRα), thyroid hormone receptor beta (TRβ).

- **Clinical Relevance**: Alterations in thyroid hormone receptors can lead to thyroid disorders such as hypothyroidism or hyperthyroidism.

3. Retinoic Acid Receptors

- **Structure**: These receptors are nuclear receptors that include ligand-binding and DNA-binding domains.
- **Mechanism**: Retinoic acid (a metabolite of vitamin A) binds to retinoic acid receptors in the nucleus. The receptor-ligand complex regulates gene transcription by interacting with retinoic acid response elements in target gene promoters.
- **Examples**: Retinoic acid receptor alpha (RARA), retinoic acid receptor beta (RARB).
- **Clinical Relevance**: Retinoic acid receptors play a role in cell differentiation and development. Mutations can contribute to conditions like acute promyelocytic leukemia (APL).

4. Peroxisome Proliferator-Activated Receptors (PPARs)

- **Structure**: These are nuclear receptors with ligand-binding and DNA-binding domains.
- **Mechanism**: PPARs bind to fatty acids and other ligands. Upon activation, they form heterodimers with retinoid X receptors (RXRs) and bind to PPAR response elements in the DNA, regulating genes involved in metabolism and inflammation.
- **Examples**: PPAR-alpha (PPARα), PPAR-gamma (PPARγ).
- **Clinical Relevance**: PPARs are involved in regulating lipid metabolism and insulin sensitivity. They are targets for drugs used to treat diabetes and dyslipidemia.

Clinical Relevance

Understanding transcription factor-regulating receptors is crucial due to their central role in gene regulation and their involvement in various physiological processes. Abnormalities in these receptors or their pathways can lead to a range of diseases, including cancers, metabolic disorders, and endocrine diseases. Targeting these receptors with specific drugs can offer therapeutic benefits, making them important in both basic and clinical research.

4.3 Dose-Response Relationship

Therapeutic Index

Definition, Significance, and Calculation

Definition

The **therapeutic index (TI)** is a measure of a drug's safety and efficacy. It is defined as the ratio between the dose of a drug that produces a therapeutic effect and the dose that causes toxicity. Essentially, the TI helps to determine the relative safety of a drug by comparing the effective dose (ED) to the toxic dose (TD). A higher therapeutic index indicates a larger margin between effective and toxic doses, suggesting that the drug is safer to use. Conversely, a lower TI implies a narrower margin of safety and a higher risk of adverse effects.

Significance

The therapeutic index is a crucial parameter in pharmacology for several reasons:

1. **Safety Assessment**: The TI provides an estimate of the safety of a drug. A high TI means that there is a substantial difference between the effective dose and the toxic dose, reducing the likelihood of adverse effects when the drug is used as prescribed. Drugs with a low TI require careful monitoring and dosing adjustments to avoid toxicity.
2. **Dosing Guidelines**: The TI aids in establishing appropriate dosing regimens. Drugs with a high TI can be administered with greater flexibility, whereas those with a low TI require precise dosing and regular monitoring to ensure that the drug remains within the therapeutic range.
3. **Drug Comparison**: The TI allows for the comparison of the safety profiles of different drugs. Drugs with higher TIs are generally preferred for their lower risk of causing adverse effects, whereas drugs with lower TIs may be used only when necessary and with close supervision.
4. **Clinical Decision-Making**: In clinical practice, the TI informs decisions about drug selection, dosing strategies, and monitoring protocols. It is especially important for drugs used in chronic conditions or those with a high potential for adverse effects.

Calculation

The therapeutic index can be calculated using the following formula:

Therapeutic Index$_0$ (TI)= TD_{50}/ ED_{50}

Where:

- **TD_5^0** is the dose at which 50% of the population experiences a toxic effect.
- **ED_5^0** is the dose at which 50% of the population experiences the desired therapeutic effect.

Example Calculation

Consider a hypothetical drug with the following values:

- **ED_5^0** = 50 mg
- **TD_5^0** = 200 mg

Using the formula:

$TI = TD_{50} / ED_{50}$

200 mg/50 mg =4

This result indicates that the therapeutic index of the drug is 4, meaning that the toxic dose is four times higher than the effective dose.

Practical Implications

- **High TI**: Drugs such as **acetaminophen** have a relatively high TI, meaning they are generally safe when used at recommended doses. However, even these drugs can be dangerous if overdosed, as the difference between therapeutic and toxic doses can still be significant.
- **Low TI**: Drugs such as **warfarin** (an anticoagulant) have a low TI. This means careful monitoring of blood levels is necessary to avoid complications such as bleeding, which can occur if the drug level exceeds the therapeutic range.

4.3 Dose-Response Relationship

Combined Effects of Drugs

Synergism, Antagonism, and Potentiation

Synergism

Definition and Mechanism

Synergism refers to a situation where the combined effect of two drugs is greater than the sum of their individual effects. This means that when two drugs are administered together, their combined effect is more significant than what would be expected if each drug's effect were simply added together.

Example

An example of **synergism** is the combination of **aspirin** and **clopidogrel** in the treatment of cardiovascular diseases. Aspirin inhibits platelet aggregation by blocking **cyclooxygenase-1 (COX-1)**, while clopidogrel inhibits **ADP-mediated platelet aggregation**. When used together, these drugs have a greater effect on preventing blood clots compared to each drug used alone, enhancing their therapeutic efficacy.

Clinical Implications

- **Enhanced Therapeutic Effects**: Synergistic combinations are often used to maximize therapeutic outcomes. For instance, combining drugs with different mechanisms of action can achieve better disease control than using a single drug.
- **Reduced Dosage**: Synergism allows for lower doses of each drug, potentially reducing the risk of side effects while maintaining effectiveness.

Antagonism

Definition and Mechanism

Antagonism occurs when one drug counteracts or diminishes the effect of another drug. This can happen when one drug inhibits the action of another by binding to the same receptor or by opposing the physiological effects of the other drug.

Example

An example of **antagonism** is the use of **naloxone** to counteract opioid overdose. Naloxone is an opioid antagonist that binds to opioid receptors, blocking the effects of opioid agonists like **morphine** or **heroin**. This action reverses the respiratory depression caused by opioid overdose, thereby saving lives.

Clinical Implications

- **Therapeutic Use**: Antagonistic drug interactions are employed to reverse the effects of toxic or unintended drug effects. For example, antagonists are used in emergency situations to negate the effects of overdoses.
- **Potential Drug Interactions**: It is crucial to be aware of potential antagonistic interactions between drugs, as they can lead to reduced

therapeutic efficacy and unintended outcomes.

Potentiation

Definition and Mechanism

Potentiation refers to the increase in the effect of one drug due to the presence of another drug. Unlike synergism, where the combined effect is greater than the sum, potentiation involves one drug enhancing the effect of another drug without necessarily having an effect on its own.

Example

An example of **potentiation** is the combination of **levodopa** and **carbidopa** in the treatment of **Parkinson's disease**. Levodopa is converted to dopamine in the brain, while carbidopa inhibits the peripheral metabolism of levodopa, thereby increasing the amount of levodopa available to cross the blood-brain barrier. Carbidopa does not have an effect on its own but significantly enhances the effectiveness of levodopa.

Clinical Implications

- **Improved Efficacy**: Potentiation can lead to enhanced therapeutic outcomes with drugs that have limited effects when used alone.
- **Dosing Considerations**: Potentiation may allow for reduced doses of the primary drug, potentially minimizing side effects and improving patient compliance.

4.4 Factors Modifying Drug Action

Physiological Factors

Age, Gender, Body Weight, and Genetic Factors

Age

Definition and Impact

Age significantly influences drug action and metabolism. The body's response to drugs can vary markedly across different life stages—infancy, childhood, adulthood, and old age.

Infants and Children: In young children, drug absorption, distribution, metabolism, and excretion may differ from adults due to their developing organ systems. For instance, **renal function** in newborns is less efficient, which can lead to altered drug clearance rates and necessitate dosage adjustments.

Elderly: In older adults, physiological changes such as decreased liver and kidney function, reduced blood flow, and changes in body composition can affect drug metabolism and excretion. This can increase the risk of **adverse drug reactions** and **drug interactions**, requiring careful dosing and monitoring.

Clinical Implications

- **Dose Adjustments**: Dosage and frequency adjustments are often needed based on age to ensure effective and safe drug therapy.
- **Monitoring**: Regular monitoring for drug effectiveness and side effects is crucial, especially in elderly patients who may experience slower drug clearance and increased sensitivity to medications.

Gender

Definition and Impact

Gender differences can also influence drug action. Variations in **hormone levels**, body composition, and enzymatic activity between males and females can affect drug metabolism.

Hormonal Differences: For example, **estrogen** and **progesterone** can influence the metabolism of certain drugs, such as **antidepressants** and **anticonvulsants**.

Body Composition: Females generally have a higher body fat percentage compared to males, which can affect the volume of distribution for lipophilic drugs.

Clinical Implications

- **Pharmacokinetic Variations**: Gender-specific differences in drug metabolism may require adjustments in dosing or the choice of medication.
- **Gender-Based Research**: Ensuring that clinical trials include both genders helps to understand these differences and optimize drug therapy for all patients.

Body Weight

Definition and Impact

Body weight is a crucial factor influencing drug dosage and action. The distribution and metabolism of drugs can vary with changes in body mass, particularly in obese or underweight individuals.

Obesity: In obese patients, drugs that are lipophilic may have an increased volume of distribution, which could necessitate dose adjustments to achieve therapeutic levels.

Underweight: Conversely, individuals with low body weight may require lower doses due to a reduced volume of distribution and potentially increased drug concentrations.

Clinical Implications

- **Dose Calculation**: Dosing may need to be adjusted based on body weight to ensure efficacy and minimize side effects.
- **Monitoring**: Patients with significant changes in body weight should be monitored closely to adjust doses as needed.

Genetic Factors

Definition and Impact

Genetic variations can significantly impact drug metabolism, efficacy, and risk of adverse reactions. This field of study is known as **pharmacogenomics.**

Enzyme Variants: Genetic polymorphisms in drug-metabolizing enzymes, such as **cytochrome P450 enzymes**, can alter the metabolism of drugs. For example, individuals with certain genetic variants may metabolize drugs faster or slower, affecting drug levels and therapeutic outcomes.

Genetic Disorders: Specific genetic disorders can also influence drug action. For example, patients with **glucose-6-phosphate dehydrogenase (G6PD) deficiency** may experience hemolysis when exposed to certain drugs like **sulfonamides.**

Clinical Implications

- **Personalized Medicine**: Genetic testing can guide the selection and dosing of medications, improving therapeutic outcomes and reducing adverse effects.
- **Adverse Reactions**: Awareness of genetic factors can help predict and manage potential drug reactions, leading to more personalized and effective treatment plans.

Summary

Age, gender, body weight, and **genetic factors** are critical physiological aspects that modify drug action. Understanding these factors is essential for optimizing drug therapy and achieving the desired therapeutic outcomes while minimizing the risk of adverse effects. Adjustments in drug dosage and careful monitoring based on these physiological variables ensure safe and effective treatment across diverse patient populations.

4.4 Factors Modifying Drug Action

Pathological Factors

Disease States, Organ Function, and Concurrent Medications

Disease States

Definition and Impact

Various disease states can profoundly affect how drugs are absorbed, metabolized, distributed, and excreted in the body. Diseases can alter physiological functions and biochemical pathways, thus impacting drug efficacy and safety.

Chronic Diseases: Conditions like **diabetes**, **hypertension**, and **chronic renal disease** can affect drug metabolism and require adjustments in therapy. For instance, **diabetic patients** may experience altered glucose metabolism due to drug interactions, while **hypertensive individuals** may require modified dosing of antihypertensive medications to manage blood pressure effectively.

Infectious Diseases: **Infections** and **inflammatory conditions** can influence drug pharmacokinetics. For example, **sepsis** can alter blood flow and organ function, impacting drug distribution and clearance.

Clinical Implications

- **Drug-Disease Interactions**: The presence of a disease may necessitate changes in drug choice or dosage. For instance, drugs that are primarily metabolized by the liver may need to be adjusted in patients with **liver disease**.
- **Monitoring and Adjustment**: Regular monitoring is crucial to assess the impact of disease states on drug therapy and adjust treatment as needed to maintain efficacy and safety.

Organ Function

Definition and Impact

The function of various organs, particularly the **liver** and **kidneys**, plays a critical role in drug metabolism and excretion. Impairment in organ function can lead to altered drug levels and increased risk of toxicity.

Liver Function: The liver is responsible for the biotransformation of many drugs. **Liver diseases** such as **cirrhosis** or **hepatitis** can impair drug metabolism, leading to increased drug concentrations and potential toxicity.

Renal Function: The kidneys are vital for the excretion of many drugs and their metabolites. **Renal impairment** or **chronic kidney disease** can reduce drug clearance, necessitating dose adjustments to prevent accumulation and toxicity.

Clinical Implications

- **Dosing Adjustments**: Drugs that are extensively metabolized by the liver or excreted by the kidneys often require dose adjustments in patients with compromised organ function.
- **Safety Monitoring**: Monitoring organ function through laboratory tests (e.g., liver function tests, serum creatinine) helps ensure safe and effective drug therapy.

Concurrent Medications

Definition and Impact

The use of multiple medications, or **polypharmacy**, can lead to drug interactions that modify the effectiveness and safety of therapy. Concurrent medications can affect drug absorption, metabolism, and excretion.

Drug Interactions: **Pharmacokinetic interactions** can occur when one drug alters the absorption, metabolism, or excretion of another. For example, some drugs may induce or inhibit **cytochrome P450 enzymes**, impacting the metabolism of co-administered drugs.

Additive or Synergistic Effects: Certain drug combinations can lead to enhanced effects (synergism) or increased risk of adverse reactions (additive effects). For instance, combining **anticoagulants** with **NSAIDs** can increase the risk of bleeding.

Clinical Implications

- **Interaction Monitoring**: Healthcare providers should review patients' medication lists to identify potential interactions and adjust therapy accordingly.
- **Patient Education**: Educating patients about potential interactions and the importance of informing healthcare providers about all medications, including over-the-counter drugs and supplements, is crucial for preventing adverse effects.

Table 4.1: **Types of Receptors**

Type	Description	Exa
Ionotropic	Ligand-gated ion channels	Nic
Metabotropic	G-protein coupled receptors	Mu

Table 4.2: **Signal Transduction Mechanisms**

Mechanism	Description
G-Protein-Coupled Receptors	Activation of second messeng
Ion Channel Receptors	Direct ion flow into cells

Table 4.3: **Dose-Response Relationships**

Term	Description
Therapeutic Index	Ratio of toxic dose to therapeutic dose
Potency	Amount of drug needed for a desired effect

Table 4.4: **Classification of Receptors**

Class	Description
Enzyme-linked Receptors	Receptors that activate enzymes
Intracellular Receptors	Receptors within the cell

Table 4.5: **Combined Effects of Drugs**

Effect	Description
Synergism	Combined effect greater than the sum of individual eff
Antagonism	One drug reduces or blocks the effect of another

Table 4.6: **Factors Modifying Drug Action**

Factor	Description
Age	Elderly may have decreased metabolism
Gender	Hormonal differences can affect drug action

Lock and Key Model for Interaction between Drug and Receptor

CHAPTER V

Adverse Drug Reactions and Drug Interactions

Adverse Drug Reactions (**ADRs**) are unexpected and harmful responses that occur when medications are taken under normal conditions. These reactions can vary greatly in severity and manifestation, ranging from mild side effects such as **nausea and headaches** to more severe and life-threatening conditions like **anaphylaxis, organ failure, or even death**. The significance of ADRs lies in their impact on patient safety and healthcare costs, as they are a leading cause of morbidity and mortality worldwide. It is estimated that ADRs account for up to **5% of all hospital admissions** and can occur in **10% to 20% of hospitalized patients**, making them a critical area of concern for healthcare professionals, patients, and pharmaceutical companies alike.

5.1 Types of Adverse Drug Reactions

ADRs are broadly classified into two main types: **Type A (Augmented) Reactions** and **Type B (Bizarre) Reactions.**

- **Type A Reactions** are **predictable and dose-dependent**. These reactions are often an extension of the drug's pharmacological action. For instance, the blood-thinning effect of warfarin can lead to bleeding, which is an expected reaction if the dose is too high. Since these reactions are predictable, they can often be managed by adjusting the dosage or switching to an alternative medication. Type A reactions account for approximately **80% of all ADRs.**
- **Type B Reactions** are **unpredictable and not dose-dependent**. These reactions are often related to the patient's unique genetic makeup or an immune response. Examples include an allergic reaction to penicillin or a rash caused by carbamazepine. Since Type B reactions are unpredictable, they are generally more serious and can be life-threatening, necessitating immediate discontinuation of the drug.

Other Classifications of Adverse Drug Reactions

In addition to the primary classification of **Type A** and **Type B** reactions, **ADRs** can be further categorized based on their specific characteristics and the context in which they occur. These include **Type C (Chronic)**

Reactions, Type D (Delayed) Reactions, Type E (End-of-use) Reactions, and **Type F (Failure of therapy) Reactions.**

- **Type C (Chronic) Reactions** are those that occur as a result of long-term medication use. These reactions are typically dose-related and manifest over extended periods. For instance, the prolonged use of corticosteroids can lead to conditions such as **osteoporosis**, **cataracts**, or **adrenal suppression.** Managing Type C reactions often requires regular monitoring of the patient's condition and adjusting the medication regimen to minimize harm.
- **Type D (Delayed) Reactions** are those that appear after a long time following exposure to a medication. They may occur weeks, months, or even years after the initial drug administration. A well-known example is the teratogenic effects of **thalidomide**, which were not evident until after exposure during pregnancy. Another example is the increased risk of cancer associated with certain chemotherapy drugs, which may manifest years later.
- **Type E (End-of-use) Reactions** occur when a medication is abruptly discontinued. These reactions are also known as withdrawal reactions. For example, stopping **beta-blockers** suddenly can lead to a rebound effect, causing elevated heart rate and blood pressure. **Benzodiazepines** are another class of drugs known for causing withdrawal symptoms, such as anxiety and insomnia, if stopped suddenly. Gradual tapering of the medication dose is often required to mitigate these effects.
- **Type F (Failure of Therapy) Reactions** represent the failure of a drug to produce the desired therapeutic effect. This can occur due to drug interactions, improper dosage, or individual patient factors such as genetic differences affecting drug metabolism. An example of this is the failure of certain **antibiotics** to treat infections due to bacterial resistance.

5.2 Mechanisms of Adverse Drug Reactions

The mechanisms underlying **ADRs** can be complex and multifaceted, involving pharmacokinetic and pharmacodynamic interactions, as well as immune-mediated responses.

Pharmacokinetic Interactions refer to changes in the absorption, distribution, metabolism, or excretion of a drug, leading to altered drug concentrations in the body. For instance, the concomitant use of drugs that induce liver enzymes, such as **rifampicin**, can accelerate the metabolism of other drugs, reducing their efficacy. Conversely, drugs that inhibit liver enzymes, like **ketoconazole**, can lead to increased concentrations and potential toxicity of other medications.

Pharmacodynamic Interactions occur when two or more drugs interact at the same receptor site or influence the same physiological pathway, potentially leading to additive, synergistic, or antagonistic effects. For example, the concurrent use of **warfarin** and **aspirin** can increase the risk of bleeding due to their additive anticoagulant effects.

Immune-mediated Responses are often unpredictable and can lead to allergic reactions, ranging from mild skin rashes to severe anaphylaxis. These reactions are typically caused by the formation of drug-protein complexes that trigger an immune response. Penicillin and sulfa drugs are common culprits in drug allergies.

5.3 Risk Factors for Adverse Drug Reactions

Several factors can increase the risk of **ADRs** in patients, including **age, gender, genetics, existing medical conditions, and polypharmacy**.

- **Age**: Both very young and older adults are more susceptible to ADRs. In children, immature organ systems can affect drug metabolism and elimination, while in older adults, age-related changes in liver and kidney function can lead to altered drug handling.
- **Gender**: Some studies suggest that women are more prone to certain ADRs than men, possibly due to differences in body composition, hormone levels, and metabolic enzyme activity.
- **Genetics**: Genetic polymorphisms can affect drug metabolism and response. For example, variations in the **CYP450** enzyme system can lead to differences in how individuals metabolize drugs, influencing both efficacy and the likelihood of adverse effects.
- **Existing Medical Conditions**: Patients with certain medical conditions, such as **liver or kidney disease**, may have altered drug metabolism or excretion, increasing the risk of toxicity.
- **Polypharmacy**: The use of multiple medications, common in patients with chronic diseases, can increase the risk of drug interactions and ADRs.

5.4 Identification and Reporting of Adverse Drug Reactions

The identification and reporting of **ADRs** are crucial for patient safety and the ongoing evaluation of drug safety profiles. Healthcare professionals play a vital role in detecting ADRs and reporting them to regulatory authorities and pharmacovigilance centers.

Spontaneous Reporting Systems allow healthcare providers and patients to report suspected ADRs to national regulatory agencies, such as the **Pharmacovigilance Programme of India (PvPI)** or the **US Food and Drug Administration (FDA)**. These reports contribute to post-marketing surveillance and help identify new safety concerns that may not have been evident during clinical trials.

Electronic Health Records (EHRs) and **Data Mining Techniques** are increasingly being used to identify potential ADRs through the analysis of large datasets. These technologies can help detect patterns and correlations that may indicate previously unrecognized ADRs.

5.4 Prevention and Management of Adverse Drug Reactions

Preventing and managing **ADRs** requires a multi-faceted approach, including careful drug selection, dose adjustment, patient education, and ongoing monitoring.

Careful Drug Selection involves choosing medications with a favorable safety profile and considering patient-specific factors, such as age, gender, genetics, and co-existing conditions, to minimize the risk of ADRs.

Dose Adjustment is often necessary to account for individual variability in drug metabolism and response. For instance, patients with liver or kidney impairment may require lower doses to prevent accumulation and toxicity.

Patient Education is crucial in preventing ADRs. Educating patients about the potential side effects of their medications, the importance of adhering to prescribed doses, and recognizing early signs of ADRs can empower them to take an active role in their healthcare.

Ongoing Monitoring through regular follow-up appointments and laboratory tests can help detect ADRs early and allow for timely intervention. Monitoring is especially important for drugs with narrow therapeutic indices, such as **digoxin** or **lithium**.

CHAPTER VI

Drug Discovery and Clinical Evaluation

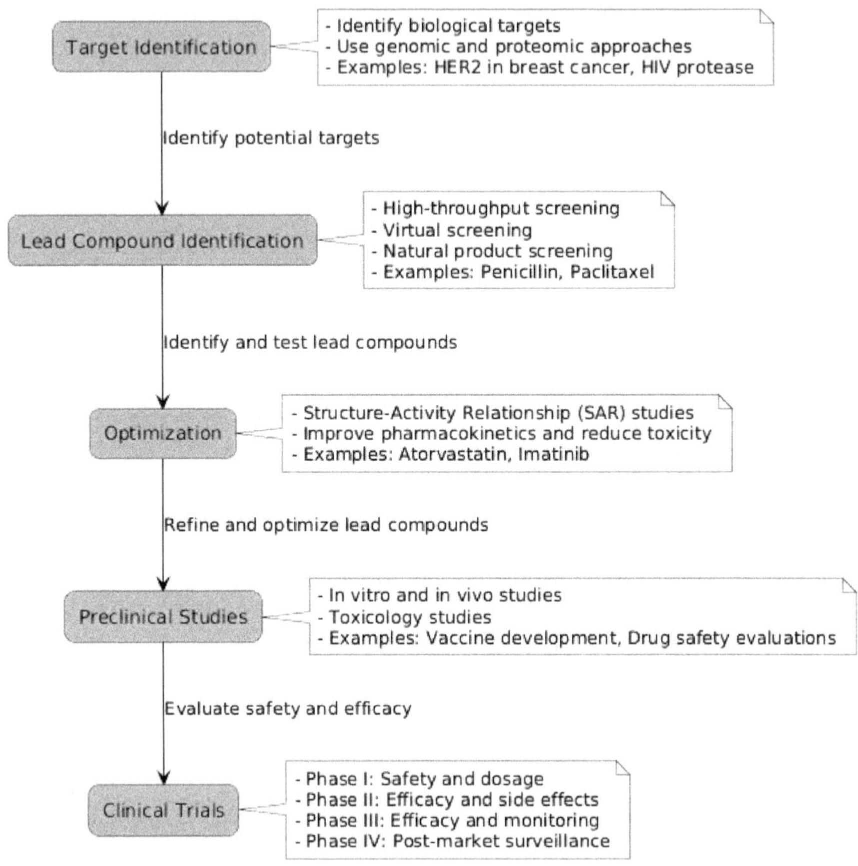

Key Steps in Drug Discovery

Steps in Drug Discovery

Target Identification

Definition and Importance

Target identification is the initial and crucial step in the drug discovery process where specific biological molecules or pathways associated with a disease are identified as potential targets for therapeutic intervention.

These targets are typically proteins, enzymes, or receptors that play a key role in the disease pathology.

Process and Techniques

1. **Understanding Disease Mechanisms**: Researchers study the underlying mechanisms of a disease to identify key molecular players. This involves understanding the disease pathology at a molecular level and identifying molecules that are crucial for disease progression.
2. **Genomic and Proteomic Approaches**: High-throughput **genomic** and **proteomic** technologies are used to identify potential targets. Genomic approaches may include **gene expression profiling** and **genome-wide association studies (GWAS)**, while proteomic approaches involve analyzing protein expression and interactions.
3. **Bioinformatics**: **Bioinformatics** tools and databases help in predicting and validating potential drug targets by analyzing large datasets and identifying molecules that are involved in disease pathways.

Examples and Applications

- **Cancer**: **HER2** (Human Epidermal Growth Factor Receptor 2) is a well-known target for breast cancer therapy. The identification of HER2 as a target led to the development of **trastuzumab** (Herceptin), a drug that specifically targets HER2-positive cancer cells.
- **HIV/AIDS**: **HIV protease** was identified as a target for HIV therapy, leading to the development of **protease inhibitors** that interfere with viral replication.

Lead Compound Identification

Definition and Importance

Lead compound identification involves discovering and selecting small molecules or compounds that have the potential to interact with the identified target and produce a therapeutic effect. These compounds are termed "lead compounds" and serve as the starting point for drug development.

Process and Techniques

1. **High-Throughput Screening (HTS)**: **HTS** is a method used to rapidly test thousands of compounds for their ability to interact with the target.

This involves using automated systems to assess the biological activity of compounds in various assays.

2. **Virtual Screening: Virtual screening** uses computational methods to predict which compounds are likely to bind to the target based on their structure. This approach helps in narrowing down the number of compounds for experimental testing.
3. **Natural Product Screening:** Natural sources, such as plants, animals, and microorganisms, are screened for bioactive compounds that may act as lead candidates.

Examples and Applications

- **Antibiotics: Penicillin** was discovered as a lead compound from the mold **Penicillium notatum**, which led to its development as a widely used antibiotic.
- **Anticancer Agents: Taxol** (paclitaxel), derived from the Pacific yew tree, was identified as a lead compound with potential anticancer properties.

Optimization

Definition and Importance

Optimization involves modifying and refining the lead compounds to improve their efficacy, selectivity, and pharmacokinetic properties. The goal is to enhance the compound's potential as a therapeutic agent while minimizing undesirable side effects.

Process and Techniques

1. **Structure-Activity Relationship (SAR) Studies: SAR** studies involve systematically modifying the chemical structure of lead compounds to determine which changes enhance their activity or reduce toxicity.
2. **Pharmacokinetics and Toxicology:** Assessing the **pharmacokinetic** properties (absorption, distribution, metabolism, excretion) and **toxicity** of lead compounds is crucial for optimizing their suitability as drugs.
3. **In Vivo Studies:** Testing optimized compounds in animal models to evaluate their therapeutic potential and safety profile.

Examples and Applications

- **Statins: Atorvastatin** was optimized from initial lead compounds to improve its efficacy in lowering cholesterol and reducing cardiovascular risk.
- **Anticancer Drugs: Imatinib** (Gleevec) underwent optimization to enhance its selectivity and effectiveness in treating chronic myeloid leukemia.

Preclinical Studies

Definition and Importance

Preclinical studies are conducted to evaluate the safety, efficacy, and pharmacokinetics of the optimized lead compounds before they are tested in humans. These studies provide essential data to support the transition to clinical trials.

Process and Techniques

1. **In Vitro Studies:** Laboratory studies conducted in cell cultures to assess the biological activity and toxicity of the compound.
2. **In Vivo Studies:** Animal studies to evaluate the pharmacokinetics, pharmacodynamics, and potential side effects of the compound. This includes testing in multiple animal models to ensure broad applicability.
3. **Toxicology Studies:** Comprehensive assessment of the compound's potential to cause adverse effects, including acute, subchronic, and chronic toxicity studies.

Examples and Applications

- **Vaccine Development: Preclinical studies** on vaccine candidates, such as those for COVID-19, involve extensive animal testing to ensure safety and efficacy before human trials.
- **Drug Safety: Thalidomide** is a notable example where preclinical studies failed to predict teratogenic effects in humans, leading to significant regulatory changes in drug testing.

6.2 Preclinical Evaluation

In Vitro Studies

Cell Culture Models

Definition and Importance

Cell culture models involve growing cells outside their natural environment, typically in a laboratory setting, to study the biological effects of compounds. These models are crucial for assessing the preliminary efficacy and safety of drug candidates before advancing to animal studies.

Types of Cell Culture Models

1. **Primary Cell Cultures**: Derived directly from tissues, these cultures retain many characteristics of the original tissue. They are used to study specific cell types and their responses to drugs. For example, primary hepatocyte cultures are used to assess liver metabolism.
2. **Cell Lines**: Established from cancerous or immortalized cells, these lines provide a consistent and reproducible model. Common examples include **HeLa cells** (derived from cervical cancer) and **HEK293 cells** (derived from human embryonic kidney).
3. **3D Cell Cultures**: Unlike traditional 2D cultures, **3D cultures** mimic the complex structure of tissues and organs. They offer more accurate representations of drug effects and are used to study tumor growth and drug resistance.

Applications and Examples

- **Drug Toxicity**: **Cell culture models** are used to assess cytotoxicity by measuring cell viability, proliferation, and apoptosis. For instance, the **MTT assay** evaluates cell metabolic activity and viability.
- **Mechanism of Action**: Researchers use cell cultures to study how drugs interact with specific cellular targets. For example, testing inhibitors of cell signaling pathways in cancer cell lines can elucidate their potential as anticancer agents.

Biochemical Assays

Definition and Importance

Biochemical assays are laboratory techniques used to measure the biochemical activity of compounds, including their effects on enzymes, proteins, and other biomolecules. These assays help determine the mechanism of action and potential therapeutic effects of drug candidates.

Types of Biochemical Assays

1. **Enzyme Activity Assays:** Measure the impact of a drug on enzyme activity. For example, the **enzymatic assay** for **acetylcholinesterase** inhibition can be used to test potential treatments for Alzheimer's disease.
2. **Binding Assays:** Assess the binding affinity of a compound to its target. **Radiolabeled binding assays** and **fluorescence resonance energy transfer (FRET)** are commonly used to study drug-receptor interactions.
3. **Reporter Gene Assays:** Utilize cells that contain a reporter gene, such as **luciferase**, to measure gene expression changes in response to drug treatment. These assays are useful for studying transcriptional regulation and signaling pathways.

Applications and Examples

- **Drug Efficacy: Biochemical assays** help determine the efficacy of a drug by measuring its ability to inhibit or activate specific enzymes or receptors. For instance, **enzyme-linked immunosorbent assays (ELISA)** are used to quantify cytokine levels in response to drug treatment.
- **Mechanistic Studies:** Understanding how drugs affect cellular processes at a molecular level can provide insights into their therapeutic potential and help optimize their structure.

6.2 Preclinical Evaluation

In Vivo Studies

Animal Models

Definition and Importance

Animal models are living organisms used in research to study the effects of drug candidates in a whole-body context. These models are essential for evaluating the pharmacokinetics, pharmacodynamics, efficacy, and safety of new drugs before they are tested in humans.

Types of Animal Models

1. **Rodent Models:** Mice and rats are commonly used due to their well-characterized genetics, short lifespans, and low cost. They are ideal for studying general pharmacological effects, toxicity, and basic mechanisms of action. For example, **C57BL/6 mice** are frequently used

in immunology studies.

2. **Non-Rodent Models**: Larger animals like rabbits, guinea pigs, and dogs are used for studies requiring more complex physiology. For instance, **beagle dogs** are often used in preclinical toxicology studies due to their physiological similarities to humans.
3. **Genetically Modified Models**: Animals genetically engineered to express or lack specific genes are valuable for studying diseases and drug effects at a molecular level. For example, **knockout mice** lacking specific genes are used to understand the role of those genes in drug responses.

Applications and Examples

- **Pharmacokinetics**: In animal models, **pharmacokinetic studies** involve administering the drug and monitoring its absorption, distribution, metabolism, and excretion. This helps in understanding how the drug behaves in the body and predicting its behavior in humans.
- **Toxicology**: **Toxicity studies** assess the safety of a drug by observing adverse effects and determining dose limits. For instance, acute toxicity studies in rodents help identify the maximum tolerated dose and potential side effects.
- **Disease Models**: Animal models of diseases, such as **diabetic rats** or **Alzheimer's disease mice**, are used to test the efficacy of new treatments and understand disease mechanisms.

Pharmacokinetic Studies

Definition and Importance

Pharmacokinetic studies in vivo involve assessing how a drug is absorbed, distributed, metabolized, and excreted in a living organism. These studies provide crucial data on the drug's behavior in the body, including its **bioavailability**, **half-life**, and **clearance**.

Types of Pharmacokinetic Studies

1. **Absorption Studies**: Evaluate how well and how quickly a drug is absorbed into the bloodstream from the site of administration. For example, oral absorption studies may involve measuring drug levels in plasma over time.
2. **Distribution Studies**: Investigate how a drug is distributed throughout the body's tissues and organs. This involves measuring **volume of**

distribution and **protein binding**. For example, studies might track the distribution of a drug labeled with a radioactive tracer.

3. **Metabolism Studies:** Determine how a drug is metabolized in the body, including the identification of **metabolites** and the enzymes involved. This helps in understanding the drug's **half-life** and potential interactions with other drugs.
4. **Excretion Studies:** Assess how a drug and its metabolites are eliminated from the body, primarily through urine and feces. This includes measuring the **renal clearance** and the rate of elimination.

Applications and Examples

- **Bioavailability Assessment:** Studies measure how much of the drug reaches systemic circulation and how it compares to the dose administered. For example, measuring plasma drug levels after oral and intravenous administration provides insights into the drug's **bioavailability.**
- **Drug-Drug Interactions:** Pharmacokinetic studies help identify how a drug may affect the metabolism of other drugs, potentially leading to **interaction effects.** For instance, enzyme inhibition studies assess how one drug might inhibit the metabolism of another.
- **Dosing Regimens:** Data from pharmacokinetic studies inform the optimal dosing regimen, including dosage, frequency, and route of administration, to achieve therapeutic effects while minimizing side effects.

6.3 Clinical Trials

Phases of Clinical Trials

Introduction

Clinical trials are structured research studies conducted to evaluate the safety, efficacy, and optimal use of new drugs or therapies in human subjects. The clinical trial process is divided into four distinct phases, each designed to address different aspects of drug development and ensure that new treatments are both effective and safe for use. Understanding these phases is crucial for comprehending how new drugs progress from initial development to routine clinical use.

Phase I Studies

Objective and Design

Phase I studies are the first stage of clinical trials where a new drug or therapy is tested in humans for the first time. The primary aim is to assess the drug's safety profile and determine its appropriate dosage.

Key Characteristics

- **Participants**: Typically involve a small group of healthy volunteers (20-100 participants), though sometimes patients with specific conditions may be included.
- **Focus**: Safety, dosage, and pharmacokinetics. Researchers closely monitor the subjects for adverse effects, determine the maximum tolerated dose, and gather data on how the drug is absorbed, distributed, metabolized, and excreted.
- **Design**: Often a dose-escalation study, where doses are gradually increased to find the highest dose that can be safely administered.

Examples

- Testing a new chemotherapy agent to determine safe dosage levels and observe any immediate side effects.
- Evaluating a new drug's pharmacokinetics and pharmacodynamics in healthy volunteers.

Phase II Studies

Objective and Design

Phase II studies focus on assessing the efficacy of the drug for treating a specific disease or condition, while continuing to monitor its safety.

Key Characteristics

- **Participants**: Involve a larger group of patients (100-300) who have the condition the drug is intended to treat.
- **Focus**: Effectiveness and safety in patients. This phase aims to determine whether the drug has a therapeutic benefit and to refine dosage guidelines.
- **Design**: Often includes randomized controlled trials (RCTs) and may be divided into multiple sub-phases to test various dosages or treatment regimens.

Examples

- Evaluating the effectiveness of a new antihypertensive drug in lowering blood pressure compared to a placebo or existing treatment.
- Assessing the efficacy of a new antidepressant in reducing symptoms of depression in patients.

Phase III Studies

Objective and Design

Phase III studies are conducted to confirm the drug's efficacy, monitor side effects, and compare it to standard or existing treatments.

Key Characteristics

- **Participants**: Enroll a large group of patients (1,000-3,000 or more) across multiple centers, often including diverse patient populations.
- **Focus**: Confirm efficacy and safety in a broad patient population. This phase provides the most comprehensive data on the drug's benefit-risk profile.
- **Design**: Typically involves randomized controlled trials with blinding, where patients are randomly assigned to receive either the new drug, a placebo, or an existing standard treatment.

Examples

- Comparing the effectiveness of a new antidiabetic medication against current standard treatments in controlling blood glucose levels.
- Testing a new vaccine in a large cohort to assess its protective effect against a specific infectious disease.

Phase IV Studies

Objective and Design

Phase IV studies, also known as post-marketing surveillance, are conducted after a drug has been approved and is available for use by the general public. The aim is to monitor long-term effects and gather additional data on the drug's performance in real-world settings.

Key Characteristics

- **Participants**: Involve a wide range of patients using the drug in everyday clinical practice.

- **Focus**: Long-term safety, efficacy, and optimal use. These studies can detect rare or long-term adverse effects not observed in earlier phases and provide information on the drug's performance in various populations.
- **Design**: Includes ongoing observational studies, registry studies, and post-marketing trials. Data collected from real-world use are analyzed to identify any new safety concerns or to assess the drug's long-term benefits.

Examples

- Monitoring the long-term safety of a new cholesterol-lowering drug in the general population after its market release.
- Evaluating the effectiveness of a recently approved drug in different patient demographics or in combination with other treatments.

6.3 Clinical Trials

Phases of Clinical Trials

Introduction

Clinical trials are critical steps in the drug development process, designed to evaluate the safety, efficacy, and optimal use of new drugs or therapies. They are conducted in a series of phases, each with specific objectives and methodologies, to ensure that new treatments are safe and effective before they are approved for widespread use. Here, we explore the objectives, methodologies, and examples of each phase in detail.

Phase I Studies

Objectives

- **Safety Evaluation**: To assess the safety profile of the drug in humans for the first time.
- **Dosage Determination**: To establish the maximum tolerated dose (MTD) and identify any dose-limiting toxicities.
- **Pharmacokinetics**: To understand how the drug is absorbed, distributed, metabolized, and excreted.

Methodologies

- **Participants:** Involves a small group of healthy volunteers (20-100), or occasionally patients with specific conditions if the drug may not be safe for healthy individuals.
- **Study Design:** Often includes dose-escalation studies where different dose levels are tested to determine the highest dose that can be safely administered without severe adverse effects.
- **Monitoring:** Intensive monitoring for adverse effects, blood tests, and other assessments to evaluate the drug's safety.

Examples

- **New Chemotherapy Agents:** Testing a new chemotherapy drug to determine safe dosage levels and identify any immediate side effects.
- **Novel Analgesics:** Evaluating a new pain relief medication's pharmacokinetics and initial safety profile in healthy volunteers.

Phase II Studies
Objectives

- **Efficacy Assessment:** To evaluate the drug's effectiveness in treating the targeted disease or condition.
- **Safety Confirmation:** To continue monitoring safety in a larger patient population.
- **Dosage Optimization:** To refine dosing guidelines based on observed efficacy and safety data.

Methodologies

- **Participants:** Enroll a larger group of patients (100-300) who have the condition that the drug aims to treat.
- **Study Design:** Often includes randomized controlled trials (RCTs) to compare the new drug with a placebo or an existing treatment. May also include dose-ranging studies to identify the most effective dose.
- **Monitoring:** Regular monitoring of patient responses and side effects to assess therapeutic benefit and safety.

Examples

- **Antihypertensive Drugs**: Testing a new blood pressure medication in patients with hypertension to determine its effectiveness in lowering blood pressure compared to a placebo.
- **Antidiabetic Medications**: Evaluating a new drug for diabetes management in patients to assess its impact on blood glucose levels.

Phase III Studies
Objectives

- **Confirmation of Efficacy**: To confirm the drug's effectiveness and establish its therapeutic benefit in a broader patient population.
- **Safety Profiling**: To identify any rare or long-term adverse effects and confirm overall safety.
- **Comparison with Standard Treatments**: To compare the new drug's efficacy and safety with current standard treatments.

Methodologies

- **Participants**: Enroll a large number of patients (1,000-3,000 or more) across multiple sites and diverse patient populations.
- **Study Design**: Typically involves large-scale randomized controlled trials with blinding to minimize bias. Patients are randomly assigned to receive either the new drug, a placebo, or an existing standard treatment.
- **Monitoring**: Comprehensive monitoring of both efficacy and safety, including long-term follow-up to detect any delayed adverse effects.

Examples

- **New Antihyperlipidemic Drugs**: Comparing a new cholesterol-lowering drug with an existing treatment to evaluate its effectiveness in reducing cholesterol levels.
- **New Vaccines**: Assessing a new vaccine's efficacy in preventing a specific disease compared to an established vaccine or placebo.

Phase IV Studies
Objectives

- **Long-Term Safety Monitoring**: To identify any long-term or rare adverse effects that were not detected in earlier phases.
- **Effectiveness in Real-World Settings**: To evaluate how the drug performs in the general population outside of the controlled clinical trial environment.
- **Post-Marketing Surveillance**: To gather additional information on the drug's performance and any potential issues that may arise with widespread use.

Methodologies

- **Participants**: Involves a broad range of patients using the drug in everyday clinical practice.
- **Study Design**: Includes observational studies, registry studies, and additional post-marketing trials. Data is collected from routine clinical use and analyzed for new safety or efficacy information.
- **Monitoring**: Ongoing collection of adverse event reports, effectiveness data, and patient feedback.

Examples

- **Post-Market Surveillance of New Diabetes Drugs**: Monitoring the long-term safety of a new diabetes medication in a diverse patient population.
- **Registry Studies for New Anticancer Drugs**: Collecting real-world data on the effectiveness and safety of a newly approved cancer drug.

6.4 Pharmacovigilance

Importance and Methods

Introduction

Pharmacovigilance is a critical aspect of drug safety that involves the **monitoring, reporting**, and **management** of adverse drug reactions (ADRs) to ensure the safe use of pharmaceuticals. Its primary goal is to enhance patient safety by detecting, assessing, and preventing adverse effects associated with drug use. This process is essential for identifying potential risks and ensuring that the benefits of a drug outweigh its risks throughout its lifecycle.

Monitoring Adverse Drug Reactions

Definition and Objectives

Monitoring involves the systematic collection and evaluation of data on adverse drug reactions. The objectives are to detect any safety concerns that may not have been identified during clinical trials, to understand the frequency and severity of ADRs, and to assess their impact on public health.

Methods

- **Spontaneous Reporting Systems**: Healthcare professionals, patients, and drug manufacturers report ADRs through established systems, such as the FDA's MedWatch in the United States or the Yellow Card Scheme in the UK. These reports provide valuable data on unexpected or rare adverse effects.
- **Electronic Health Records (EHRs)**: EHRs can be analyzed to identify patterns of ADRs across large populations, allowing for real-time monitoring and rapid detection of safety issues.
- **Data Mining Techniques**: Advanced statistical and data mining techniques are used to analyze large datasets from clinical trials and post-marketing surveillance to identify potential safety signals that may indicate new or previously unrecognized ADRs.

Reporting Adverse Drug Reactions

Definition and Importance

Reporting involves documenting and submitting information about ADRs to regulatory authorities and relevant stakeholders. Effective reporting ensures that safety information is communicated promptly and accurately, facilitating timely regulatory actions and updates.

Methods

- **Mandatory Reporting by Healthcare Professionals**: In many countries, healthcare professionals are required to report serious or unexpected ADRs to national pharmacovigilance centers. This requirement helps to ensure that significant safety concerns are addressed quickly.
- **Pharmaceutical Companies' Responsibilities**: Drug manufacturers are obligated to report all known and suspected ADRs related to their products. They must continuously monitor safety data, conduct risk assessments, and update product labeling as needed.
- **Patient Reporting Systems**: Patients can also report ADRs directly to regulatory agencies or through patient advocacy organizations. This involvement helps capture ADRs that may not be reported by healthcare

professionals or manufacturers.

Managing Adverse Drug Reactions

Definition and Objectives

Managing ADRs involves taking appropriate actions based on the collected data to minimize risks and enhance patient safety. The objectives are to implement risk mitigation strategies, update drug labeling, and communicate safety information effectively to healthcare professionals and patients.

Methods

- **Risk Assessment and Risk Management**: Regulatory agencies conduct thorough risk assessments to evaluate the severity and likelihood of ADRs. Based on these assessments, they may implement risk management strategies such as risk communication, restricted use, or even market withdrawal of the drug if necessary.
- **Labeling Changes**: If new safety information emerges, drug labeling is updated to include warnings, contraindications, and precautionary measures. This ensures that healthcare providers and patients are informed about the potential risks associated with the drug.
- **Safety Alerts and Communication**: Regulatory authorities issue safety alerts and warnings to inform healthcare professionals and the public about significant safety concerns. This includes updating the product information and issuing public health advisories as needed.

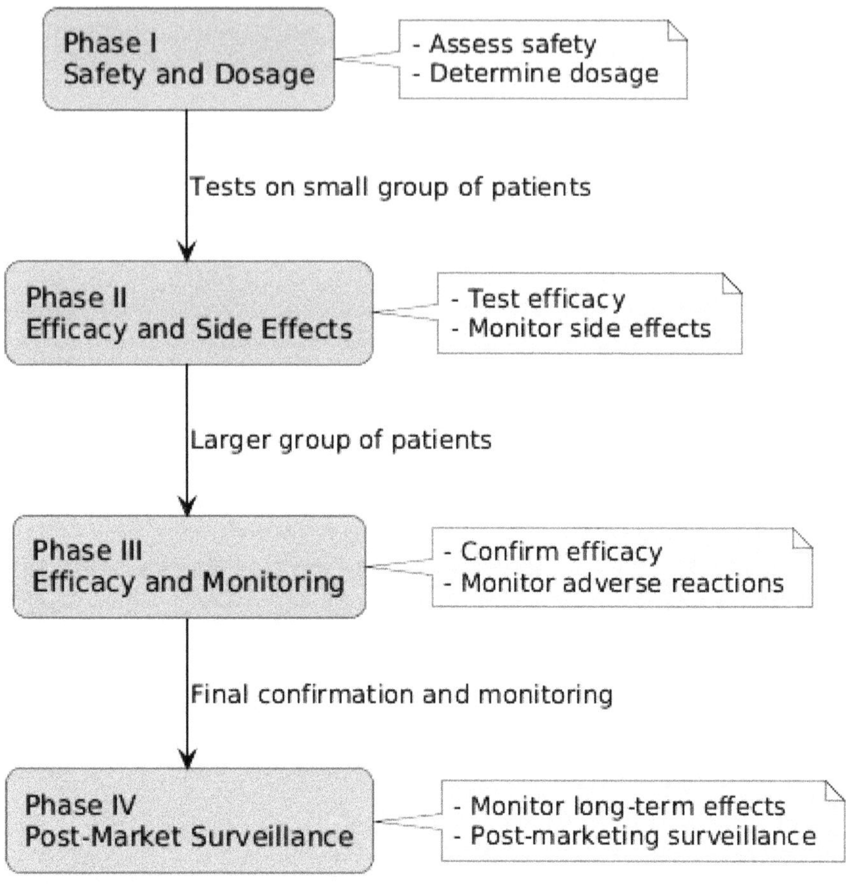

Phases of Clinical Trials: A Comprehensive Overview

CHAPTER VII

Pharmacology of the Peripheral Nervous System

7.1 Organization and Function of ANS

Structure and Functions

The **Autonomic Nervous System (ANS)** is a crucial part of the peripheral nervous system responsible for regulating involuntary physiological functions. It controls essential functions such as heart rate, digestion, respiratory rate, and pupil dilation, operating largely outside conscious control. The ANS is divided into two primary branches: the **sympathetic** and **parasympathetic** divisions. Each division has distinct roles and utilizes different neurotransmitters to achieve its effects.

Sympathetic Division

Structure and Functions

The sympathetic division is often described as the "fight or flight" system due to its role in preparing the body for stressful or emergency situations. Its primary function is to mobilize the body's resources in response to acute stressors. This division is characterized by:

- **Neurotransmitters**: The sympathetic division primarily uses **norepinephrine** (noradrenaline) as its neurotransmitter at the postganglionic nerve endings. At the preganglionic level, **acetylcholine** is used.
- **Ganglia**: Sympathetic ganglia are located near the spinal cord in a chain-like structure known as the sympathetic chain or trunk. This arrangement allows for a rapid and widespread response to stimuli.
- **Effects**: Activation of the sympathetic division results in increased heart rate, dilation of bronchial passages, dilation of the pupils (mydriasis), increased blood flow to muscles, and mobilization of energy stores. These responses collectively prepare the body to react to stressful situations by enhancing physical performance and alertness.

Parasympathetic Division

Structure and Functions

The parasympathetic division is often referred to as the "rest and digest" system. It counteracts the effects of the sympathetic division and promotes restorative processes. Key features include:

- **Neurotransmitters**: The primary neurotransmitter used by the parasympathetic division is **acetylcholine**. It is employed both at the ganglionic and postganglionic levels.
- **Ganglia**: Parasympathetic ganglia are located closer to or within the target organs. This localized arrangement facilitates more specific and targeted responses.
- **Effects**: Activation of the parasympathetic division leads to decreased heart rate, constriction of bronchial passages, constriction of the pupils (miosis), stimulation of digestive processes, and enhancement of salivation. These effects support processes that promote relaxation, digestion, and energy conservation.

Neurotransmitters and Their Functions

Sympathetic Neurotransmitters:

- **Norepinephrine**: Acts primarily on adrenergic receptors, which are divided into alpha and beta subtypes. For example, beta-1 receptors in the heart increase heart rate and force of contraction, while alpha-1 receptors in blood vessels cause vasoconstriction.
- **Epinephrine**: Secreted by the adrenal medulla and acts similarly to norepinephrine, enhancing the sympathetic response throughout the body.

Parasympathetic Neurotransmitters:

- **Acetylcholine**: Acts on muscarinic receptors in various organs. For instance, muscarinic receptors in the heart decrease heart rate, while those in the gastrointestinal tract enhance motility and secretions.

Interaction and Balance

The sympathetic and parasympathetic systems work in a coordinated manner to maintain homeostasis. They generally have opposing effects, but their actions can be complementary in certain situations. For example, while the sympathetic system prepares the body for action, the parasympathetic system helps the body recover and restore energy balance once the stressful situation has passed.

7.2 Neurohumoral Transmission and Co-Transmission

Neurotransmitters and Their Classification

Neurohumoral transmission involves the release of neurotransmitters from nerve endings to transmit signals across synapses to target cells, including neurons, muscle cells, or glands. These neurotransmitters play a critical role in modulating various physiological processes and maintaining homeostasis. They can be classified based on their chemical structure, function, and mechanism of action. Here's an overview of the different types, their mechanisms, and examples:

Types of Neurotransmitters

1. Amino Acids

- **Glutamate**: The primary **excitatory neurotransmitter** in the central nervous system (CNS). It is involved in **learning** and **memory**.

Glutamate acts on ionotropic receptors (e.g., NMDA, AMPA) and metabotropic glutamate receptors (mGluRs), facilitating synaptic plasticity and signal transmission.

- **Gamma-Aminobutyric Acid (GABA)**: The main **inhibitory neurotransmitter** in the CNS. It reduces neuronal excitability and is crucial for maintaining the balance between excitation and inhibition in the brain. GABA acts on ionotropic GABA_A receptors, which are linked to chloride ion channels, and metabotropic GABA_B receptors.

2. Monoamines

- **Dopamine**: Involved in **motivation**, **reward**, and **motor control**. It acts on various receptors, including D1-like (D1, D5) and D2-like (D2, D3, D4) receptors. Dysregulation of dopamine is associated with **Parkinson's disease** and **schizophrenia**.
- **Norepinephrine**: Functions as both a **neurotransmitter** and **hormone**, impacting **alertness**, **arousal**, and **mood**. It acts on alpha and beta adrenergic receptors. It plays a role in **stress responses** and **blood pressure regulation**.
- **Serotonin**: Regulates **mood**, **appetite**, and **sleep**. It acts on various 5-HT receptors, including 5-HT1 to 5-HT7, influencing both excitatory and inhibitory responses. Alterations in serotonin levels are linked to **depression** and **anxiety disorders**.
- **Histamine**: Involved in **immune responses**, **gastric acid secretion**, and **neurotransmission**. It acts on H1, H2, H3, and H4 receptors. Histamine is also crucial in regulating **sleep-wake cycles** and **allergic reactions**.

3. Peptides

- **Substance P**: Involved in **pain transmission** and **inflammation**. It acts on neurokinin receptors (NK1) and plays a role in the **central processing of pain**.
- **Endorphins**: Act as **endogenous opioids**, modulating **pain** and **pleasure**. They bind to opioid receptors (μ, δ, κ) and are involved in **pain relief** and **euphoria**.

4. Purines

- **Adenosine**: Functions as an **inhibitory neurotransmitter** that modulates **sleep** and **cardiovascular function**. It acts on adenosine receptors (A1, A2A, A2B, A3), influencing both central and peripheral effects.

5. Acetylcholine

- **Acetylcholine (ACh)**: A crucial neurotransmitter in both the central and peripheral nervous systems. It acts on nicotinic receptors (nAChRs) and muscarinic receptors (mAChRs). ACh is involved in **muscle contraction**, **cognitive functions**, and **autonomic nervous system** regulation.

Mechanisms of Neurotransmitter Action

1. Ionotropic Receptors

These receptors are directly linked to ion channels. When neurotransmitters bind to these receptors, they cause the opening or closing of ion channels, leading to changes in the membrane potential of the target cell. Examples include:

- **NMDA and AMPA Receptors** (for glutamate)
- **GABA_A Receptor** (for GABA)

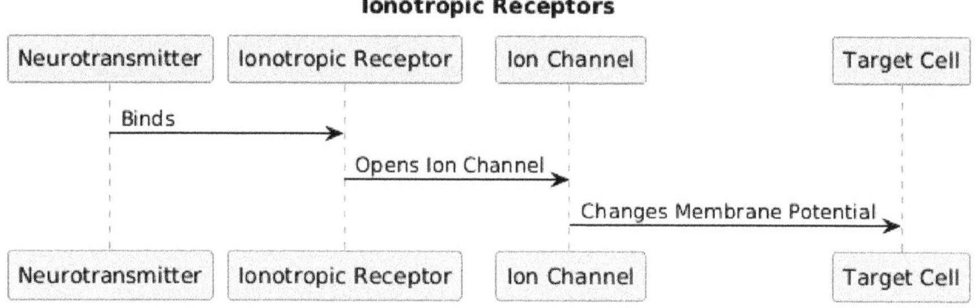

2. Metabotropic Receptors

These receptors are linked to intracellular signaling pathways through G-proteins. Binding of neurotransmitters to metabotropic receptors activates these G-proteins, which then influence various intracellular signaling cascades, such as cyclic AMP (cAMP) or phosphatidylinositol turnover. Examples include:

- **Dopamine Receptors** (D1-D5)
- **Muscarinic Acetylcholine Receptors** (M1-M5)

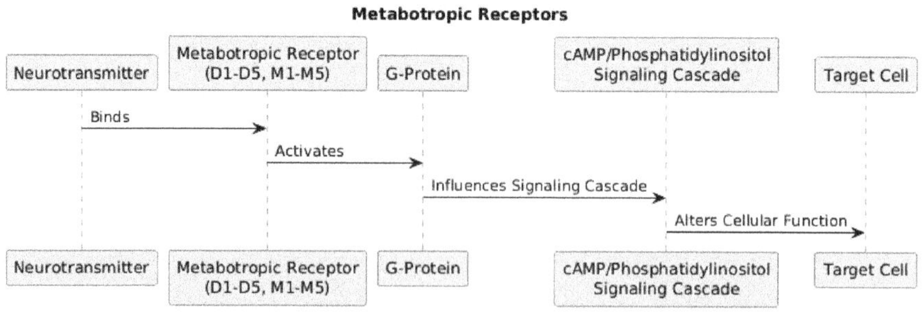

3. Autoreceptors

Autoreceptors are located on the presynaptic neuron and regulate neurotransmitter release. They provide feedback inhibition by reducing the release of neurotransmitters when levels are high. Examples include:

- **α2-Adrenergic Receptors** (for norepinephrine)
- **5-HT1A Receptors** (for serotonin)

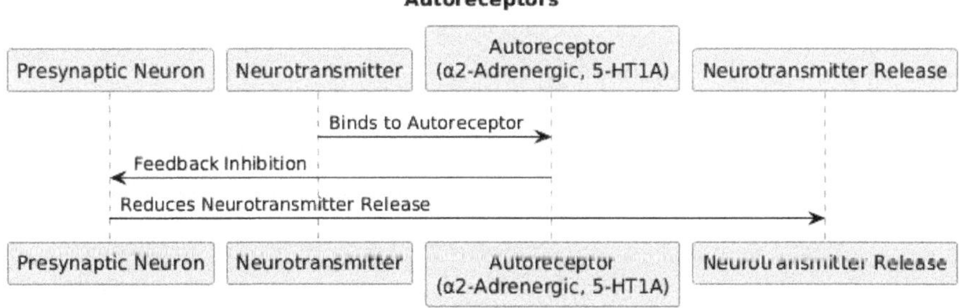

4. Transporters

Transporters are responsible for the reuptake of neurotransmitters from the synaptic cleft back into the presynaptic neuron. This process terminates the neurotransmitter's action and recycles it. Examples include:

- **Serotonin Transporter (SERT)**
- **Dopamine Transporter (DAT)**

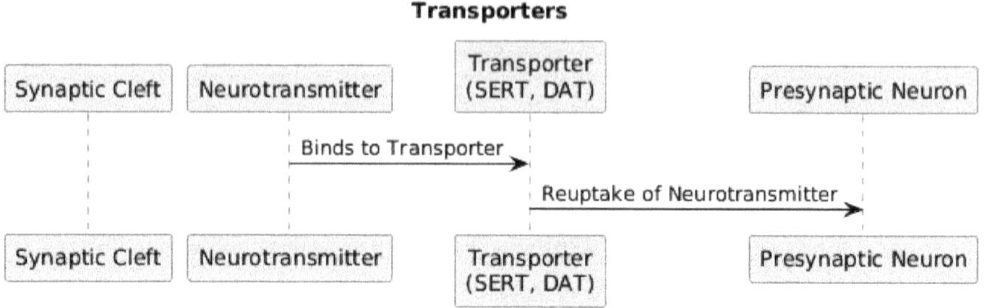

5. Enzymatic Degradation

Neurotransmitters can also be broken down by enzymes in the synaptic cleft, thus terminating their action. Examples include:

- **Acetylcholinesterase**: Breaks down acetylcholine.
- **Monoamine Oxidase (MAO)**: Degrades monoamines like dopamine, norepinephrine, and serotonin.

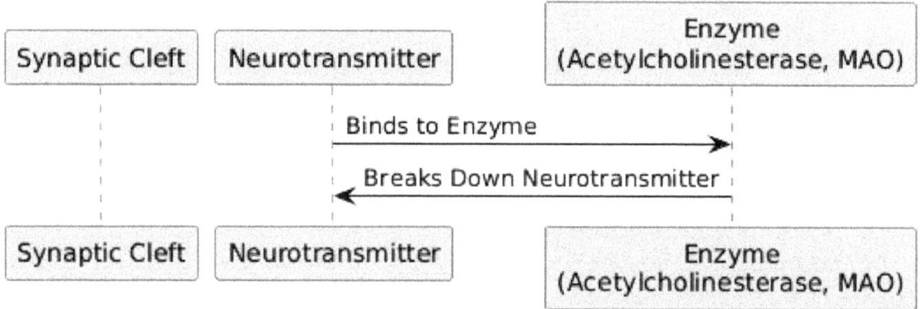

Examples

- **Glutamate**: Involved in cognitive functions such as learning and memory. Dysregulation can lead to neurological disorders such as Alzheimer's disease.
- **Dopamine**: Central to the reward system and movement control. Abnormalities are linked to diseases like Parkinson's disease and

schizophrenia.

- **Serotonin**: Regulates mood and emotions. Imbalances are associated with depression and anxiety.

7.3 Drugs Acting on the Parasympathetic System

Parasympathomimetics

Parasympathomimetics, also known as **cholinomimetics**, are drugs that mimic the effects of the parasympathetic nervous system. They enhance or replicate the action of the neurotransmitter **acetylcholine** (ACh) at muscarinic and nicotinic receptors. These drugs are utilized to treat various conditions where the stimulation of the parasympathetic system is beneficial.

Mechanisms of Action

1. Direct-Acting Parasympathomimetics

Direct-acting parasympathomimetics act as agonists at muscarinic and/or nicotinic receptors, directly stimulating these receptors as acetylcholine would. This results in the activation of the parasympathetic nervous system, leading to various physiological effects. They can be classified into:

- **Muscarinic Agonists**: These drugs specifically activate muscarinic receptors, which are present in various tissues including the heart, smooth muscles, and glands. Their activation leads to effects such as decreased heart rate, increased glandular secretions, and smooth muscle contraction.
- **Nicotinic Agonists**: These drugs target nicotinic receptors, which are found in the neuromuscular junctions and autonomic ganglia. Their action can result in muscle contraction and increased neurotransmitter release in the autonomic ganglia.

2. Indirect-Acting Parasympathomimetics

Indirect-acting parasympathomimetics, also known as **anticholinesterase agents**, do not directly activate the parasympathetic receptors but instead inhibit the enzyme **acetylcholinesterase** (AChE). This enzyme is responsible for the breakdown of acetylcholine in the synaptic cleft. By inhibiting AChE, these drugs increase the concentration and duration of action of acetylcholine, thereby enhancing parasympathetic activity.

Examples and Clinical Uses

1. Direct-Acting Parasympathomimetics

- **Bethanechol**: A **muscarinic agonist** used primarily to treat urinary retention by stimulating bladder contraction. It is also used in managing gastrointestinal atony.
- **Pilocarpine**: Another **muscarinic agonist** that is used in the treatment of **glaucoma** to reduce intraocular pressure by increasing aqueous humor outflow. It is also used to manage **xerostomia** (dry mouth) in patients with Sjögren's syndrome.
- **Nicotine**: A **nicotinic agonist** that stimulates nicotinic receptors in the autonomic ganglia and neuromuscular junctions. It is used in smoking cessation therapies and as a part of nicotine replacement therapy.

2. Indirect-Acting Parasympathomimetics

- **Physostigmine**: A reversible **anticholinesterase** agent used in the treatment of **anticholinergic toxicity** and **glaucoma**. It crosses the blood-brain barrier and is used in central nervous system disorders to improve cognitive function.

- **Neostigmine**: Another reversible **anticholinesterase** used primarily in the management of **myasthenia gravis**, a condition characterized by muscle weakness due to impaired neuromuscular transmission. It is also used to reverse neuromuscular blockades induced by non-depolarizing muscle relaxants in anesthesia.
- **Donepezil**: A reversible **anticholinesterase** used in the treatment of **Alzheimer's disease** to improve cognitive function and slow disease progression. It increases acetylcholine levels in the brain, which is beneficial in managing symptoms of dementia.

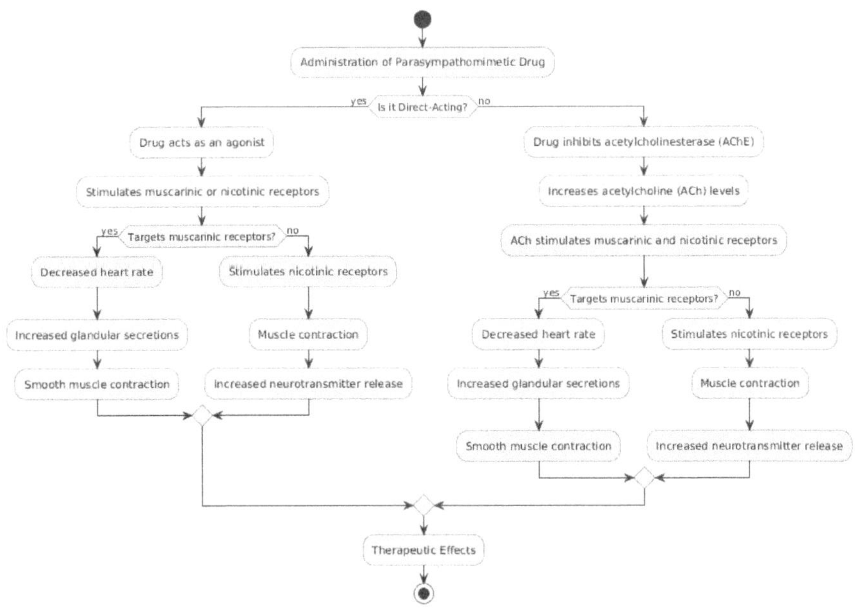

Flowchart illustrating the Mechanism of Action and Therapeutic Effects of Parasympathomimetic Drugs"

Clinical Uses

1. **Urinary and Gastrointestinal Disorders**: Drugs like bethanechol are used to treat conditions involving bladder and gastrointestinal tract dysfunction, promoting contraction and improving function.

2. **Glaucoma**: Pilocarpine is used to manage elevated intraocular pressure, providing relief from glaucoma.

3. **Neuromuscular Disorders:** Physostigmine and neostigmine are utilized in the management of conditions such as myasthenia gravis and for reversing neuromuscular blockades during surgical procedures.

4. **Cognitive Disorders:** Donepezil is used to alleviate symptoms of Alzheimer's disease and improve cognitive function in patients with dementia.

5. **Smoking Cessation:** Nicotine replacement therapies help individuals quit smoking by mimicking the effects of nicotine and reducing withdrawal symptoms.

7.3 Drugs Acting on the Parasympathetic System

Parasympatholytics

Parasympatholytics, also known as **anticholinergics** or **muscarinic antagonists**, are drugs that inhibit the effects of the parasympathetic nervous system. They work by blocking the action of **acetylcholine** (ACh) at muscarinic receptors, which are a type of cholinergic receptor found in various tissues throughout the body. By doing so, these drugs decrease the activity of the parasympathetic nervous system, leading to effects that are often the opposite of those produced by parasympathomimetics.

Mechanisms of Action

1. Muscarinic Receptor Blockade

Parasympatholytics primarily exert their effects by antagonizing muscarinic receptors, which are widely distributed in the body, including in the heart, smooth muscles, and glands. By blocking these receptors, parasympatholytics reduce the influence of the parasympathetic nervous system on these tissues, leading to various physiological effects:

- **Inhibition of Glandular Secretion:** Anticholinergics decrease secretions from salivary, gastric, and bronchial glands, leading to dry mouth, reduced gastric acid secretion, and decreased mucus production in the airways.
- **Smooth Muscle Relaxation:** By blocking muscarinic receptors on smooth muscles, parasympatholytics can lead to relaxation of muscles in the gastrointestinal tract and the urinary bladder, reducing motility and relieving spasm.
- **Increased Heart Rate:** Anticholinergics reduce the parasympathetic tone on the heart, which can result in an increased heart rate (tachycardia).

- **Dilation of Pupils**: Muscarinic antagonists induce **mydriasis** (pupil dilation) by preventing parasympathetic stimulation of the iris sphincter muscle.

Examples and Clinical Uses
1. Atropine

- **Mechanism**: Atropine is a non-selective muscarinic antagonist that blocks all subtypes of muscarinic receptors. It inhibits the effects of acetylcholine at these sites, leading to a variety of physiological effects.
- **Clinical Uses**: Atropine is used to increase heart rate in bradycardia (slow heart rate) by blocking vagal effects. It is also used as a pre-anesthetic to reduce salivation and bronchial secretions, and to dilate pupils for ocular examinations (mydriasis). Additionally, atropine is employed in the treatment of organophosphate poisoning, where it counteracts the excessive cholinergic activity caused by these toxic substances.

2. Scopolamine

- **Mechanism**: Scopolamine, like atropine, is a non-selective muscarinic antagonist. It also acts on the central nervous system, particularly affecting the vestibular system.
- **Clinical Uses**: Scopolamine is used primarily for its antiemetic properties to prevent motion sickness and postoperative nausea and vomiting. It is administered as a transdermal patch or orally. Additionally, scopolamine is used in the management of irritable bowel syndrome (IBS) due to its antispasmodic effects on the gastrointestinal tract.

3. Ipratropium Bromide

- **Mechanism**: Ipratropium is a muscarinic antagonist with a preference for M3 receptors found in the bronchial tissues. It is less likely to cross the blood-brain barrier compared to other anticholinergics.
- **Clinical Uses**: Ipratropium is used as an inhaled medication for the management of chronic obstructive pulmonary disease (COPD) and asthma. By inhibiting muscarinic receptors in the airways, it helps to

reduce bronchoconstriction and mucus production, leading to improved airflow and respiratory function.

4. Tiotropium

- **Mechanism**: Tiotropium is a long-acting muscarinic antagonist (LAMA) with a high affinity for M3 receptors, similar to ipratropium but with a longer duration of action.
- **Clinical Uses**: Tiotropium is used for the long-term management of COPD and asthma. Its extended duration of action allows for once-daily dosing, providing sustained relief from bronchoconstriction and improving lung function over time.

Clinical Implications

1. **Treatment of Respiratory Disorders**: Drugs like ipratropium and tiotropium are crucial in managing chronic respiratory conditions by reducing airway inflammation and improving breathing.
2. **Management of Gastrointestinal and Urological Conditions**: Parasympatholytics help alleviate symptoms of gastrointestinal disorders such as IBS by reducing smooth muscle contractions and managing urinary incontinence by decreasing bladder contractions.
3. **Preoperative and Emergency Settings**: Atropine is valuable in preoperative settings to manage excessive secretions and in emergencies to treat bradycardia.
4. **Motion Sickness and Nausea**: Scopolamine is effective in preventing nausea associated with motion sickness and postoperative conditions.

7.4 Drugs Acting on the Sympathetic System

Sympathomimetics

Sympathomimetics, also known as **adrenergic agonists**, are drugs that mimic the effects of the sympathetic nervous system by stimulating adrenergic receptors. These drugs either directly activate adrenergic receptors or indirectly enhance the release of **norepinephrine** and **epinephrine**, which are the primary neurotransmitters of the sympathetic nervous system. By stimulating these receptors, sympathomimetics produce effects similar to those of sympathetic nervous system activation, such as increased heart rate, vasoconstriction, and bronchodilation.

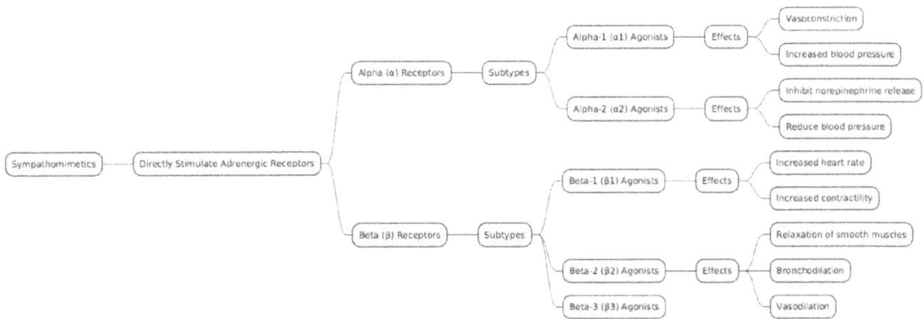

Mechanisms of Action

1. Direct Receptor Agonism

Sympathomimetics directly stimulate adrenergic receptors, which are classified into two main types: alpha (α) and beta (β) receptors. These receptors are further divided into subtypes, including α1, α2, β1, β2, and β3. The specific effects of sympathomimetics depend on the receptor subtype they target:

- **Alpha-1 Agonists**: Activate α1 receptors, leading to vasoconstriction and increased blood pressure.
- **Alpha-2 Agonists**: Activate α2 receptors, which inhibit norepinephrine release and can reduce blood pressure.
- **Beta-1 Agonists**: Stimulate β1 receptors in the heart, resulting in increased heart rate and contractility.
- **Beta-2 Agonists**: Activate β2 receptors, leading to relaxation of smooth muscles, particularly in the bronchi, and vasodilation.

2. Indirect Mechanisms

Some sympathomimetics work indirectly by increasing the release of norepinephrine or preventing its reuptake. These drugs enhance the effects of endogenous catecholamines (norepinephrine and epinephrine) by:

- **Increasing Norepinephrine Release**: Drugs that stimulate the release of norepinephrine from nerve terminals enhance sympathetic activity.

- **Inhibiting Norepinephrine Reuptake**: Certain drugs prevent the reuptake of norepinephrine, prolonging its action at adrenergic receptors.

Examples and Clinical Uses

1. Phenylephrine

- **Mechanism**: Phenylephrine is a selective α1-adrenergic agonist. It predominantly activates α1 receptors, leading to vasoconstriction.
- **Clinical Uses**: Phenylephrine is commonly used as a decongestant in nasal sprays and oral medications to relieve nasal congestion. It is also used as a vasopressor to increase blood pressure in cases of hypotension and as a mydriatic agent to dilate pupils during eye examinations.

2. Clonidine

- **Mechanism**: Clonidine is an α2-adrenergic agonist. It stimulates α2 receptors in the central nervous system, reducing sympathetic outflow and lowering blood pressure.
- **Clinical Uses**: Clonidine is used to manage hypertension, particularly in patients who do not respond to other antihypertensive medications. It is also used in the treatment of withdrawal symptoms from opioids and alcohol, and as an adjunct therapy in attention deficit hyperactivity disorder (ADHD).

3. Dobutamine

- **Mechanism**: Dobutamine is a β1-adrenergic agonist that primarily stimulates β1 receptors in the heart, leading to increased cardiac output.
- **Clinical Uses**: Dobutamine is used in the treatment of acute heart failure and cardiogenic shock. It enhances cardiac contractility and improves heart function in patients with compromised cardiac output.

4. Albuterol

- **Mechanism**: Albuterol is a β2-adrenergic agonist that selectively activates β2 receptors in the bronchial smooth muscle, causing bronchodilation.

- **Clinical Uses**: Albuterol is widely used as a bronchodilator in the management of asthma and chronic obstructive pulmonary disease (COPD). It provides rapid relief of bronchospasm and improves airflow in patients with obstructive lung diseases.

5. Ephedrine

- **Mechanism**: Ephedrine is a mixed-acting sympathomimetic. It has both direct agonistic effects on α and β receptors and indirect effects by promoting norepinephrine release.
- **Clinical Uses**: Ephedrine is used as a vasopressor to increase blood pressure during hypotensive episodes. It is also used as a bronchodilator in the treatment of asthma and to alleviate nasal congestion.

Clinical Implications

1. **Management of Cardiovascular Conditions**: Drugs like dobutamine and ephedrine are essential in treating acute heart failure and hypotension, helping to stabilize patients in critical conditions.

2. **Treatment of Respiratory Disorders**: β2-adrenergic agonists, such as albuterol, play a crucial role in managing asthma and COPD by providing symptomatic relief of bronchospasm.

3. **Use in Nasal Congestion**: Phenylephrine and other α1-agonists are effective in treating nasal congestion and improving breathing comfort in patients with respiratory infections or allergies.

4. **Control of Hypertension and Withdrawal Symptoms**: Clonidine is used not only for controlling high blood pressure but also for managing withdrawal symptoms and as part of ADHD treatment strategies.

7.4 Drugs Acting on the Sympathetic System

Sympatholytics

Sympatholytics, also known as **adrenergic antagonists**, are drugs that inhibit the effects of the sympathetic nervous system by blocking adrenergic receptors. Unlike **sympathomimetics**, which stimulate these receptors to mimic sympathetic activity, sympatholytics reduce sympathetic output and counteract the actions of endogenous catecholamines like **norepinephrine** and **epinephrine**. This class of drugs is used to manage conditions associated with excessive sympathetic activity, such as hypertension, anxiety, and certain types of heart disease.

Mechanisms of Action

1. Receptor Blockade

Sympatholytics exert their effects primarily through the blockade of adrenergic receptors. These drugs can be classified based on the type of adrenergic receptor they target:

- **Alpha-1 Blockers**: Block α1 receptors, which are primarily involved in vasoconstriction. By inhibiting these receptors, alpha-1 blockers lead to vasodilation and reduced blood pressure.
- **Alpha-2 Blockers**: Block α2 receptors, which are involved in the inhibition of norepinephrine release. Blocking these receptors can increase norepinephrine release and sympathetic outflow, but the clinical use of alpha-2 antagonists is less common due to this effect.
- **Beta Blockers**: Block β-adrenergic receptors. β1 blockers primarily affect the heart, reducing heart rate and contractility, while β2 blockers can affect the lungs and other tissues. Non-selective beta blockers block both β1 and β2 receptors.

2. Reduction of Sympathetic Outflow

Some sympatholytics work by reducing sympathetic outflow from the central nervous system. These drugs typically act on central adrenergic receptors to decrease overall sympathetic tone, resulting in lower blood pressure and heart rate.

Examples and Clinical Uses

1. Alpha-1 Blockers

a. Prazosin

- **Mechanism**: Prazosin is a selective α1-adrenergic blocker. It inhibits α1 receptors on vascular smooth muscle, leading to vasodilation and reduced blood pressure.
- **Clinical Uses**: Prazosin is used to treat hypertension and symptoms of benign prostatic hyperplasia (BPH), such as urinary obstruction. It helps relax smooth muscle in the prostate and bladder neck, improving urinary flow.

b. Doxazosin

- **Mechanism:** Doxazosin is similar to prazosin in that it blocks α1 receptors, resulting in vasodilation and reduced blood pressure.
- **Clinical Uses:** Doxazosin is used in the management of hypertension and BPH. It improves symptoms associated with urinary obstruction and is effective in lowering blood pressure.

2. Alpha-2 Blockers
a. Yohimbine

- **Mechanism:** Yohimbine is an α2-adrenergic antagonist. By blocking α2 receptors, it increases the release of norepinephrine and enhances sympathetic activity.
- **Clinical Uses:** Yohimbine is used in the treatment of erectile dysfunction and as a diagnostic tool for assessing certain autonomic disorders. It is less commonly used due to its potential to increase blood pressure and heart rate.

3. Beta Blockers
a. Propranolol

- **Mechanism:** Propranolol is a non-selective β-adrenergic antagonist, blocking both β1 and β2 receptors. This reduces heart rate and myocardial contractility while also causing bronchodilation.
- **Clinical Uses:** Propranolol is used for hypertension, angina, arrhythmias, and in the prevention of migraine headaches. It is also used in the management of essential tremor and hyperthyroidism.

b. Metoprolol

- **Mechanism:** Metoprolol is a selective β1-adrenergic antagonist. It specifically blocks β1 receptors in the heart, reducing heart rate and myocardial contractility.
- **Clinical Uses:** Metoprolol is used in the treatment of hypertension, heart failure, angina, and certain types of arrhythmias. Its selective action makes it suitable for patients with respiratory conditions where non-selective beta blockers might be contraindicated.

c. Atenolol

- **Mechanism:** Atenolol is another selective β1-adrenergic blocker, similar to metoprolol. It lowers heart rate and blood pressure by blocking β1 receptors.
- **Clinical Uses:** Atenolol is used in managing hypertension, angina, and heart attack recovery. It is often chosen for its relative selectivity and favorable side effect profile.

Clinical Implications

1. **Management of Hypertension:** Alpha-1 blockers like prazosin and beta blockers like propranolol and metoprolol are commonly used to manage hypertension by reducing vascular resistance and cardiac output.
2. **Treatment of Benign Prostatic Hyperplasia (BPH):** Alpha-1 blockers help relieve urinary symptoms associated with BPH by relaxing smooth muscle in the prostate and bladder neck.
3. **Control of Cardiac Conditions:** Beta blockers are essential in managing conditions such as angina, arrhythmias, and heart failure by decreasing heart rate and myocardial workload.
4. **Use in Anxiety and Migraine Prevention:** Beta blockers like propranolol are used to prevent migraines and manage anxiety due to their calming effect on the cardiovascular system.

7.5 Neuromuscular Blocking Agents and Skeletal Muscle Relaxants

Neuromuscular Blocking Agents

Neuromuscular blocking agents are drugs used to induce muscle relaxation during surgical procedures, facilitate endotracheal intubation, and manage certain medical conditions requiring muscle paralysis. These agents act at the neuromuscular junction, where they interfere with the transmission of nerve impulses to skeletal muscles, leading to muscle paralysis. They are critical in anesthesia for ensuring adequate muscle relaxation and preventing unintended movements during surgery.

Types of Neuromuscular Blockers

Neuromuscular blocking agents are broadly classified into two main types based on their mechanism of action: **depolarizing** and **non-depolarizing** neuromuscular blockers.

1. Depolarizing Neuromuscular Blockers

a. Succinylcholine

- **Mechanism of Action**: Succinylcholine is a depolarizing neuromuscular blocker that mimics acetylcholine (ACh) at the neuromuscular junction. It binds to the nicotinic receptors on the motor end plate, causing an initial depolarization or muscle twitch (fasciculation). This is followed by prolonged muscle relaxation due to its inability to be metabolized quickly, leading to persistent depolarization and muscle paralysis.
- **Clinical Uses**: Succinylcholine is used for rapid sequence induction of anesthesia, particularly for intubation due to its fast onset and short duration of action. It is also used in emergency situations where quick muscle relaxation is required.
- **Adverse Effects**: Common side effects include muscle soreness, hyperkalemia, and in rare cases, malignant hyperthermia. Caution is required in patients with conditions that predispose them to hyperkalemia or malignant hyperthermia.

2. Non-Depolarizing Neuromuscular Blockers
a. Curare

- **Mechanism of Action**: Curare, a classic non-depolarizing neuromuscular blocker, acts as a competitive antagonist at the neuromuscular junction. It binds to nicotinic receptors on the motor end plate without activating them, thereby blocking the action of acetylcholine and preventing muscle contraction.
- **Clinical Uses**: Although not commonly used today, curare served as a prototype for understanding neuromuscular blocking mechanisms and paved the way for modern non-depolarizing agents.

b. Rocuronium

- **Mechanism of Action**: Rocuronium is a non-depolarizing neuromuscular blocker that competes with acetylcholine for binding to nicotinic receptors on the neuromuscular junction. It prevents acetylcholine from binding and thereby inhibits muscle contraction.
- **Clinical Uses**: Rocuronium is used for muscle relaxation during surgical procedures and endotracheal intubation. It has a relatively rapid onset and intermediate duration of action.
- **Adverse Effects**: Potential side effects include hypotension and respiratory depression. It is generally well-tolerated but requires careful

dosing and monitoring.

c. Vecuronium

- **Mechanism of Action**: Vecuronium, like other non-depolarizing blockers, competes with acetylcholine for binding to nicotinic receptors. It prevents muscle contraction by blocking acetylcholine from binding to its receptor.
- **Clinical Uses**: Vecuronium is used to induce and maintain muscle relaxation during surgeries. It is preferred for its intermediate duration of action and minimal cardiovascular effects.
- **Adverse Effects**: Adverse effects can include muscle weakness, prolonged paralysis, and respiratory depression. Careful monitoring is essential to manage these risks.

Skeletal Muscle Relaxants

Skeletal muscle relaxants are drugs used to alleviate muscle spasticity, reduce muscle tone, and relieve muscle spasms associated with various conditions. They act centrally or peripherally to produce their effects.

Types of Skeletal Muscle Relaxants

1. Central Muscle Relaxants

a. Baclofen

- **Mechanism of Action**: Baclofen acts on the central nervous system as a GABA-B receptor agonist. It reduces muscle spasticity by inhibiting excitatory neurotransmitter release in the spinal cord, thereby decreasing muscle tone and spasms.
- **Clinical Uses**: Baclofen is used to treat spasticity associated with multiple sclerosis, spinal cord injuries, and cerebral palsy.
- **Adverse Effects**: Side effects include drowsiness, dizziness, and muscle weakness. Abrupt discontinuation can lead to withdrawal symptoms and exacerbation of spasticity.

b. Diazepam

- **Mechanism of Action:** Diazepam, a benzodiazepine, enhances the effect of the neurotransmitter GABA at the GABA-A receptor. This action increases the inhibitory effect in the central nervous system, leading to reduced muscle spasticity.

- **Clinical Uses:** Diazepam is used for muscle spasticity, anxiety, and as an adjunct in the management of seizures. It is particularly effective for short-term relief of muscle spasms.
- **Adverse Effects:** Potential side effects include sedation, muscle weakness, and dependence. Long-term use can lead to tolerance and withdrawal symptoms.

2. Peripheral Muscle Relaxants

a. Dantrolene

- **Mechanism of Action:** Dantrolene acts directly on skeletal muscle by interfering with calcium release from the sarcoplasmic reticulum, thus reducing muscle contraction.
- **Clinical Uses:** Dantrolene is used to treat malignant hyperthermia and certain types of muscle spasticity. It is the only muscle relaxant effective in treating this life-threatening condition.
- **Adverse Effects:** Side effects may include muscle weakness, drowsiness, and hepatotoxicity. Regular liver function tests are recommended during treatment.

Clinical Implications

1. **Surgical Procedures:** Neuromuscular blockers are essential in providing muscle relaxation during surgery, facilitating endotracheal intubation, and ensuring patient immobility.

2. **Management of Spasticity:** Skeletal muscle relaxants are used to manage spasticity associated with neurological disorders, improving patient comfort and function.

3. **Emergency Situations:** Depolarizing neuromuscular blockers like succinylcholine are preferred for rapid onset and short duration, making them suitable for emergency intubation.

7.5 Neuromuscular Blocking Agents and Skeletal Muscle Relaxants

Neuromuscular Blocking Agents

Neuromuscular blocking agents are crucial in various medical and surgical settings due to their ability to induce muscle relaxation and paralysis. They are essential tools in anesthesia and critical care, facilitating surgical procedures and managing respiratory support.

Clinical Applications

1. **Surgical Procedures**: Neuromuscular blockers are widely used during surgery to provide muscle relaxation, which is crucial for optimal surgical conditions. They allow surgeons to perform delicate operations by minimizing muscle contractions and reducing patient movement. This is particularly important in procedures requiring precise control, such as neurosurgery, orthopedic surgery, and abdominal surgeries.

2. **Endotracheal Intubation**: During emergency situations or elective surgeries, neuromuscular blockers are employed to facilitate endotracheal intubation. By inducing rapid and complete muscle relaxation, these agents make it easier to insert an endotracheal tube into the trachea, ensuring proper airway management and ventilation.

3. **Mechanical Ventilation**: In critical care settings, neuromuscular blockers may be used to assist with mechanical ventilation. They help in synchronizing the patient's breathing with the ventilator, reducing the risk of ventilator-induced lung injury, and improving overall ventilation efficiency.

4. **Management of Spasticity**: While neuromuscular blockers are not the primary treatment for spasticity, they may be used in specific cases to manage severe muscle spasms and spasticity that do not respond to other treatments. This use is more common in acute settings or as a short-term solution to alleviate severe symptoms.

Skeletal Muscle Relaxants

Skeletal muscle relaxants play a significant role in managing conditions associated with muscle spasticity and spasm. They are used to improve mobility, reduce pain, and enhance the quality of life for patients with various neuromuscular disorders.

Clinical Applications

1. **Management of Spasticity**: Skeletal muscle relaxants are frequently used to treat spasticity resulting from conditions such as multiple sclerosis, cerebral palsy, and spinal cord injuries. By reducing muscle tone and spasms, these medications help improve functional mobility and alleviate discomfort.

2. **Acute Muscle Spasms**: For patients experiencing acute muscle spasms, skeletal muscle relaxants provide relief by targeting the central nervous system or directly acting on the muscle. Conditions such as back pain, tension headaches, and neck pain can be managed effectively with these medications.

3. **Preoperative and Postoperative Care**: In the perioperative setting, skeletal muscle relaxants are used to relieve muscle tension and discomfort before and after surgical procedures. This application helps in reducing postoperative pain and promoting faster recovery.

4. **Management of Malignant Hyperthermia**: Dantrolene, a specific skeletal muscle relaxant, is crucial in treating malignant hyperthermia, a life-threatening condition triggered by certain anesthetics. Dantrolene works by reducing excessive calcium release in muscle cells, thereby alleviating the symptoms of malignant hyperthermia and preventing further complications.

5. **Muscle Spasticity in Neurodegenerative Disorders**: In patients with neurodegenerative disorders such as amyotrophic lateral sclerosis (ALS) and Parkinson's disease, skeletal muscle relaxants help manage muscle spasticity and rigidity. This management improves patient comfort and functional ability, supporting overall quality of life.

7.6 Local Anesthetic Agents

Local anesthetic agents are used to induce a reversible loss of sensation in a specific area of the body, making them essential in various medical and dental procedures. They work by blocking nerve conduction in the targeted region, providing pain relief without affecting consciousness. Local anesthetics can be categorized into two primary types based on their chemical structure: **ester** and **amide** local anesthetics.

Ester Local Anesthetics

Ester local anesthetics are characterized by their ester linkage between the aromatic ring and the amine group. These agents are metabolized primarily by plasma esterases, leading to relatively rapid breakdown and shorter duration of action compared to amide local anesthetics.

Examples:

1. **Procaine (Novocain)**: One of the first local anesthetics developed, procaine is commonly used in dental procedures and minor surgical interventions. It is known for its relatively short duration of action.
2. **Cocaine**: Historically significant as one of the first local anesthetics, cocaine has a dual action as a local anesthetic and a vasoconstrictor. Its use has been largely replaced by other agents due to its potential for abuse and significant side effects.
3. **Benzocaine**: Used primarily in topical preparations, benzocaine is employed to relieve pain and itching caused by minor skin irritations,

sunburn, and teething.

Mechanism of Action: Ester local anesthetics work by blocking voltage-gated sodium channels in the neuronal membrane. This inhibition prevents the influx of sodium ions, thereby blocking the propagation of action potentials along the nerve fibers. The selective block of sensory fibers results in the loss of pain sensation without affecting motor function if used appropriately.

Metabolism: Ester local anesthetics are rapidly hydrolyzed by plasma esterases into non-active metabolites. This rapid metabolism reduces the risk of systemic toxicity but also limits the duration of their anesthetic effect.

Amide Local Anesthetics

Amide local anesthetics have an amide linkage between the aromatic ring and the amine group. They are metabolized primarily in the liver by hepatic enzymes, resulting in a longer duration of action compared to ester local anesthetics.

Examples:

1. **Lidocaine (Xylocaine)**: One of the most widely used local anesthetics, lidocaine is employed in various procedures including dental work, minor surgical interventions, and as a topical anesthetic for pain relief. It provides a moderate duration of action.
2. **Bupivacaine (Marcaine)**: Known for its prolonged duration of action, bupivacaine is often used in regional anesthesia, including epidural and nerve block anesthesia during labor and major surgeries.
3. **Ropivacaine**: Similar to bupivacaine but with a slightly shorter duration, ropivacaine is used for regional anesthesia and pain management. It has a lower risk of cardiotoxicity compared to bupivacaine.

Mechanism of Action: Amide local anesthetics, like their ester counterparts, block voltage-gated sodium channels in the neuronal membrane. This blockade prevents sodium ion influx, thereby inhibiting nerve impulse conduction. The effects of amide anesthetics are generally more prolonged due to their slower metabolism.

Metabolism: Amide local anesthetics are metabolized in the liver by cytochrome P450 enzymes. This process is slower than the hydrolysis seen with ester local anesthetics, contributing to their longer duration of action and the need for careful dosing to avoid systemic toxicity.

7.6 Local Anesthetic Agents

Local anesthetic agents are crucial in providing targeted pain relief by inducing a reversible loss of sensation in a specific area. They work primarily by interfering with the normal functioning of nerve cells in the targeted region. The **mechanisms of action** for local anesthetics are central to understanding how they achieve their effects and how their properties influence their clinical use.

Mechanisms of Action

Local anesthetics act by blocking **voltage-gated sodium channels** on the neuronal membrane, which is essential for the propagation of action potentials in nerves. This action can be broken down into several key steps:

1. **Binding to Sodium Channels:**
    - **Local anesthetics** bind specifically to the **sodium channels** in their inactive or open states. The **sodium channels** are integral membrane proteins responsible for the influx of sodium ions into the neuron, which is crucial for initiating and conducting nerve impulses.
    - The binding of local anesthetics occurs in the **cytoplasmic** part of the sodium channel. The drug crosses the neuronal membrane in its uncharged (neutral) form and then binds to the channel in its charged (cationic) form.

2. **Blockade of Sodium Ion Influx:**
    - Once bound, local anesthetics inhibit the flow of **sodium ions** through the channel. This blockade prevents the depolarization of the neuronal membrane, which is necessary for generating and transmitting nerve impulses.
    - By blocking the influx of sodium ions, the local anesthetics effectively **interrupt the action potential propagation** along the nerve fiber, leading to a loss of sensation in the affected area.

3. **Differential Blockade:**
    - Local anesthetics affect different types of nerve fibers with varying selectivity. **Small, unmyelinated C fibers** (which carry pain and

temperature sensations) are more sensitive to local anesthetics compared to **large, myelinated A fibers** (which carry motor and proprioceptive signals).
- The **degree of blockade** can be influenced by the concentration of the anesthetic, the type of nerve fiber, and the location of administration.

4. **Reversibility:**

    - The blockade caused by local anesthetics is reversible. As the drug is metabolized or diffuses away from the site of action, **sodium channels** return to their normal state, allowing nerve function to gradually return.

5. **Pharmacokinetics Influence:**

    - The onset and duration of action are influenced by the **pH of the tissue**, the **lipid solubility** of the anesthetic, and its **protein binding properties.**
    - **Lipid solubility** affects the drug's ability to cross the neuronal membrane, while **protein binding** determines the drug's duration of action by influencing its availability at the site of action.

Types of Local Anesthetics and Their Mechanisms
Ester Local Anesthetics:

- Ester local anesthetics, such as **procaine** and **cocaine**, are hydrolyzed by **plasma esterases.** Their relatively short duration of action is due to rapid hydrolysis, which limits their systemic exposure and reduces the risk of toxicity.

Amide Local Anesthetics:

- Amide local anesthetics, such as **lidocaine** and **bupivacaine**, are metabolized primarily in the **liver** by **cytochrome P450 enzymes.** They generally have a longer duration of action due to slower metabolism, making them suitable for prolonged procedures.

7.7 Drugs for Myasthenia Gravis and Glaucoma

Myasthenia Gravis (MG) and **glaucoma** are two distinct conditions that require specific pharmacological interventions. The drugs used to manage these conditions operate through different mechanisms to alleviate symptoms and improve patient outcomes. Below is a detailed exploration of the types of drugs used for these conditions, their mechanisms, and therapeutic uses.

Drugs for Myasthenia Gravis

Myasthenia Gravis is an autoimmune disorder characterized by the **destruction of acetylcholine receptors** at the neuromuscular junction, leading to muscle weakness. The primary treatment goals are to enhance **acetylcholine levels** at the neuromuscular junction and modulate the immune response.

1. **Acetylcholinesterase Inhibitors:**
    - **Mechanism:**
        - These drugs work by inhibiting the enzyme **acetylcholinesterase** (AChE), which is responsible for breaking down **acetylcholine** in the synaptic cleft. By inhibiting AChE, these drugs increase the concentration of acetylcholine, thereby improving neuromuscular transmission.
    - **Examples:**
        - **Pyridostigmine:** Often used as a first-line treatment for MG. It provides symptomatic relief by increasing acetylcholine levels at the neuromuscular junction.
        - **Neostigmine:** Similar to pyridostigmine but with a shorter duration of action. It is also used in combination with other drugs for MG management.
    - **Therapeutic Uses:**
        - These drugs help to alleviate muscle weakness and improve muscle strength in patients with MG. They are used in conjunction with immunosuppressive agents for comprehensive management.

2. **Immunosuppressants:**
    - **Mechanism:**
        - Immunosuppressants help to reduce the abnormal immune response that attacks acetylcholine receptors. By modulating the immune system, these drugs decrease the production of antibodies against these receptors.
    - **Examples:**
        - **Prednisone:** A corticosteroid that suppresses the immune response. It is used to reduce inflammation and autoimmunity in MG.
        - **Azathioprine:** An immunosuppressive agent that inhibits lymphocyte proliferation, helping to reduce antibody production against acetylcholine receptors.
    - **Therapeutic Uses:**
        - These drugs are used for long-term management of MG, particularly in patients who do not respond adequately to acetylcholinesterase inhibitors alone.
3. **Monoclonal Antibodies:**
    - **Mechanism:**
        - Monoclonal antibodies target specific components of the immune system involved in the autoimmune response. They can help to reduce the production of pathogenic antibodies against acetylcholine receptors.
    - **Examples:**
        - **Rituximab:** A monoclonal antibody that targets B-cells, which are involved in the production of anti-acetylcholine receptor antibodies.

- **Therapeutic Uses:**
  - Rituximab is used for patients with severe or refractory MG, often in combination with other treatments.

4. **Thymectomy:**
   - **Mechanism:**
     - Thymectomy involves the surgical removal of the thymus gland, which is believed to play a role in the pathogenesis of MG. Removing the thymus can help to reduce the production of autoantibodies.
   - **Therapeutic Uses:**
     - It is used in certain cases of MG, especially in patients with thymomas or those who have not responded to medical therapy.

Drugs for Glaucoma

Glaucoma is a group of eye diseases characterized by elevated intraocular pressure (IOP) that can damage the optic nerve and lead to vision loss. The primary treatment goal is to lower IOP to prevent damage to the optic nerve.

1. **Prostaglandin Analogs:**
   - **Mechanism:**
     - These drugs increase the outflow of aqueous humor from the eye, thereby reducing IOP. They work by enhancing the uveoscleral outflow pathway.
   - **Examples:**
     - **Latanoprost:** A commonly used prostaglandin analog that effectively reduces IOP and is well-tolerated.

- **Bimatoprost:** Similar to latanoprost but may also affect the trabecular meshwork, further aiding in IOP reduction.

◦ **Therapeutic Uses:**

- They are often used as first-line treatment for glaucoma due to their efficacy and relatively few side effects.

2. **Beta-Adrenergic Blockers:**

◦ **Mechanism:**

- These drugs reduce the production of aqueous humor by blocking β-adrenergic receptors in the ciliary body.

◦ **Examples:**

- **Timolol:** A widely used beta-blocker for glaucoma that effectively lowers IOP.
- **Betaxolol:** A selective beta-1 blocker with fewer systemic side effects.

◦ **Therapeutic Uses:**

- They are used to manage IOP in both open-angle and angle-closure glaucoma.

3. **Alpha-Adrenergic Agonists:**

◦ **Mechanism:**

- These drugs reduce aqueous humor production and increase its outflow. They act on α-adrenergic receptors in the eye.

◦ **Examples:**

- **Brimonidine:** An alpha-2 agonist that lowers IOP by reducing aqueous humor production and increasing uveoscleral outflow.

- **Therapeutic Uses:**
    - Brimonidine is used as an adjunctive therapy for glaucoma when monotherapy is insufficient.

4. **Carbonic Anhydrase Inhibitors:**
    - **Mechanism:**
        - These drugs reduce the production of aqueous humor by inhibiting the enzyme carbonic anhydrase, which is involved in the secretion of aqueous humor.
    - **Examples:**
        - **Dorzolamide:** An example of a topical carbonic anhydrase inhibitor used to lower IOP.
        - **Acetazolamide:** An oral carbonic anhydrase inhibitor used for short-term management and in acute cases.
    - **Therapeutic Uses:**
        - They are used to manage elevated IOP in glaucoma, particularly when other treatments are inadequate.

5. **Cholinergic Agents:**
    - **Mechanism:**
        - These drugs increase the outflow of aqueous humor by stimulating the contraction of the ciliary muscle and opening the trabecular meshwork.
    - **Examples:**
        - **Pilocarpine:** A classic cholinergic agent that reduces IOP by improving aqueous humor drainage.

- **Therapeutic Uses:**
  - Pilocarpine is used as an adjunctive therapy for glaucoma, especially in acute situations.

7.7 Drugs for Myasthenia Gravis and Glaucoma

Myasthenia Gravis (MG) and **glaucoma** are conditions that require targeted pharmacological interventions to manage symptoms and improve patient outcomes. The following section explores the mechanisms of action and clinical applications of drugs used for these conditions.

Drugs for Myasthenia Gravis

Myasthenia Gravis is an autoimmune disorder where antibodies attack acetylcholine receptors at the neuromuscular junction, resulting in muscle weakness. The treatment strategy involves enhancing neuromuscular transmission and modulating the immune response.

1. **Acetylcholinesterase Inhibitors:**
   - **Mechanism of Action:**
     - Acetylcholinesterase inhibitors, such as **pyridostigmine** and **neostigmine**, work by blocking the enzyme **acetylcholinesterase**. This enzyme is responsible for breaking down **acetylcholine** in the synaptic cleft. By inhibiting its action, these drugs increase the concentration of acetylcholine available at the neuromuscular junction, which enhances neuromuscular transmission and improves muscle strength.
   - **Clinical Applications:**
     - These drugs are primarily used to manage muscle weakness in patients with MG. They provide symptomatic relief and are often the first-line treatment. Pyridostigmine is commonly used due to its effectiveness and long duration of action. Neostigmine is used in various clinical scenarios, including in combination with other therapies for more severe cases.
2. **Immunosuppressants:**

- **Mechanism of Action:**
  - **Prednisone** and **azathioprine** are used to suppress the overactive immune response in MG. Prednisone, a corticosteroid, reduces inflammation and suppresses the immune system's activity, decreasing the production of antibodies against acetylcholine receptors. Azathioprine, an immunosuppressive agent, inhibits lymphocyte proliferation, thus reducing the immune response that targets acetylcholine receptors.
- **Clinical Applications:**
  - These drugs are used for long-term management of MG, particularly in patients who do not respond adequately to acetylcholinesterase inhibitors alone. Prednisone is used to quickly control symptoms, while azathioprine is employed for sustained immunosuppression.

3. **Monoclonal Antibodies:**
   - **Mechanism of Action:**
     - **Rituximab** is a monoclonal antibody that targets **B-cells**, which are responsible for producing the autoantibodies against acetylcholine receptors. By depleting these B-cells, rituximab reduces the levels of these harmful antibodies, thereby alleviating symptoms of MG.
   - **Clinical Applications:**
     - Rituximab is used in patients with severe or refractory MG, often when conventional treatments are insufficient. It is typically considered when other treatments fail or in cases with significant disease activity.
4. **Thymectomy:**
   - **Mechanism of Action:**

- Thymectomy involves the surgical removal of the **thymus gland**, which is believed to contribute to the pathogenesis of MG by supporting the production of autoantibodies. Removing the thymus can help reduce the autoimmunity by eliminating this source of abnormal immune activity.

◦ **Clinical Applications:**

- Thymectomy is considered for patients with thymomas (tumors of the thymus gland) or those with generalized MG who do not respond well to medical therapy. It is often used in conjunction with other treatments for better outcomes.

Drugs for Glaucoma

Glaucoma is characterized by elevated intraocular pressure (IOP), which can lead to optic nerve damage and vision loss. The treatment aims to reduce IOP to prevent such damage.

1. **Prostaglandin Analogs:**

◦ **Mechanism of Action:**

- Prostaglandin analogs, such as **latanoprost** and **bimatoprost**, work by increasing the outflow of aqueous humor through the **uveoscleral pathway**. These drugs mimic the effects of natural prostaglandins, which enhance the drainage of aqueous humor and reduce IOP.

◦ **Clinical Applications:**

- These drugs are often used as first-line therapy for open-angle glaucoma due to their effectiveness in lowering IOP and their favorable side effect profile. They are typically administered once daily.

2. **Beta-Adrenergic Blockers:**

◦ **Mechanism of Action:**

    - **Timolol** and **betaxolol** reduce the production of aqueous humor by blocking **β-adrenergic receptors** in the ciliary body. This decreases the secretion of aqueous humor, leading to a reduction in IOP.

  - **Clinical Applications:**

    - Beta-blockers are commonly used in the treatment of open-angle glaucoma and are effective in lowering IOP. They are often used in combination with other medications for better control of IOP.

3. **Alpha-Adrenergic Agonists:**

  - **Mechanism of Action:**

    - **Brimonidine** and similar agents work by decreasing the production of aqueous humor and increasing its outflow. They act on **α-adrenergic receptors**, leading to reduced aqueous humor production and enhanced drainage through the uveoscleral pathway.

  - **Clinical Applications:**

    - These drugs are used as adjunctive therapy in glaucoma management, particularly when IOP is not adequately controlled with other medications.

4. **Carbonic Anhydrase Inhibitors:**

  - **Mechanism of Action:**

    - **Dorzolamide** and **acetazolamide** inhibit the enzyme **carbonic anhydrase**, which is involved in the production of aqueous humor. By blocking this enzyme, these drugs reduce aqueous humor production, thereby lowering IOP.

  - **Clinical Applications:**

- These inhibitors are used for short-term management of elevated IOP and in acute cases of glaucoma. They are also used as adjunctive therapy in combination with other drugs for better control of IOP.

5. **Cholinergic Agents:**

   - **Mechanism of Action:**

     - **Pilocarpine**, a cholinergic agent, increases the outflow of aqueous humor by stimulating the contraction of the **ciliary muscle** and opening the trabecular meshwork. This facilitates the drainage of aqueous humor and reduces IOP.

   - **Clinical Applications:**

     - Pilocarpine is used in the management of acute glaucoma and as an adjunctive therapy for chronic glaucoma. It helps in reducing IOP by improving aqueous humor drainage.

CHAPTER VIII

Pharmacology of the Central Nervous System

8.1 Neurohumoral Transmission in CNS

Neurohumoral transmission in the **central nervous system (CNS)** is a complex process involving various **neurotransmitters** that mediate communication between neurons. These neurotransmitters play crucial roles in regulating mood, cognition, motor function, and other essential CNS activities. The primary neurotransmitters include **GABA**, **glutamate**, **glycine**, **serotonin**, and **dopamine**. Each of these neurotransmitters has distinct functions and mechanisms of action, contributing to the overall balance and functionality of the CNS.

GABA (Gamma-Aminobutyric Acid)

GABA is the principal **inhibitory neurotransmitter** in the CNS. It plays a crucial role in maintaining the balance between excitatory and inhibitory signals, thereby modulating neuronal excitability and preventing excessive neuronal firing.

- **Mechanism of Action:**
  - GABA exerts its effects by binding to **GABA_A** and **GABA_B** receptors. The **GABA_A** receptors are ionotropic receptors that mediate inhibitory neurotransmission through the influx of **chloride ions** (Cl^-), leading to hyperpolarization of the neuron. The **GABA_B** receptors are metabotropic receptors that activate **G-proteins**, which in turn open potassium channels and close calcium channels, resulting in a decrease in neuronal excitability.
- **Clinical Relevance:**
  - GABAergic dysfunction is associated with various neurological and psychiatric disorders, including **epilepsy**, **anxiety disorders**, and **insomnia**. Drugs that enhance GABAergic activity, such as **benzodiazepines** and **barbiturates**, are used to treat these conditions by increasing inhibitory neurotransmission.

Glutamate

Glutamate is the primary **excitatory neurotransmitter** in the CNS and is involved in various cognitive functions, including learning and memory.

- **Mechanism of Action:**
  - Glutamate acts on several types of receptors, including **NMDA** (N-Methyl-D-Aspartate), **AMPA** (Alpha-Amino-3-Hydroxy-5-Methyl-4-Isoxazolepropionic Acid), and **kainate** receptors. The NMDA receptors are ionotropic and allow the influx of calcium (Ca^{2+}) and sodium (Na^{+}) ions when activated, which is crucial for synaptic plasticity and learning. AMPA and kainate receptors are also ionotropic but primarily mediate fast excitatory synaptic transmission by allowing sodium ions to enter the neuron.
- **Clinical Relevance:**
  - Excessive glutamate activity can lead to excitotoxicity and neuronal damage, contributing to neurodegenerative diseases such as **Alzheimer's disease**, **Parkinson's disease**, and **amyotrophic lateral sclerosis (ALS)**. Drugs that modulate glutamate activity, such as **NMDA receptor antagonists** like **memantine**, are used in the treatment of these conditions.

Glycine

Glycine is another **inhibitory neurotransmitter** in the CNS, primarily found in the spinal cord and brainstem.

- **Mechanism of Action:**
  - Glycine acts on **glycine receptors**, which are ionotropic and mediate inhibitory neurotransmission by allowing chloride ions to enter the neuron, leading to hyperpolarization. This helps to regulate motor and sensory functions.
- **Clinical Relevance:**

- Dysregulation of glycinergic neurotransmission can result in disorders such as **startle disease** and **hyperekplexia**. Glycine receptor agonists and antagonists can be used to modulate these conditions, although therapeutic options are still under investigation.

Serotonin (5-Hydroxytryptamine, 5-HT)

Serotonin is a monoamine neurotransmitter involved in mood regulation, sleep, appetite, and pain perception.

- **Mechanism of Action:**
  - Serotonin acts on multiple types of receptors, including **5-HT_1**, **5-HT_2**, **5-HT_3**, and **5-HT_4** receptors. The 5-HT_1 receptors are involved in inhibitory neurotransmission, while 5-HT_2 receptors mediate excitatory responses. The 5-HT_3 receptors are ionotropic and mediate fast excitatory synaptic transmission by allowing sodium and calcium ions to enter the neuron.
- **Clinical Relevance:**
  - Abnormalities in serotonin levels are linked to **depression**, **anxiety disorders**, and **schizophrenia**. Selective serotonin reuptake inhibitors (SSRIs) like **fluoxetine** and **sertraline** are commonly used to treat depression and anxiety by increasing serotonin levels in the synaptic cleft.

Dopamine

Dopamine is a monoamine neurotransmitter that plays a crucial role in movement, motivation, and reward.

- **Mechanism of Action:**
  - Dopamine acts on **D1** and **D2** receptors, among others. The D1 receptors are coupled with **adenylate cyclase** and increase **cAMP** levels, leading to excitatory effects. In contrast, D2 receptors are coupled with **Gi-proteins** that decrease cAMP levels and have inhibitory effects.

- **Clinical Relevance:**
  - Dopamine dysregulation is associated with various neurological and psychiatric disorders, including **Parkinson's disease**, **schizophrenia**, and **drug addiction**. **Dopamine agonists** like **pramipexole** are used to manage Parkinson's disease, while **antipsychotic drugs** targeting dopamine receptors are used in the treatment of schizophrenia.

8.1 Neurohumoral Transmission in CNS

Neurohumoral transmission in the **central nervous system (CNS)** is crucial for maintaining proper neuronal function and communication. It involves neurotransmitters such as **GABA**, **glutamate**, **glycine**, **serotonin**, and **dopamine**, each playing distinct roles in modulating neural activity. Here, we delve into their **mechanisms** and **functions**.

GABA (Gamma-Aminobutyric Acid)

Mechanisms:

- **GABA** functions primarily as an **inhibitory neurotransmitter**. It acts through **GABA_A** and **GABA_B** receptors.
  - **GABA_A Receptors**: These are **ionotropic receptors** that facilitate **chloride ion (Cl^-)** influx into the neuron. This influx hyperpolarizes the neuron, making it less likely to fire an action potential.
  - **GABA_B Receptors**: These are **metabotropic receptors** linked to **G-proteins**. Activation of GABA_B receptors leads to the opening of potassium channels and the closing of calcium channels, resulting in reduced neuronal excitability.

Functions:

- **GABA** helps balance **excitatory** signals within the CNS, preventing overactivity and **seizures**. It plays a role in **regulating muscle tone**, **anxiety**, and **sleep**. Dysregulation of GABAergic neurotransmission is implicated in disorders like **epilepsy**, **anxiety disorders**, and **insomnia**.

Glutamate

Mechanisms:

- **Glutamate** is the principal **excitatory neurotransmitter** in the CNS, acting through **NMDA**, **AMPA**, and **kainate** receptors.
    - **NMDA Receptors**: These are **ionotropic receptors** that mediate the influx of **calcium (Ca^{2+})** and **sodium (Na^{+})** ions. NMDA receptor activation is critical for **synaptic plasticity** and **learning**.
    - **AMPA Receptors**: These are also **ionotropic**, but they primarily mediate fast **excitatory** neurotransmission through sodium ion influx.
    - **Kainate Receptors**: Similar to AMPA receptors, they facilitate excitatory neurotransmission but also play roles in modulating synaptic transmission.

Functions:

- **Glutamate** is essential for **cognitive functions** such as **memory** and **learning**. However, excessive glutamate activity can lead to **excitotoxicity**, contributing to neurodegenerative diseases like **Alzheimer's disease** and **Parkinson's disease**.

Glycine
Mechanisms:

- **Glycine** is an **inhibitory neurotransmitter** mainly in the spinal cord and brainstem. It acts through **glycine receptors**, which are **ionotropic** and facilitate the entry of **chloride ions (Cl^{-})** into the neuron, leading to hyperpolarization.

Functions:

- **Glycine** helps regulate **motor and sensory functions** by inhibiting excessive neuronal firing. Imbalances in glycinergic neurotransmission can lead to disorders such as **hyperekplexia** and **startle disease**.

Serotonin (5-Hydroxytryptamine, 5-HT)
Mechanisms:

- **Serotonin** acts through various receptors including **5-HT_1**, **5-HT_2**, **5-HT_3**, and **5-HT_4**.

  - **5-HT_1 Receptors**: These are **metabotropic receptors** that usually lead to decreased cAMP levels, producing inhibitory effects.
  - **5-HT_2 Receptors**: These are **metabotropic** and often mediate excitatory effects by activating phospholipase C.
  - **5-HT_3 Receptors**: These are **ionotropic receptors** that mediate fast excitatory neurotransmission through sodium and calcium ion influx.

Functions:

- **Serotonin** regulates mood, **appetite**, **sleep**, and **pain perception**. Alterations in serotonin levels are associated with **depression**, **anxiety**, and **schizophrenia**. SSRIs (Selective Serotonin Reuptake Inhibitors) increase serotonin levels and are commonly used to treat mood disorders.

Dopamine
Mechanisms:

- **Dopamine** acts on various receptors including **D1** and **D2** receptors.

  - **D1 Receptors**: These are **metabotropic** and activate **adenylate cyclase**, increasing **cAMP** levels and leading to excitatory effects.
  - **D2 Receptors**: These are **metabotropic** but inhibit **adenylate cyclase**, reducing cAMP levels and producing inhibitory effects.

Functions:

- **Dopamine** is crucial for **movement**, **motivation**, and **reward**. Dysregulation can lead to **Parkinson's disease** (due to dopamine deficiency) and **schizophrenia** (due to excessive dopamine activity). Dopamine agonists and antagonists are used to manage these conditions.

8.2 General Anesthetics and Pre-Anesthetics

General anesthetics are agents used to induce a state of **unconsciousness** and **analgesia** to perform surgical procedures without pain or awareness. They are categorized into **inhalational** and **intravenous** anesthetics, each with distinct mechanisms of action and clinical applications. **Pre-anesthetics** are drugs used before the administration of general anesthetics to prepare the patient for anesthesia and surgery.

Inhalational Anesthetics

Types and Mechanisms:

- **Inhalational anesthetics** are administered via inhalation and include agents such as **nitrous oxide, halothane, isoflurane, sevoflurane**, and **desflurane**.
    - **Nitrous Oxide (N_2O)**: Commonly known as "laughing gas," nitrous oxide is used for its **analgesic** and **anxiolytic** effects. It works by diffusing into the nitrogen-filled spaces of the body, leading to a reduction in pain perception. Nitrous oxide is often used in combination with other anesthetics due to its minimal effect on cardiovascular stability.
    - **Halothane**: An early inhalational anesthetic with a non-flammable, volatile nature. It is known for its **potent anesthetic** properties but has been largely replaced by newer agents due to its potential for **hepatotoxicity** and **cardiovascular effects.**
    - **Isoflurane**: A widely used volatile anesthetic with a **pleasant** odor and **minimal** effects on cardiovascular function. It is used for **maintenance** of anesthesia and provides **muscle relaxation** and **analgesia.**
    - **Sevoflurane**: Known for its **rapid onset** and **recovery**, sevoflurane is often used in outpatient procedures. It has a **low** blood-gas partition coefficient, allowing for quick adjustments in anesthetic depth.
    - **Desflurane**: A very **potent** inhalational anesthetic with a **low** blood-gas partition coefficient, providing rapid **induction** and **emergence** from anesthesia. It is commonly used for **long surgeries** and **quick recovery.**

Mechanisms:

- Inhalational anesthetics primarily act by **modulating** the activity of **neurotransmitter systems** in the brain, particularly enhancing **GABA_A receptor activity** and inhibiting **NMDA receptor activity.** This results in **central nervous system depression**, loss of consciousness, and suppression of **pain**.

Intravenous Anesthetics
Types and Mechanisms:

- **Intravenous anesthetics** are administered directly into the bloodstream and include drugs such as **propofol**, **thiopental**, **etomidate**, and **ketamine**.
    - **Propofol**: A popular intravenous anesthetic known for its **rapid onset** and **short duration** of action. It is commonly used for **induction** and **maintenance** of anesthesia due to its **antiemetic** properties and minimal **cardiovascular effects**.
    - **Thiopental**: An ultra-short-acting barbiturate used for **induction** of anesthesia. It rapidly induces a state of **unconsciousness** by enhancing **GABA_A receptor activity**. Its use has declined due to the availability of newer agents with more favorable side-effect profiles.
    - **Etomidate**: A non-barbiturate anesthetic with **minimal** cardiovascular and respiratory effects, making it ideal for **induction** in patients with compromised cardiac function. It works by enhancing **GABA_A receptor activity** but has limited analgesic effects.
    - **Ketamine**: A dissociative anesthetic that provides **analgesia** and **dissociative anesthesia**. It acts primarily as an **NMDA receptor antagonist**, leading to a unique state of **conscious sedation** and **analgesia**. Ketamine is useful for **emergency** procedures and **pain management**.

Mechanisms:

- **Intravenous anesthetics** generally act by enhancing the activity of **GABA_A receptors** or inhibiting **NMDA receptors**. This results in rapid **central nervous system depression**, leading to loss of consciousness and pain suppression.

Pre-Anesthetics
Types and Uses:

- **Pre-anesthetics** are medications given before the induction of general anesthesia to facilitate the anesthetic process and minimize complications. Common pre-anesthetics include:

    - **Benzodiazepines** (e.g., **midazolam**): Used for their **anxiolytic** and **amnesic** effects. They help to calm the patient and reduce anxiety before surgery.
    - **Opioids** (e.g., **fentanyl**): Provide **analgesia** and help reduce the required dose of general anesthetics. They are used to manage pain and enhance the overall anesthetic experience.
    - **Anticholinergics** (e.g., **atropine**): Used to reduce **salivation** and **secretions** during surgery. They help prevent complications related to excessive secretions.
    - **H2 Antagonists** (e.g., **ranitidine**): Administered to reduce **gastric acid secretion** and decrease the risk of **aspiration pneumonia** during surgery.

Mechanisms:

- Pre-anesthetics act through various mechanisms to prepare the patient for anesthesia. **Benzodiazepines** enhance **GABA_A receptor activity**, leading to sedation and anxiolysis. **Opioids** act on **opioid receptors** to provide analgesia. **Anticholinergics** inhibit **acetylcholine** activity to reduce secretions, while **H2 antagonists** block **histamine H2 receptors** to decrease acid production in the stomach.

8.2 General Anesthetics and Pre-Anesthetics

General anesthetics are essential for inducing a state of **unconsciousness** and **analgesia** during surgical procedures. They are classified into **inhalational** and **intravenous** anesthetics, each with unique mechanisms of action. **Pre-anesthetics** are administered before general anesthesia to optimize patient preparation and minimize potential complications.

Inhalational Anesthetics

Types and Mechanisms:

- **Nitrous Oxide (N_2O):**

- **Mechanism of Action:** Nitrous oxide primarily acts as an **NMDA receptor antagonist**, which contributes to its **analgesic** and **anxiolytic** properties. By blocking these receptors, it reduces the perception of pain and anxiety. Additionally, nitrous oxide affects the **GABA_A receptors**, contributing to its anesthetic effects.

- **Halothane:**
  - **Mechanism of Action:** Halothane acts by enhancing the activity of **GABA_A receptors** and inhibiting **NMDA receptors**. This dual action leads to **CNS depression**, resulting in loss of consciousness and analgesia. Halothane's potency as an anesthetic is partly due to its ability to modulate these neurotransmitter systems.
- **Isoflurane:**
  - **Mechanism of Action:** Isoflurane enhances **GABA_A receptor** activity, increasing **chloride ion influx** into neurons, which leads to hyperpolarization and reduced neuronal excitability. It also inhibits **NMDA receptors**, further contributing to its anesthetic effects.
- **Sevoflurane:**
  - **Mechanism of Action:** Sevoflurane, like other inhalational anesthetics, works by increasing **GABA_A receptor** activity and decreasing **NMDA receptor** activity. Its rapid onset and recovery are due to its low **blood-gas partition coefficient**, allowing it to quickly equilibrate between the blood and the brain.
- **Desflurane:**
  - **Mechanism of Action:** Desflurane has a similar mechanism to other inhalational anesthetics, enhancing **GABA_A receptor** activity and inhibiting **NMDA receptors**. Its low **blood-gas partition coefficient** allows for rapid changes in anesthetic depth and quick recovery.

Intravenous Anesthetics
Types and Mechanisms:

- **Propofol:**
  - **Mechanism of Action:** Propofol acts primarily by enhancing the activity of **GABA_A receptors**, leading to increased **chloride ion influx** and neuronal inhibition. This results in rapid induction and maintenance of anesthesia. It also has some **antagonistic** effects on the **NMDA receptors**, contributing to its overall anesthetic profile.
- **Thiopental:**
  - **Mechanism of Action:** Thiopental, a barbiturate, enhances **GABA_A receptor** activity, increasing **chloride ion conductance** into the neuron, leading to hyperpolarization and decreased neuronal excitability. Its rapid onset and short duration are due to its high lipid solubility, allowing it to quickly cross the blood-brain barrier.
- **Etomidate:**
  - **Mechanism of Action:** Etomidate primarily enhances **GABA_A receptor** activity, similar to other anesthetics. It has minimal cardiovascular and respiratory effects, making it suitable for induction in patients with compromised organ function. It does not provide analgesia but is effective for inducing anesthesia.
- **Ketamine:**
  - **Mechanism of Action:** Ketamine is a dissociative anesthetic that acts as an **NMDA receptor antagonist**, disrupting **glutamate** transmission in the central nervous system. This leads to a state of **dissociative anesthesia**, characterized by analgesia and a form of consciousness where the patient is detached from their surroundings.

Pre-Anesthetics
Types and Mechanisms:

- **Benzodiazepines (e.g., Midazolam):**

- **Mechanism of Action:** Benzodiazepines enhance the activity of **GABA_A receptors**, increasing **chloride ion influx** into neurons and leading to **sedation, anxiolysis**, and **amnesia**. They help to calm the patient and reduce anxiety before surgical procedures.

- **Opioids (e.g., Fentanyl):**
  - **Mechanism of Action:** Opioids act on **opioid receptors** (μ, κ, δ) in the central nervous system, primarily the μ-opioid receptors, to produce **analgesia** and sedation. They are effective in reducing pain and often used in conjunction with general anesthetics.

- **Anticholinergics (e.g., Atropine):**
  - **Mechanism of Action:** Anticholinergics block **acetylcholine** action at **muscarinic receptors**, leading to decreased **salivation** and **secretions**. This helps to minimize the risk of airway complications during anesthesia.

- **H2 Antagonists (e.g., Ranitidine):**
  - **Mechanism of Action:** H2 antagonists block **histamine H2 receptors** in the stomach lining, reducing **gastric acid secretion**. This decreases the risk of **aspiration pneumonia** during anesthesia by minimizing stomach acid content.

8.3 Sedatives, Hypnotics, and Centrally Acting Muscle Relaxants

Sedatives and **hypnotics** are medications that influence the central nervous system to induce a calming effect or sleep. They are used to manage various conditions such as anxiety, insomnia, and muscle spasms. **Centrally acting muscle relaxants** target muscle tone and are employed to relieve muscle spasticity and pain. Understanding the types, mechanisms, and uses of these drugs is essential for their effective application in clinical practice.

Types of Sedatives and Hypnotics

Sedatives are drugs that reduce **nervousness** and **excitability**, inducing a calming effect. **Hypnotics**, on the other hand, are specifically used to induce and maintain **sleep**. Both classes of drugs often overlap in their effects and can be categorized based on their mechanisms of action and duration of effect.

- **Benzodiazepines:**
    - **Mechanism of Action:** Benzodiazepines enhance the activity of **GABA_A receptors** by increasing the frequency of **chloride ion channel** opening. This leads to increased **hyperpolarization** of neurons, producing a calming effect, reduced anxiety, and sedation. Benzodiazepines are commonly used for their **anxiolytic**, **sedative**, **hypnotic**, and **muscle relaxant** properties.
    - **Examples:Diazepam**, **Lorazepam**, **Alprazolam**, and **Temazepam**.
    - **Uses:** They are used to treat **anxiety disorders**, **insomnia**, **muscle spasms**, and **seizure disorders**. Due to their broad spectrum of effects, they are often used as first-line treatment for anxiety and sleep disturbances.

- **Barbiturates:**
    - **Mechanism of Action:** Barbiturates enhance **GABA_A receptor** activity similarly to benzodiazepines but also prolong the duration of **chloride ion channel** opening. They can induce sleep and have **anxiolytic** effects. However, barbiturates have a higher risk of **tolerance**, **dependence**, and **overdose** compared to benzodiazepines.
    - **Examples:Phenobarbital**, **Secobarbital**, and **Pentobarbital**.
    - **Uses:** Historically used for **sedation** and **anesthesia**, they are now less commonly used due to the risk of dependence and the availability of safer alternatives. They are occasionally used in the management of **seizure disorders**.

- **Non-Benzodiazepine Sleep Aids:**
    - **Mechanism of Action:** These drugs selectively bind to specific subtypes of the **GABA_A receptor**, resulting in **sedation** without the broad-spectrum effects of benzodiazepines. They typically have a shorter duration of action.
    - **Examples:Zolpidem**, **Zaleplon**, and **Eszopiclone**.
    - **Uses:** Primarily used for the short-term management of **insomnia**. They are preferred for their lower risk of dependence and adverse

effects compared to benzodiazepines.

- **Melatonin Receptor Agonists:**
  - **Mechanism of Action:** These agents mimic the action of **melatonin**, a hormone that regulates the sleep-wake cycle, by binding to **melatonin receptors** (MT1 and MT2) in the brain. They help to regulate **circadian rhythms** and promote sleep.
  - **Examples:Ramelteon.**
  - **Uses:** Used to manage **insomnia** related to sleep onset difficulties and disturbances in the circadian rhythm.

- **Antihistamines:**
  - **Mechanism of Action:** Some antihistamines, particularly the first-generation ones, have **sedative** properties due to their ability to cross the blood-brain barrier and block **H1 histamine receptors** in the central nervous system.
  - **Examples:Diphenhydramine, Hydroxyzine.**
  - **Uses:** Often used for their **sedative** effect in the short-term management of **insomnia** or **anxiety**.

Centrally Acting Muscle Relaxants

Centrally acting muscle relaxants work by acting on the central nervous system rather than directly on the muscle. They are used to relieve muscle spasticity and associated pain.

- **Benzodiazepines:**
  - **Mechanism of Action:** Benzodiazepines, as previously mentioned, enhance **GABA_A receptor** activity, leading to **muscle relaxation** in addition to their anxiolytic and hypnotic effects.
  - **Examples:Diazepam, Clonazepam.**
  - **Uses:** Used to treat **muscle spasticity** and **spasms** associated with conditions such as **multiple sclerosis** or **cerebral palsy**.

- **Cyclobenzaprine:**

- **Mechanism of Action:** Cyclobenzaprine primarily acts as a **muscle relaxant** by influencing **muscarinic** receptors and indirectly modulating **serotonin** levels in the central nervous system, which helps reduce muscle spasm.
- **Examples:Cyclobenzaprine.**
- **Uses:** Commonly prescribed for the short-term management of **muscle spasms** and **pain** associated with musculoskeletal conditions.

- **Methocarbamol:**

  - **Mechanism of Action:** Methocarbamol acts centrally to relieve muscle spasm and pain. Its exact mechanism is not well understood but is believed to involve **CNS depressant** effects that reduce muscle tone.
  - **Examples:Methocarbamol.**
  - **Uses:** Used for **muscle relaxation** in conditions such as **muscle strain** and **spasm.**

- **Tizanidine:**

  - **Mechanism of Action:** Tizanidine acts as an **alpha-2 adrenergic agonist**, leading to reduced **muscle tone** through decreased central excitatory input to motor neurons.
  - **Examples:Tizanidine.**
  - **Uses:** Used to manage **muscle spasticity** and **pain** in conditions like **multiple sclerosis** and **spinal cord injury**.

8.3 Sedatives, Hypnotics, and Centrally Acting Muscle Relaxants

Sedatives, hypnotics, and **centrally acting muscle relaxants** play crucial roles in managing a variety of medical conditions related to anxiety, sleep disturbances, and muscle spasticity. Each class of drugs has specific clinical applications based on its pharmacological effects, mechanisms of action, and safety profiles.

Clinical Applications of Sedatives and Hypnotics

1. Benzodiazepines:

- **Anxiety Disorders:** Benzodiazepines are frequently prescribed for the short-term management of **generalized anxiety disorder (GAD), panic**

disorder, and **social anxiety disorder**. They provide rapid relief from symptoms by enhancing **GABA_A receptor** activity, which reduces neuronal excitability and anxiety.

- **Insomnia:** These medications are effective for managing **insomnia**, particularly when it is related to anxiety or stress. They help to induce and maintain sleep by facilitating the calming effects of **GABA**.
- **Muscle Spasms:** In conditions like **cerebral palsy** or **multiple sclerosis**, benzodiazepines help relieve **muscle spasticity** and **muscle spasms** due to their central muscle relaxant properties.
- **Seizure Disorders:** Benzodiazepines are used in the acute management of **seizures** and in the treatment of **epilepsy** due to their **antiepileptic** properties.

2. Barbiturates:

- **Sedation and Anesthesia:** Barbiturates are used for their **sedative** and **anesthetic** properties in various medical procedures. They are effective in producing **deep sedation** and **general anesthesia**.
- **Seizure Disorders:** Despite being less commonly used today, barbiturates can be prescribed for **seizure control** in cases where other antiepileptic drugs are ineffective.

3. Non-Benzodiazepine Sleep Aids:

- **Short-Term Insomnia Treatment:** These drugs are prescribed for the short-term management of **insomnia**, particularly in patients who have difficulty falling asleep. They are preferred over benzodiazepines due to their lower risk of dependence.
- **Circadian Rhythm Disorders:** Non-benzodiazepine sleep aids can be beneficial for individuals with **circadian rhythm sleep disorders**, such as **shift work sleep disorder** or **jet lag**.

4. Melatonin Receptor Agonists:

- **Insomnia:** Melatonin receptor agonists are used to treat **insomnia**, particularly in patients with **sleep-onset difficulties**. They help regulate the sleep-wake cycle by mimicking the action of **melatonin**.

- **Circadian Rhythm Disorders:** These agents are useful in managing **circadian rhythm disorders** and are often used in patients with irregular sleep patterns due to shift work or time zone changes.

5. Antihistamines:

- **Short-Term Insomnia:** Antihistamines with sedative properties are sometimes used for **short-term insomnia** or **sleep disturbances**. They are less commonly used as a first-line treatment due to their anticholinergic side effects.

Clinical Applications of Centrally Acting Muscle Relaxants
1. Benzodiazepines:

- **Muscle Spasms:** In addition to their use in anxiety and sleep disorders, benzodiazepines are used to relieve **muscle spasms** associated with conditions like **back pain**, **musculoskeletal injuries**, and **spinal cord injuries**.

2. Cyclobenzaprine:

- **Acute Muscle Spasms:** Cyclobenzaprine is used for the short-term management of **acute muscle spasms** and **muscle pain** resulting from musculoskeletal injuries or conditions such as **fibromyalgia**.
- **Muscle Spasticity:** It is sometimes used in the management of **muscle spasticity** related to **neurological conditions**.

3. Methocarbamol:

- **Muscle Spasms and Strains:** Methocarbamol is prescribed for the relief of **muscle spasms**, **muscle strains**, and **musculoskeletal pain**. It is useful in acute conditions and can be combined with rest and physical therapy.

4. Tizanidine:

- **Muscle Spasticity:** Tizanidine is used for the management of **muscle spasticity** associated with conditions such as **multiple sclerosis**, **spinal cord injury**, and **stroke**. It is effective in reducing muscle tone and improving mobility.

8.4 Anti-Epileptics

Anti-epileptic drugs (AEDs) are essential in the management of **epilepsy**, a neurological disorder characterized by recurrent seizures. These drugs work through various mechanisms to stabilize neuronal activity and prevent seizures. Understanding the mechanisms of action of different anti-epileptic drugs is crucial for effective treatment and individualized patient care.

Mechanisms of Action of Various Anti-Epileptics

1. Sodium Channel Blockers

Phenytoin:

- **Mechanism:** Phenytoin stabilizes neuronal membranes by binding to **voltage-gated sodium channels** in their inactive state. This prevents the rapid firing of neurons and inhibits the spread of abnormal electrical activity.
- **Clinical Use:** It is effective in controlling **partial seizures, generalized tonic-clonic seizures**, and **status epilepticus.**

Carbamazepine:

- **Mechanism:** Similar to phenytoin, carbamazepine inhibits **voltage-gated sodium channels**, reducing neuronal excitability and preventing the propagation of seizure activity.
- **Clinical Use:** It is commonly used for **partial seizures** and **generalized tonic-clonic seizures**, as well as **trigeminal neuralgia**.

Lamotrigine:

- **Mechanism:** Lamotrigine inhibits **sodium channels** and also modulates **glutamate** release. By stabilizing the neuronal membrane, it reduces the likelihood of seizure generation.
- **Clinical Use:** It is effective for **partial seizures**, **generalized seizures**, and **bipolar disorder**.

2. Calcium Channel Blockers

Ethosuximide:

- **Mechanism:** Ethosuximide inhibits **T-type calcium channels** in the **thalamic neurons**, which reduces the rhythmic bursting activity that characterizes **absence seizures.**
- **Clinical Use:** It is specifically used for **absence seizures** and is effective in reducing their frequency and severity.

3. GABAergic Agents
Benzodiazepines (e.g., Diazepam, Lorazepam):

- **Mechanism:** Benzodiazepines enhance the action of **gamma-aminobutyric acid (GABA)** at the **GABA_A receptors**, leading to increased neuronal inhibition and reduced seizure activity.
- **Clinical Use:** They are used for **acute seizure control**, **status epilepticus**, and **short-term management** of seizures.

Valproate (Valproic Acid):

- **Mechanism:** Valproate increases **GABA levels** by inhibiting its breakdown and also blocks **sodium channels.** This dual mechanism helps stabilize neuronal activity.
- **Clinical Use:** Valproate is used for **generalized tonic-clonic seizures**, **absence seizures**, and **bipolar disorder.**

4. Glutamate Receptor Antagonists
Topiramate:

- **Mechanism:** Topiramate inhibits **glutamate receptors** and **sodium channels**, and enhances **GABAergic transmission.** These actions help prevent seizure activity by stabilizing the neuronal membrane.
- **Clinical Use:** It is effective for **partial seizures**, **generalized seizures**, and as an adjunct in **bipolar disorder.**

5. Other Mechanisms
Gabapentin:

- **Mechanism:** Gabapentin binds to the **2 (alpha-2-delta) subunit** of voltage-gated calcium channels, reducing excitatory neurotransmitter release. It also modulates **GABAergic activity.**

- **Clinical Use:** It is used for **partial seizures, neuropathic pain**, and **postherpetic neuralgia**.

Pregabalin:

- **Mechanism:** Pregabalin binds to the **alpha-2-delta subunit** of voltage-gated calcium channels, reducing **glutamate** release and stabilizing neuronal activity.
- **Clinical Use:** It is used for **partial seizures, neuropathic pain**, and **generalized anxiety disorder**.

Levetiracetam:

- **Mechanism:** Levetiracetam binds to the **synaptic vesicle protein SV2A**, modulating neurotransmitter release and stabilizing neuronal activity.
- **Clinical Use:** It is effective for **partial seizures, generalized tonic-clonic seizures**, and **myoclonic seizures**.

8.4 Anti-Epileptics

Anti-epileptic drugs (AEDs) are vital in managing **epilepsy**, a condition characterized by recurrent and uncontrolled seizures. The effectiveness and appropriateness of each drug depend on its specific mechanism of action, the type of seizures being treated, and individual patient factors. Here is an overview of the clinical applications of various anti-epileptic drugs:

1. Sodium Channel Blockers

Phenytoin:

- **Clinical Applications:** Phenytoin is primarily used for the management of **partial seizures** and **generalized tonic-clonic seizures**. It is also used in the treatment of **status epilepticus** and has a long history of use in epilepsy management. Its role in preventing **post-traumatic seizures** and **seizure prophylaxis** during neurosurgery is also well established. Phenytoin is often chosen for its efficacy in controlling generalized tonic-clonic seizures and for its relatively favorable side-effect profile.

Carbamazepine:

- **Clinical Applications:** Carbamazepine is effective for **partial seizures** and **generalized tonic-clonic seizures.** It is also used in the management of **trigeminal neuralgia**, a condition characterized by severe facial pain, and **bipolar disorder**. Carbamazepine is often selected for its effectiveness in managing complex partial seizures and its ability to stabilize mood in bipolar disorder.

Lamotrigine:

- **Clinical Applications:** Lamotrigine is used for **partial seizures**, **generalized seizures**, and **bipolar disorder**. It is particularly effective in **absence seizures** and **myoclonic seizures.** Lamotrigine is valued for its broad-spectrum efficacy and is often used as an adjunctive therapy in cases where other AEDs are insufficient.

2. Calcium Channel Blockers
Ethosuximide:

- **Clinical Applications:** Ethosuximide is specifically indicated for **absence seizures.** It is the first-line treatment for this type of seizure, effectively reducing the frequency and severity of absence seizures. It is not typically used for other types of seizures, making it a specialized treatment for this particular seizure disorder.

3. GABAergic Agents
Benzodiazepines (e.g., Diazepam, Lorazepam):

- **Clinical Applications:** Benzodiazepines are primarily used for **acute seizure control** and **status epilepticus.** They are effective in rapidly terminating prolonged seizures and are often used in emergency settings. These drugs are also used for **short-term management** of seizures and as adjuncts to other AEDs in the management of chronic epilepsy.

Valproate (Valproic Acid):

- **Clinical Applications:** Valproate is effective for **generalized tonic-clonic seizures**, **absence seizures**, **myoclonic seizures**, and **bipolar**

disorder. It is often used as a broad-spectrum AED due to its efficacy in various types of seizures and its role in stabilizing mood in bipolar disorder. Valproate is also used in cases where multiple seizure types are present.

4. Glutamate Receptor Antagonists
Topiramate:

- **Clinical Applications:** Topiramate is used for **partial seizures**, **generalized seizures**, and **bipolar disorder**. It is also used as an adjunctive therapy in patients with **refractory seizures**. Topiramate is valued for its broad spectrum of activity and its effectiveness in reducing seizure frequency.

5. Other Mechanisms
Gabapentin:

- **Clinical Applications:** Gabapentin is used for **partial seizures** and **neuropathic pain**. It is commonly prescribed for conditions like **postherpetic neuralgia** and **diabetic neuropathy**. Gabapentin's role in epilepsy is particularly important in managing seizures that are resistant to other treatments.

Pregabalin:

- **Clinical Applications:** Pregabalin is used for **partial seizures**, **neuropathic pain**, and **generalized anxiety disorder**. It is effective in managing **neuropathic pain** conditions and is sometimes used in conjunction with other AEDs for optimal seizure control.

Levetiracetam:

- **Clinical Applications:** Levetiracetam is used for **partial seizures**, **generalized tonic-clonic seizures**, and **myoclonic seizures**. It is often chosen for its efficacy and favorable side-effect profile. Levetiracetam is also used as an adjunctive therapy for patients with refractory seizures.

8.5 Alcohols and Disulfiram

Pharmacology of Alcohol

Alcohol, specifically **ethanol**, is one of the most widely consumed psychoactive substances globally. Its pharmacology is complex, involving multiple mechanisms and effects on various body systems. Here's an in-depth look at the pharmacology of alcohol:

1. Mechanism of Action

Ethanol primarily acts on the **central nervous system (CNS)**, where it influences neurotransmitter systems and modulates brain function. Its effects are mediated through several key mechanisms:

- **GABA-A Receptor Modulation:** Ethanol enhances the activity of the **gamma-aminobutyric acid (GABA)** neurotransmitter at GABA-A receptors. This leads to increased inhibitory effects in the CNS, contributing to its **sedative** and **anxiolytic** properties.
- **NMDA Receptor Antagonism:** Ethanol inhibits the activity of the **N-methyl-D-aspartate (NMDA)** receptors, which are involved in **glutamate** neurotransmission. This antagonism contributes to its **cognitive impairments** and **memory disturbances**.
- **Dopamine Release:** Ethanol stimulates the release of **dopamine** in the brain's reward pathways. This action is associated with the **euphoric** effects of alcohol and its potential for **addiction.**
- **Serotonin Modulation:** Ethanol can alter serotonin levels, which may influence mood, behavior, and **aggression.**

2. Pharmacokinetics

- **Absorption:** Ethanol is rapidly absorbed from the **gastrointestinal tract**. It is absorbed quickly in the stomach and small intestine, with peak blood levels typically reached within **30 to 90 minutes** after consumption.
- **Distribution:** Ethanol is widely distributed throughout the body. It is **lipophilic**, allowing it to cross the **blood-brain barrier** and other cellular membranes easily. Its distribution is influenced by factors such as body water content, fat content, and the presence of food in the stomach.
- **Metabolism:** Ethanol is metabolized primarily in the liver. The main enzyme responsible for its metabolism is **alcohol dehydrogenase (ADH)**, which converts ethanol to **acetaldehyde**. Acetaldehyde is further metabolized to **acetic acid** by **aldehyde dehydrogenase**

(ALDH). Ethanol metabolism follows **zero-order kinetics** at high doses, meaning that the rate of metabolism is constant and independent of ethanol concentration.

- **Excretion:** A small fraction of ethanol is excreted unchanged through the **urine**, **sweat**, and **breath**. The **breath alcohol concentration** is commonly used for detecting alcohol use and impairment.

3. Effects

- **CNS Effects:** Ethanol produces a range of CNS effects, including **euphoria**, **drowsiness**, **impaired motor coordination**, and **cognitive dysfunction**. At higher doses, it can lead to **sedation**, **hypnosis**, and **anesthesia**.
- **Behavioral Effects:** Alcohol can affect mood and behavior, leading to **disinhibition**, **aggressiveness**, and impaired **judgment**. Long-term use may result in **alcohol dependence** and **addiction**.
- **Physiological Effects:** Acute alcohol consumption can lead to **vasodilation**, causing a feeling of warmth. Chronic use can lead to serious health issues such as **liver disease**, **gastritis**, **cardiomyopathy**, and **neuropathy**.
- **Tolerance and Dependence:** Regular use of ethanol can lead to the development of **tolerance**, where increasing amounts are required to achieve the same effects. Dependence may develop, leading to withdrawal symptoms when alcohol use is reduced or stopped.

Disulfiram

Disulfiram is a medication used to support the treatment of **chronic alcoholism** by deterring alcohol consumption. It is not a treatment for alcoholism per se but works as a deterrent to drinking.

1. Mechanism of Action

Disulfiram works by inhibiting the enzyme **aldehyde dehydrogenase (ALDH)**, which is crucial for metabolizing acetaldehyde, a toxic byproduct of ethanol metabolism. When disulfiram is taken and alcohol is consumed, acetaldehyde accumulates, leading to unpleasant reactions:

- **Acetaldehyde Accumulation:** The inhibition of ALDH results in the buildup of acetaldehyde, causing symptoms such as **flushing**, **nausea**, **vomiting**, **palpitations**, and **headaches**. This reaction is commonly referred to as the **disulfiram-alcohol reaction.**

2. Clinical Uses

- **Alcohol Deterrent:** Disulfiram is used in the management of **alcohol dependence** to discourage drinking by making the consumption of alcohol unpleasant. It is used as part of a comprehensive treatment program that includes counseling and support.
- **Adjunct to Alcohol Treatment Programs:** Disulfiram is most effective when used in conjunction with psychosocial therapies and support groups. It is intended to complement other treatment strategies rather than serve as a standalone solution.

3. Administration and Monitoring

- **Administration:** Disulfiram is typically administered orally in tablet form. The dosage is usually adjusted based on individual patient needs and tolerance.
- **Monitoring:** Patients on disulfiram should be monitored for adherence to the treatment regimen and any adverse effects. It is important to ensure that patients understand the potential reactions and avoid alcohol consumption during therapy.

Disulfiram: Mechanism of Action and Clinical Uses

Mechanism of Disulfiram

Disulfiram is a medication used to assist in the treatment of chronic alcoholism. Its primary action is to deter alcohol consumption by causing unpleasant reactions when alcohol is ingested. The mechanism of disulfiram involves the inhibition of the enzyme **aldehyde dehydrogenase (ALDH),** which plays a crucial role in the metabolism of alcohol.

1. **Inhibition of Aldehyde Dehydrogenase (ALDH):**

    - **Normal Ethanol Metabolism:** When ethanol (alcohol) is consumed, it is first metabolized in the liver by the enzyme **alcohol dehydrogenase (ADH)** into **acetaldehyde**, a toxic substance. Acetaldehyde is then further metabolized to **acetic acid** by **aldehyde dehydrogenase (ALDH)**, which is a less toxic compound that is eventually broken down into water and carbon dioxide.

- **Disulfiram's Action:** Disulfiram inhibits ALDH, leading to the accumulation of acetaldehyde in the blood. As a result, when alcohol is consumed, acetaldehyde levels rise significantly, causing a range of unpleasant symptoms due to its toxic effects.

2. **Disulfiram-Alcohol Reaction:**

   - **Symptoms:** The accumulation of acetaldehyde produces a set of symptoms known as the **disulfiram-alcohol reaction**. These symptoms include **flushing**, **nausea**, **vomiting**, **palpitations**, **headaches**, and **breathing difficulties**. The severity of these reactions can vary based on the amount of alcohol consumed and individual sensitivity.
   - **Mechanism:** The disulfiram-alcohol reaction is an adverse interaction that serves as a deterrent for drinking alcohol. The unpleasant symptoms act as a strong negative reinforcement against alcohol consumption.

Clinical Uses of Disulfiram

Disulfiram is primarily used as a part of a comprehensive treatment program for alcohol dependence. Its clinical uses include:

1. **Deterrence of Alcohol Consumption:**

   - **Objective:** The main clinical use of disulfiram is to help individuals with chronic alcoholism abstain from drinking by inducing a highly unpleasant reaction if alcohol is consumed. This deterrent effect is intended to encourage individuals to avoid alcohol and maintain sobriety.
   - **Administration:** Disulfiram is administered orally, usually in the form of tablets. The typical dose is 250 to 500 mg daily, adjusted based on patient tolerance and response.

2. **Adjunctive Therapy:**

   - **Comprehensive Treatment Programs:** Disulfiram is most effective when used in conjunction with other treatment strategies, including behavioral therapy, counseling, and support groups. It is not a standalone treatment but rather an adjunct to a broader alcoholism treatment program.

- **Behavioral Support:** Patients receiving disulfiram should be engaged in ongoing behavioral support and counseling to address the psychological and social aspects of alcohol dependence.

3. **Patient Education and Monitoring:**

   - **Patient Education:** Patients prescribed disulfiram must be thoroughly educated about the potential reactions with alcohol and the importance of avoiding alcohol-containing products. This education helps prevent accidental ingestion and enhances the effectiveness of the treatment.
   - **Monitoring:** Regular monitoring is essential to ensure adherence to the treatment regimen and to manage any side effects or adverse reactions. Healthcare providers should also monitor for any potential drug interactions and assess the overall progress of alcohol dependence treatment.

CHAPTER IX

Psychopharmacology

Table 9.1: **Types of Antipsychotic Agents**

Type	Mechanism of Action	Example
Typical Antipsychotics	Block dopamine receptors	Haloperidol, Chlorpromazine
Atypical Antipsychotics	Block dopamine and serotonin receptors	Risperidone, Clozapine

Table 9.2: **Classes of Antidepressants**

Class	Mechanism of Action	Example
SSRIs	Selective serotonin reuptake inhibitors	Fluoxetine, Sertraline
SNRIs	Serotonin and norepinephrine reuptake inhibitors	Venlafaxine, Duloxetine

Table 9.3: **Types of Anti-Anxiety Agents**

Type	Mechanism of Action	Example
Benzodiazepines	Enhance GABA effects	Diazepam, Alprazolam
Non-Benzodiazepines	Bind to serotonin receptors	Buspirone

Table 9.4: **Drug Classes for Bipolar Disorder**

Class	Mechanism of Action	Example
Mood Stabilizers	Stabilize mood	Lithium
Antipsychotics	Block dopamine receptors	Olanzapine

Table 9.5: **Drugs for Obsessive-Compulsive Disorder (OCD)**

Class	Mechanism of Action	Example
SSRIs	Inhibit serotonin reuptake	Fluoxetine
Tricyclic Antidepressants	Inhibit reuptake of norepinephrine and serotonin	Clomipramine

Table 9.6: **Pharmacological Management of PTSD**

Class	Mechanism of Action	Example
SSRIs	Inhibit serotonin reuptake	Sertraline
Alpha-1 Blockers	Block alpha-1 adrenergic receptors	Prazosin

Antipsychotic Agents: Types and Mechanisms

Antipsychotic agents are primarily used to manage symptoms of psychotic disorders, such as **schizophrenia** and **bipolar disorder**. These drugs are categorized into two main classes: **typical** (or first-generation) and **atypical** (or second-generation) antipsychotics. Each class has distinct mechanisms of action, clinical applications, and side effect profiles.

Typical Antipsychotics

Typical antipsychotics, introduced in the 1950s, are primarily known for their ability to alleviate **positive symptoms** of schizophrenia, such as **hallucinations** and **delusions**. They work mainly by antagonizing **dopamine D2 receptors** in the **mesolimbic** and **mesocortical pathways**.

1. **Mechanism of Action:**

   - **Dopamine D2 Receptor Antagonism:** Typical antipsychotics block dopamine D2 receptors in the central nervous system, particularly in the **mesolimbic** system. This blockade reduces dopaminergic overactivity that is associated with positive symptoms of schizophrenia.
   - **Effect on Other Neurotransmitter Systems:** Some typical antipsychotics also affect other neurotransmitter systems, including serotonin and norepinephrine, but their primary action remains the blockade of dopamine receptors.

2. **Examples of Typical Antipsychotics:**

   - **Chlorpromazine:** One of the earliest antipsychotics, used for its efficacy in treating acute psychotic episodes. It is also used to manage agitation and severe anxiety.
   - **Haloperidol:** Known for its potent dopamine D2 receptor antagonism. It is used in the treatment of acute psychotic states and agitation.

3. **Side Effects:**

- **Extrapyramidal Symptoms (EPS):** Includes **tremors**, **rigidity**, **bradykinesia**, and **akathisia**, which are associated with disturbances in the basal ganglia.
- **Tardive Dyskinesia:** A condition characterized by repetitive, involuntary movements, often occurring after prolonged use of the medication.
- **Neuroleptic Malignant Syndrome (NMS):** A rare but serious side effect involving high fever, muscle rigidity, and autonomic instability.

Atypical Antipsychotics

Atypical antipsychotics, introduced in the 1990s, offer a broader spectrum of treatment, addressing both **positive** and **negative symptoms** of schizophrenia, such as **social withdrawal** and **apathy**. They have a more favorable side effect profile compared to typical antipsychotics.

1. **Mechanism of Action:**

   - **Dopamine D2 Receptor Antagonism:** Atypical antipsychotics also antagonize D2 receptors, but they tend to bind with a lower affinity compared to typical antipsychotics. This may contribute to a reduced risk of extrapyramidal side effects.
   - **Serotonin 5-HT2A Receptor Antagonism:** Atypical antipsychotics exhibit significant antagonism at serotonin 5-HT2A receptors. This action is thought to counteract some of the dopaminergic blockade, reducing the risk of EPS and improving the management of negative symptoms.

2. **Examples of Atypical Antipsychotics:**

   - **Risperidone:** Effective in treating both positive and negative symptoms of schizophrenia. It is also used for bipolar disorder and irritability associated with autism.
   - **Olanzapine:** Known for its efficacy in managing acute psychotic episodes and bipolar disorder. It has a favorable effect on both positive and negative symptoms.
   - **Quetiapine:** Used in the treatment of schizophrenia, bipolar disorder, and as an adjunct in depression. It is noted for its sedative effects, which can be beneficial in managing agitation.

3. **Side Effects:**

    - **Metabolic Syndrome:** Atypical antipsychotics are associated with weight gain, hyperglycemia, and dyslipidemia, leading to an increased risk of diabetes and cardiovascular conditions.
    - **Sedation:** Many atypical antipsychotics can cause sedation due to their antihistaminic properties.
    - **Less Extrapyramidal Symptoms:** Compared to typical antipsychotics, atypicals have a lower incidence of EPS but may still cause **tardive dyskinesia** and other movement disorders.

Antipsychotic Agents: Mechanisms of Action

Antipsychotic agents are used to treat various psychotic disorders, including **schizophrenia** and **bipolar disorder**. Their primary mechanisms of action are centered around modulating neurotransmitter systems in the brain, particularly those involving **dopamine** and **serotonin**.

Typical Antipsychotics

Typical antipsychotics, also known as first-generation antipsychotics, primarily target the **dopaminergic system**. Their mechanisms of action are mainly characterized by the following:

1. **Dopamine D2 Receptor Antagonism:**

    - **Blocking Dopamine D2 Receptors:** Typical antipsychotics work by binding to and blocking dopamine D2 receptors in the **mesolimbic** and **mesocortical pathways**. This receptor antagonism reduces the overactivity of dopamine, which is thought to be responsible for the **positive symptoms** of schizophrenia, such as **hallucinations** and **delusions**.
    - **Receptor Binding:** These drugs exhibit a high affinity for D2 receptors, leading to significant dopaminergic blockade. This blockade is effective in alleviating positive symptoms but can also lead to **extrapyramidal symptoms** (EPS) and other side effects due to interference with normal dopamine transmission in motor pathways.

2. **Other Neurotransmitter Effects:**

- **Serotonin:** Although the primary mechanism is through dopamine antagonism, some typical antipsychotics also affect serotonin receptors, particularly 5-HT2 receptors. This can contribute to their therapeutic effects and may help balance the side effect profile.

Atypical Antipsychotics

Atypical antipsychotics, or second-generation antipsychotics, offer a broader spectrum of action and a different side effect profile compared to typical antipsychotics. Their mechanisms of action include:

1. **Dopamine D2 Receptor Antagonism:**

   - **Partial Agonism and Antagonism:** Atypical antipsychotics typically have a lower affinity for D2 receptors compared to typical antipsychotics. They often act as **partial agonists** at these receptors, which means they can modulate dopaminergic activity rather than completely blocking it. This approach helps alleviate positive symptoms while reducing the risk of EPS.

2. **Serotonin 5-HT2A Receptor Antagonism:**

   - **Blocking Serotonin 5-HT2A Receptors:** Atypical antipsychotics have a significant effect on serotonin receptors, especially the 5-HT2A subtype. This antagonism helps counterbalance the dopamine D2 blockade and contributes to the management of both positive and negative symptoms of schizophrenia. By affecting serotonin transmission, these drugs can improve mood and cognitive functions, as well as reduce the risk of EPS.

3. **Effects on Other Neurotransmitter Systems:**

   - **Dopamine D1 and D4 Receptors:** Some atypical antipsychotics also have actions on other dopamine receptor subtypes, such as D1 and D4, which can contribute to their overall therapeutic effects and side effect profiles.
   - **Histamine H1 Receptors:** Many atypical antipsychotics interact with histamine H1 receptors, leading to sedative effects. This can be beneficial in managing agitation but may also cause sedation as a side

effect.

Antidepressants: Types and Mechanisms

Antidepressants are a class of medications used to treat **depression** and other mood disorders. They work by altering neurotransmitter levels in the brain to improve mood and emotional state. The main classes of antidepressants include **Selective Serotonin Reuptake Inhibitors (SSRIs)**, **Serotonin-Norepinephrine Reuptake Inhibitors (SNRIs)**, **Tricyclic Antidepressants (TCAs)**, and **Monoamine Oxidase Inhibitors (MAOIs)**. Each class has a unique mechanism of action, which influences its therapeutic effects and side effect profile.

Selective Serotonin Reuptake Inhibitors (SSRIs)

SSRIs are among the most commonly prescribed antidepressants due to their efficacy and relatively favorable side effect profile. They primarily function by:

1. **Selective Inhibition of Serotonin Reuptake:**
   - **Mechanism:** SSRIs inhibit the reuptake of **serotonin** (5-HT) into the presynaptic neuron. By blocking the serotonin transporter (SERT), SSRIs increase the concentration of serotonin in the synaptic cleft, thereby enhancing serotonergic neurotransmission.
   - **Effect:** This increase in serotonin levels helps improve mood and alleviate symptoms of depression. SSRIs are also effective in treating **anxiety disorders**, **obsessive-compulsive disorder (OCD)**, and **panic disorder**.
2. **Examples:** Common SSRIs include **fluoxetine**, **sertraline**, **paroxetine**, **citalopram**, and **escitalopram**.

Serotonin-Norepinephrine Reuptake Inhibitors (SNRIs)

SNRIs are another class of antidepressants that affect both serotonin and norepinephrine levels. Their mechanisms include:

1. **Inhibition of Serotonin and Norepinephrine Reuptake:**
   - **Mechanism:** SNRIs inhibit the reuptake of both **serotonin** and **norepinephrine** by blocking their respective transporters (SERT and

NET). This dual inhibition increases the availability of these neurotransmitters in the synaptic cleft.
    - **Effect:** The combined increase in serotonin and norepinephrine levels enhances mood, alleviates depression, and can help with chronic pain conditions. SNRIs are used in treating **major depressive disorder (MDD)** and **generalized anxiety disorder (GAD)**.

2. **Examples:** Notable SNRIs include **venlafaxine**, **duloxetine**, **desvenlafaxine**, and **levomilnacipran**.

Tricyclic Antidepressants (TCAs)

TCAs are an older class of antidepressants with a broader range of effects on neurotransmitters compared to SSRIs and SNRIs. Their mechanisms include:

1. **Inhibition of Reuptake of Serotonin and Norepinephrine:**

    - **Mechanism:** TCAs inhibit the reuptake of both serotonin and norepinephrine, similar to SNRIs. They also affect other neurotransmitter systems, including **histamine**, **acetylcholine**, and **adrenergic** receptors.
    - **Effect:** By increasing levels of serotonin and norepinephrine, TCAs help improve mood. However, their interaction with other neurotransmitter systems can lead to a wider range of side effects.

2. **Side Effects:** The non-selective nature of TCAs can result in anticholinergic effects (e.g., dry mouth, constipation), sedation, and cardiovascular issues. This makes them less favorable compared to newer antidepressants.
3. **Examples:** Examples of TCAs include **amitriptyline**, **nortriptyline**, **imipramine**, and **desipramine**.

Monoamine Oxidase Inhibitors (MAOIs)

MAOIs are another class of antidepressants that work by a different mechanism compared to SSRIs, SNRIs, and TCAs:

1. **Inhibition of Monoamine Oxidase:**

- ◦ **Mechanism:** MAOIs inhibit the enzyme **monoamine oxidase** (MAO), which is responsible for the breakdown of neurotransmitters such as **serotonin, norepinephrine**, and **dopamine**. By inhibiting MAO, these neurotransmitters remain in higher concentrations in the synaptic cleft.
- ◦ **Effect:** The increased levels of neurotransmitters help alleviate symptoms of depression. MAOIs can also be effective for atypical depression and certain anxiety disorders.

2. **Dietary Restrictions:** MAOIs require dietary restrictions to avoid hypertensive crises caused by the interaction with tyramine-rich foods.
3. **Examples:** Common MAOIs include **phenelzine, tranylcypromine**, and **isocarboxazid**.

Antidepressants: Mechanisms of Action

Antidepressants are a crucial class of drugs used to treat **depression** and various other mood disorders by altering neurotransmitter levels in the brain. Each type of antidepressant works through a distinct mechanism to improve mood and alleviate symptoms. The primary classes of antidepressants are **Selective Serotonin Reuptake Inhibitors (SSRIs)**, **Serotonin-Norepinephrine Reuptake Inhibitors (SNRIs)**, **Tricyclic Antidepressants (TCAs)**, and **Monoamine Oxidase Inhibitors (MAOIs)**. Below, the mechanisms of action for each class are detailed.

Selective Serotonin Reuptake Inhibitors (SSRIs)

Mechanism of Action:

- **Selective Inhibition of Serotonin Reuptake:** SSRIs specifically inhibit the reuptake of **serotonin** (5-HT) by blocking the serotonin transporter (SERT) on the presynaptic neuron. This inhibition prevents serotonin from being reabsorbed back into the presynaptic neuron, leading to increased levels of serotonin in the synaptic cleft.
- **Enhanced Serotonergic Neurotransmission:** The elevated serotonin levels in the synaptic cleft enhance serotonergic neurotransmission, which helps improve mood and alleviate symptoms of depression and anxiety.
- **Selective Effect:** SSRIs are relatively selective for serotonin and have a lower impact on other neurotransmitters, which contributes to their favorable side effect profile compared to other antidepressants.

Examples:Fluoxetine, Sertraline, Paroxetine, Citalopram, and **Escitalopram.**

Serotonin-Norepinephrine Reuptake Inhibitors (SNRIs)

Mechanism of Action:

- **Dual Inhibition of Reuptake:** SNRIs inhibit the reuptake of both **serotonin** and **norepinephrine** by blocking the serotonin transporter (SERT) and the norepinephrine transporter (NET) on the presynaptic neuron.
- **Increased Neurotransmitter Levels:** This dual inhibition leads to increased levels of serotonin and norepinephrine in the synaptic cleft, enhancing neurotransmission in both systems.
- **Broader Effect:** By increasing the availability of both neurotransmitters, SNRIs can address a wider range of symptoms and conditions, including major depressive disorder (MDD) and certain types of chronic pain.

Examples:Venlafaxine, Duloxetine, Desvenlafaxine, and **Levomilnacipran.**

Tricyclic Antidepressants (TCAs)

Mechanism of Action:

- **Inhibition of Serotonin and Norepinephrine Reuptake:** TCAs inhibit the reuptake of both **serotonin** and **norepinephrine** by blocking SERT and NET. This increases the concentration of these neurotransmitters in the synaptic cleft.
- **Impact on Other Neurotransmitter Systems:** TCAs also affect other neurotransmitter systems, including **histamine**, **acetylcholine**, and **adrenergic** receptors, which can contribute to their side effect profile.
- **Non-Selective Effects:** The non-selective nature of TCAs results in a broader range of effects and side effects compared to newer antidepressants.

Examples:Amitriptyline, Nortriptyline, Imipramine, and **Desipramine.**

Monoamine Oxidase Inhibitors (MAOIs)

Mechanism of Action:

- **Inhibition of Monoamine Oxidase:** MAOIs inhibit the enzyme **monoamine oxidase** (MAO), which is responsible for the breakdown of neurotransmitters such as **serotonin**, **norepinephrine**, and **dopamine**. This inhibition prevents the degradation of these neurotransmitters.
- **Increased Neurotransmitter Levels:** By inhibiting MAO, MAOIs increase the levels of serotonin, norepinephrine, and dopamine in the synaptic cleft, enhancing neurotransmission and improving mood.
- **Need for Dietary Restrictions:** Due to their effect on MAO, MAOIs can interact with certain foods containing tyramine, necessitating dietary restrictions to avoid hypertensive crises.

Examples:Phenelzine, **Tranylcypromine**, and **Isocarboxazid**.

Anti-Anxiety Agents: Types and Mechanisms

Anti-anxiety agents are medications used to alleviate symptoms of **anxiety** and related disorders. They work by modulating neurotransmitter activity in the brain to provide relief from excessive worry, fear, and tension. The main classes of anti-anxiety agents include **benzodiazepines** and **non-benzodiazepines**. Each class has a distinct mechanism of action and clinical applications.

Benzodiazepines

Mechanism of Action:

- **Enhancement of GABA Activity:** Benzodiazepines primarily act on the **gamma-aminobutyric acid (GABA)** neurotransmitter system. They bind to a specific site on the **GABA_A receptor**, a type of ionotropic receptor. This binding increases the frequency of chloride channel opening in response to GABA.
- **Increased Inhibitory Neurotransmission:** By enhancing the effect of GABA, benzodiazepines increase **chloride ion influx** into the neuron, leading to **hyperpolarization** of the cell membrane. This hyperpolarization makes the neuron less likely to fire, resulting in a calming effect on the central nervous system.
- **Anxiolytic Effect:** The enhanced GABAergic activity decreases neuronal excitability and provides relief from symptoms of anxiety. Benzodiazepines are effective in rapidly reducing acute anxiety symptoms.

Examples:Diazepam, **Lorazepam**, **Clonazepam**, **Alprazolam**, and **Temazepam**.

Clinical Applications:

- **Acute Anxiety:** Effective for short-term management of severe anxiety.
- **Panic Disorders:** Useful in treating panic attacks due to their rapid onset of action.
- **Insomnia:** Often prescribed for short-term treatment of sleep disturbances.

Advantages:

- Rapid onset of action.
- Effective for short-term relief of severe anxiety.

Disadvantages:

- Risk of dependence and tolerance with long-term use.
- Potential for withdrawal symptoms if used for extended periods.
- Sedation and impaired cognitive and motor functions.

Non-Benzodiazepines

Mechanism of Action:

- **Selective Serotonin Reuptake Inhibition:** Many non-benzodiazepine anti-anxiety agents work by modulating serotonin levels. For instance, **Buspirone**, a common non-benzodiazepine, acts as a partial agonist at **serotonin (5-HT_1A) receptors**. This action results in increased serotonergic neurotransmission and reduced anxiety.
- **Interaction with Other Receptors:** Some non-benzodiazepine agents, such as **beta-blockers** (e.g., **Propranolol**), can alleviate physical symptoms of anxiety by blocking **beta-adrenergic receptors**, which reduces sympathetic nervous system activity.
- **Selective and Non-Sedative:** Non-benzodiazepines are often preferred for their selective action and lower risk of sedation and dependence compared to benzodiazepines.

Examples:Buspirone, **Hydroxyzine**, **Propranolol**, and **Gabapentin**.

Clinical Applications:

- **Chronic Anxiety:** Suitable for long-term management of chronic anxiety disorders.
- **Generalized Anxiety Disorder (GAD):** Effective in treating GAD without the risk of dependence associated with benzodiazepines.
- **Physical Symptoms of Anxiety:** Beta-blockers like propranolol can help manage symptoms such as palpitations and tremors.

Advantages:

- Lower risk of dependence and tolerance compared to benzodiazepines.
- Useful for long-term management of anxiety.
- Generally non-sedative and less impairing.

Disadvantages:

- May take longer to achieve therapeutic effects compared to benzodiazepines.
- Potential for side effects such as dizziness, nausea, and headaches.

Anti-Anxiety Agents: Mechanisms of Action

Anti-anxiety agents function through various mechanisms to alleviate symptoms of anxiety, by modulating neurotransmitter systems in the central nervous system. They can be broadly categorized into **benzodiazepines** and **non-benzodiazepines**, each with distinct mechanisms of action.

Benzodiazepines

Mechanism of Action:

- **GABA_A Receptor Modulation:** Benzodiazepines primarily act on the **gamma-aminobutyric acid (GABA_A) receptors**, which are ionotropic receptors that mediate inhibitory neurotransmission in the brain. They bind to a specific site on the GABA_A receptor, distinct from the GABA binding site.
- **Allosteric Modulation:** This binding enhances the receptor's affinity for GABA, leading to an increased frequency of chloride channel openings. As a result, the influx of chloride ions into the neuron is increased.

- **Neuronal Hyperpolarization:** The influx of chloride ions causes hyperpolarization of the neuron, making it less likely to fire. This hyperpolarization reduces neuronal excitability and inhibits neurotransmission, leading to a calming effect.
- **Anxiolytic Effect:** By enhancing GABAergic activity, benzodiazepines effectively reduce anxiety. They produce a rapid onset of therapeutic effects, which makes them useful for managing acute anxiety episodes.

Examples:Diazepam, Lorazepam, Clonazepam, Alprazolam, Temazepam.

Clinical Implications:

- **Rapid Onset:** Effective for immediate relief from acute anxiety.
- **Sedative Effects:** Also produce sedative effects due to their impact on central nervous system activity, which can be beneficial or detrimental depending on the therapeutic goal.

Non-Benzodiazepines

Mechanism of Action:

- **Buspirone:**
    - **Serotonin Receptor Modulation:Buspirone** is a partial agonist at the **serotonin 5-HT_1A receptors**. By binding to these receptors, it modulates serotonin neurotransmission.
    - **Reduced Serotonin Activity:** This action leads to an increase in serotonin levels in certain brain regions, contributing to anxiolytic effects.
    - **Dopamine Receptor Interaction:** Buspirone also has partial agonist activity at dopamine D_2 receptors, which may contribute to its anxiolytic effects.
- **Beta-Blockers:**
    - **Beta-Adrenergic Receptor Blockade:Propranolol**, a non-benzodiazepine beta-blocker, works by blocking **beta-adrenergic receptors** in the heart and other tissues.

- ◦ **Reduction of Sympathetic Activity:** By blocking these receptors, beta-blockers reduce the physiological symptoms of anxiety, such as palpitations and tremors, but do not address the psychological components of anxiety.

- Hydroxyzine:

  - ◦ **Antihistamine Action:Hydroxyzine** is an antihistamine with **anticholinergic properties.** It blocks **histamine H_1 receptors** and has sedative effects that can help reduce anxiety.
  - ◦ **Central Nervous System Effects:** Its action in the central nervous system contributes to its anxiolytic effects, though it is not as targeted as benzodiazepines or selective serotonin reuptake inhibitors.

- Gabapentin:

  - ◦ **Calcium Channel Blockade:Gabapentin** binds to the **2 subunit of voltage-gated calcium channels** in the central nervous system.
  - ◦ **Neurotransmitter Modulation:** By inhibiting calcium influx, gabapentin reduces the release of excitatory neurotransmitters, which can help alleviate anxiety symptoms.

Examples:Buspirone, Propranolol, Hydroxyzine, Gabapentin.
Clinical Implications:

- **Long-Term Management:** Non-benzodiazepines are often used for long-term management of anxiety with a lower risk of dependence compared to benzodiazepines.
- **Non-Sedative Options:** Many non-benzodiazepines are less likely to cause sedation, making them suitable for patients requiring long-term anxiety control without significant sedative effects.

Anti-Anxiety Agents: Mechanisms of Action

Anti-anxiety agents are used to manage symptoms of anxiety through various mechanisms that alter neurotransmission in the central nervous system. These agents are divided into **benzodiazepines** and **non-benzodiazepines**, each with specific actions and effects.

Benzodiazepines

Mechanism of Action:

- **GABA_A Receptor Modulation:**
  - **Binding Site:** Benzodiazepines bind to a specific site on the **GABA_A receptor**, which is distinct from the site where **GABA** binds.
  - **Allosteric Modulation:** Their binding enhances the receptor's affinity for **GABA**, leading to increased frequency of **chloride ion channel openings**.
  - **Increased Chloride Influx:** This causes an influx of chloride ions into the neuron, leading to **hyperpolarization** of the neuronal membrane.
  - **Inhibition of Neuronal Excitability:** The hyperpolarization makes neurons less likely to fire, reducing overall **neurotransmission** and producing a calming effect.

Examples:Diazepam, Lorazepam, Clonazepam, Alprazolam.
Clinical Implications:

- **Rapid Onset:** Provides quick relief from acute anxiety.
- **Sedative Effects:** Can also induce sedation, useful in some cases but potentially problematic in others.

Non-Benzodiazepines
Buspirone
Mechanism of Action:

- **Serotonin Receptor Modulation:**
  - **5-HT_1A Receptor Partial Agonism:Buspirone** acts as a partial agonist at the **5-HT_1A serotonin receptors**.
  - **Increased Serotonin Activity:** This action enhances serotonin neurotransmission, which contributes to its anxiolytic effects.

- **Dopamine Receptor Interaction:**
  - **Dopamine D_2 Receptor Partial Agonism:** Buspirone also interacts with dopamine D_2 receptors, potentially modulating dopamine-related pathways involved in anxiety.

Examples:Buspirone.
Clinical Implications:

- **Gradual Onset:** Effects develop more slowly compared to benzodiazepines, making it suitable for long-term management.

Beta-Blockers
Mechanism of Action:

- **Beta-Adrenergic Receptor Blockade:**
    - **Blocking Beta-Adrenergic Receptors:Propranolol** and similar drugs block **beta-adrenergic receptors.**
    - **Reduction of Sympathetic Activity:** This reduces symptoms of anxiety related to the physiological responses like palpitations and tremors but does not address the psychological aspects.

Examples:Propranolol.
Clinical Implications:

- **Physiological Symptom Relief:** Effective for controlling physical symptoms of anxiety but less effective for psychological symptoms.

Hydroxyzine
Mechanism of Action:

- **Antihistamine Action:**
    - **Histamine H_1 Receptor Blockade:Hydroxyzine** works by blocking **H_1 histamine receptors.**
    - **Sedative Effects:** Its antihistamine activity contributes to sedation and anxiety relief.

Examples:Hydroxyzine.
Clinical Implications:

- **Sedative Effects:** Useful for short-term anxiety relief but may cause sedation.

Gabapentin
Mechanism of Action:

- **Calcium Channel Blockade:**
    - **Binding to Voltage-Gated Calcium Channels:Gabapentin** binds to the **2 subunit of voltage-gated calcium channels**.
    - **Reduction of Neurotransmitter Release:** This inhibits calcium influx, reducing the release of excitatory neurotransmitters and modulating neuronal excitability.

Examples:Gabapentin.
Clinical Implications:

- **Neurotransmitter Modulation:** Provides anxiety relief with a different mechanism from traditional anxiolytics.

Anti-Manic Agents and Hallucinogens: Mechanisms and Uses

Anti-manic agents are primarily used in the treatment of **bipolar disorder**, particularly to manage manic episodes. **Lithium** and other **mood stabilizers** play a critical role in this treatment. **Hallucinogens**, on the other hand, are a diverse class of psychoactive substances that alter perception, mood, and cognitive processes. Understanding their mechanisms and uses provides insight into their therapeutic and recreational implications.

Lithium
Mechanism of Action:

- **Inositol Monophosphatase Inhibition:**
    - **Reduction in Inositol:Lithium** inhibits **inositol monophosphatase**, an enzyme involved in the phosphoinositide signaling pathway. This inhibition decreases the levels of **inositol trisphosphate (IP3)** and **diacylglycerol (DAG)**.
    - **Downstream Effects:** The reduction in IP3 and DAG affects intracellular signaling cascades, which are thought to modulate mood and stabilize mood swings.
- **Neurotransmitter Modulation:**

  - **Serotonin and Norepinephrine:** Lithium impacts neurotransmitter systems, including **serotonin** and **norepinephrine**, which are involved in mood regulation. It enhances serotonin receptor sensitivity and affects norepinephrine release.

- **Neuroprotection:**

  - **Neurotrophic Factors:** Lithium has been shown to promote the expression of **neurotrophic factors** like **brain-derived neurotrophic factor (BDNF)**, which supports neuronal health and plasticity.

Examples:Lithium carbonate, Lithium citrate.
Clinical Implications:

- **Bipolar Disorder:** Lithium is effective in reducing the frequency and severity of manic episodes and preventing relapse. It is also used to manage depressive episodes in bipolar disorder.

Other Mood Stabilizers
Valproic Acid (Valproate)
Mechanism of Action:

- **Sodium Channel Blockade:**

  - **Voltage-Gated Sodium Channels:Valproic acid** stabilizes neuronal membranes by blocking **voltage-gated sodium channels**, which reduces the excessive neuronal firing associated with manic episodes.

- **Inhibition of GABA Transaminase:**

  - **Increased GABA Levels:** Valproate inhibits **GABA transaminase**, the enzyme responsible for the breakdown of **gamma-aminobutyric acid (GABA)**, thus increasing GABA levels and enhancing its inhibitory effects in the brain.

Examples:Valproic acid, Divalproex sodium.
Clinical Implications:

- **Bipolar Disorder:** Valproic acid is used as an alternative to lithium for mood stabilization, particularly when patients do not respond well to lithium or have contraindications.

Carbamazepine
Mechanism of Action:

- **Sodium Channel Blockade:**
    - **Voltage-Gated Sodium Channels:Carbamazepine** also blocks **voltage-gated sodium channels**, similar to valproate, which helps in stabilizing mood by reducing abnormal electrical activity in the brain.
- **Neurotransmitter Modulation:**
    - **Serotonin and Norepinephrine:** Carbamazepine influences **serotonin** and **norepinephrine** levels, contributing to its mood-stabilizing effects.

Examples:Carbamazepine.
Clinical Implications:

- **Bipolar Disorder:** Carbamazepine is used in cases where patients either do not respond to lithium or have mixed episodes. It is particularly effective in controlling manic and mixed episodes.

Hallucinogens
Mechanism of Action:

- **Serotonin Receptor Modulation:**
    - **5-HT_2A Receptor Agonism:** Many hallucinogens, such as **lysergic acid diethylamide (LSD)** and **psilocybin**, act as agonists at the **5-HT_2A serotonin receptors**. This action alters serotonin transmission and leads to changes in perception and cognition.
- **Altered Neuroplasticity:**

- **Synaptic Plasticity:** Hallucinogens can induce changes in **synaptic plasticity**, potentially enhancing the brain's ability to reorganize itself, which might contribute to their effects on consciousness and perception.

Examples:LSD, Psilocybin, Mescaline.
Clinical Implications:

- **Research and Therapy:** While hallucinogens are often associated with recreational use, there is growing interest in their potential therapeutic applications, including treatment for conditions like **depression** and **post-traumatic stress disorder (PTSD).**

Pharmacology of Hallucinogens

Hallucinogens are a diverse class of psychoactive substances that produce profound alterations in perception, mood, and cognitive processes. These drugs are characterized by their ability to induce **hallucinations** and **altered states of consciousness**. The pharmacological effects of hallucinogens are primarily mediated through their interactions with neurotransmitter systems in the brain, particularly those involving **serotonin.**

Mechanisms of Action
Serotonin Receptor Modulation:

- **5-HT_2A Receptor Agonism:**
  - **Primary Mechanism:** Most classic hallucinogens, such as **lysergic acid diethylamide (LSD)**, **psilocybin**, and **mescaline**, exert their effects mainly by agonizing the **5-HT_2A serotonin receptors**. This receptor is a subtype of the serotonin receptor family and is widely distributed in the brain, especially in regions involved in perception and cognition.
  - **Effect on Serotonin Transmission:** Agonism of 5-HT_2A receptors enhances serotonin signaling and alters normal serotonin transmission, leading to changes in sensory perception, mood, and thought processes. This interaction is believed to be crucial for the hallucinogenic effects of these substances.

- **5-HT_2C and 5-HT_1A Receptor Interaction:**
    - **Additional Receptor Binding:** Some hallucinogens also interact with other serotonin receptors, such as **5-HT_2C** and **5-HT_1A**, which can contribute to their overall effects. The interaction with 5-HT_2C receptors can affect mood and anxiety levels, while 5-HT_1A interactions might influence the perception and cognitive effects of the drug.

Altered Neuroplasticity:

- **Synaptic Plasticity:** Hallucinogens may induce changes in **synaptic plasticity**, which is the brain's ability to reorganize and adapt synaptic connections. This alteration in plasticity can contribute to the profound changes in perception and cognition experienced during hallucinogenic states.
- **Neuroplasticity and Cognition:** The effects on neuroplasticity might help explain the altered sense of self and reality, as well as the enhanced emotional experiences often reported by users.

Pharmacokinetics
Absorption:

- **Route of Administration:** Hallucinogens can be administered via various routes including oral ingestion, inhalation, and injection. For example, **LSD** is typically taken orally, while **mescaline** is often consumed as part of peyote or San Pedro cacti.
- **Onset of Action:** The onset of effects can vary depending on the route of administration. Oral ingestion usually results in a delayed onset, with effects starting within 30 to 90 minutes.

Distribution:

- **Plasma Protein Binding:** Hallucinogens typically exhibit variable plasma protein binding, affecting their distribution in the body.
- **Brain Penetration:** These substances readily cross the blood-brain barrier, allowing them to interact with central nervous system receptors and produce their psychoactive effects.

Metabolism and Excretion:

- **Metabolism:** Hallucinogens are metabolized in the liver through processes such as oxidation and conjugation. For instance, **LSD** is metabolized into several inactive metabolites.
- **Excretion:** These drugs are primarily excreted through the urine, with varying half-lives depending on the specific substance.

Pharmacological Effects
Perceptual Changes:

- **Visual and Auditory Hallucinations:** Users often report vivid visual distortions, such as altered colors, shapes, and patterns, as well as auditory hallucinations. These perceptual changes can significantly alter the user's experience of their environment.
- **Altered Sense of Time and Space:** Hallucinogens can distort the perception of time and space, leading to a sense of time dilation or contraction and altered spatial awareness.

Emotional and Cognitive Effects:

- **Enhanced Emotional Experiences:** Users may experience heightened emotions, including euphoria, fear, or introspection. The emotional state can be profoundly affected by the hallucinogenic experience.
- **Altered Thought Processes:** Cognitive functions such as thought patterns, reasoning, and problem-solving can be disrupted, leading to non-linear thinking and altered cognitive perception.

Clinical and Therapeutic Uses
Research and Therapy:

- **Psychedelic-Assisted Therapy:** There is growing interest in the use of hallucinogens in therapeutic settings, particularly for conditions like **depression**, **anxiety**, and **post-traumatic stress disorder (PTSD)**. Research into substances like **psilocybin** and **LSD** has shown potential benefits in clinical trials, although further studies are needed to fully understand their efficacy and safety.

- **Psychedelic Research:** Studies are ongoing to explore the mechanisms, therapeutic potential, and safety profiles of hallucinogens. This research aims to harness their therapeutic potential while mitigating risks associated with their use.

CHAPTER X

Pharmacology of Neurodegenerative Diseases

10.1 Drugs for Parkinson's Disease

Mechanisms and Therapeutic Uses

Parkinson's disease (PD) is a progressive neurodegenerative disorder characterized by the degeneration of dopaminergic neurons in the **substantia nigra**, leading to motor symptoms such as tremors, rigidity, bradykinesia, and postural instability. The pharmacological treatment of PD focuses on restoring dopamine levels or mimicking its action in the brain.

Levodopa

Mechanism of Action:

- **Dopamine Precursor:Levodopa (L-DOPA)** is a precursor of dopamine. It crosses the blood-brain barrier and is converted to dopamine by the enzyme **dopa decarboxylase** in the brain. This conversion increases the levels of dopamine in the **striatum**, compensating for the dopamine deficiency caused by the degeneration of dopaminergic neurons.
- **Co-administration with Carbidopa:** Levodopa is often administered with **carbidopa**, a peripheral dopa decarboxylase inhibitor. Carbidopa prevents the peripheral conversion of levodopa to dopamine, which increases the amount of levodopa that reaches the brain and reduces peripheral side effects such as nausea and cardiovascular issues.

Therapeutic Uses:

- **Motor Symptom Relief:** Levodopa is the most effective treatment for the motor symptoms of Parkinson's disease, including tremors, rigidity, bradykinesia, and postural instability.
- **Improvement in Quality of Life:** It significantly improves the quality of life for patients by enhancing mobility and reducing disability.

Dopamine Agonists

Mechanism of Action:

- **Direct Stimulation of Dopamine Receptors:** Dopamine agonists directly stimulate **dopamine receptors** in the brain. They act on D2 and, to a lesser extent, D1 and D3 receptors, mimicking the effects of dopamine without needing conversion like levodopa.
- **Reduced Dopamine Fluctuations:** Dopamine agonists have a longer half-life than levodopa, providing more stable dopaminergic stimulation and reducing motor fluctuations and dyskinesias associated with long-term levodopa use.

Examples:Pramipexole, Ropinirole, Rotigotine, Apomorphine.
Therapeutic Uses:

- **Monotherapy in Early PD:** Dopamine agonists are often used as monotherapy in the early stages of Parkinson's disease to delay the initiation of levodopa therapy.
- **Adjunct Therapy:** They are also used in combination with levodopa in advanced stages to reduce motor fluctuations and enhance the overall therapeutic effect.
- **Reduction of "Off" Periods:** Dopamine agonists help in managing "off" periods (times when the medication is not working well and symptoms return) in patients on levodopa therapy.

MAO-B Inhibitors
Mechanism of Action:

- **Inhibition of MAO-B:Monoamine oxidase B (MAO-B) inhibitors** block the action of the enzyme MAO-B, which is responsible for the breakdown of dopamine in the brain. By inhibiting MAO-B, these drugs increase the availability and prolong the action of dopamine.
- **Neuroprotection:** There is some evidence to suggest that MAO-B inhibitors may have neuroprotective effects, potentially slowing the progression of neuronal degeneration in Parkinson's disease.

Examples:Selegiline, Rasagiline, Safinamide.
Therapeutic Uses:

- **Adjunct Therapy:** MAO-B inhibitors are used as an adjunct to levodopa in patients with fluctuating symptoms to enhance and prolong the effects of levodopa.

- **Mild Symptom Relief:** They can be used as monotherapy in the early stages of Parkinson's disease to manage mild symptoms and delay the need for levodopa.
- **Neuroprotection:** While the neuroprotective effects are still under investigation, MAO-B inhibitors may offer additional benefits beyond symptom management.

10.1 Drugs for Parkinson's Disease: Mechanisms of Action

Parkinson's Disease (PD) is a neurodegenerative disorder characterized by the loss of dopaminergic neurons in the **substantia nigra**, leading to motor symptoms such as tremors, rigidity, bradykinesia, and postural instability. The pharmacological treatment aims to restore dopaminergic function and alleviate symptoms. The main classes of drugs used include **levodopa**, **dopamine agonists**, and **MAO-B inhibitors.**

Levodopa

Mechanism of Action:

- **Dopamine Precursor:Levodopa (L-DOPA)** is a direct precursor to dopamine. It is taken up by dopaminergic neurons and converted to dopamine by the enzyme **dopa decarboxylase**.
  - **Crossing the Blood-Brain Barrier:** Unlike dopamine, levodopa can cross the blood-brain barrier. Once in the brain, it is decarboxylated to dopamine, replenishing the depleted levels of dopamine in the striatum.
- **Combination with Carbidopa or Benserazide:** Levodopa is often administered with **carbidopa** or **benserazide**, which are peripheral dopa decarboxylase inhibitors. These inhibitors prevent the conversion of levodopa to dopamine in the periphery, increasing the amount of levodopa that reaches the brain and reducing peripheral side effects such as nausea and vomiting.

Therapeutic Uses:

- **Motor Symptom Relief:** Levodopa is the most effective treatment for improving motor symptoms of Parkinson's disease, including tremors, rigidity, and bradykinesia.

- **Quality of Life:** It significantly enhances the quality of life for PD patients by improving mobility and reducing disability.

Dopamine Agonists
Mechanism of Action:

- **Direct Dopamine Receptor Stimulation:** Dopamine agonists directly stimulate **dopamine receptors** (primarily D2 receptors, and to a lesser extent D1 and D3 receptors) in the brain, mimicking the effects of dopamine.
  - **Longer Half-Life:** These drugs have a longer half-life than levodopa, providing more consistent dopaminergic stimulation and reducing motor fluctuations.
  - **Neuroprotection:** Some studies suggest that dopamine agonists might have neuroprotective properties, though this is still under investigation.

Examples:**Pramipexole**, **Ropinirole**, **Rotigotine**, **Apomorphine**.
Therapeutic Uses:

- **Monotherapy in Early PD:** Used as initial monotherapy to delay the use of levodopa.
- **Adjunct Therapy:** Combined with levodopa in advanced PD to manage motor fluctuations and reduce "off" periods.
- **Management of Motor Symptoms:** Effective in reducing tremors, rigidity, and bradykinesia.

MAO-B Inhibitors
Mechanism of Action:

- **Inhibition of Monoamine Oxidase B (MAO-B):** MAO-B inhibitors block the action of the enzyme **monoamine oxidase B**, which breaks down dopamine in the brain. By inhibiting this enzyme, these drugs increase the availability of dopamine.

- ◦ **Prolonged Dopamine Action:** By preventing dopamine degradation, MAO-B inhibitors prolong the action of both endogenous dopamine and dopamine derived from levodopa.
- ◦ **Potential Neuroprotection:** There is some evidence suggesting that MAO-B inhibitors may have neuroprotective effects, potentially slowing disease progression.

Examples:Selegiline, Rasagiline, Safinamide.
Therapeutic Uses:

- **Adjunct Therapy:** Used in conjunction with levodopa to enhance and extend its effects.
- **Monotherapy in Early PD:** Can be used alone in early PD to manage mild symptoms and delay the need for levodopa.
- **Reduction of "Off" Periods:** Helps in reducing "off" periods and improving overall symptom control.

10.2 Drugs for Alzheimer's Disease: Mechanisms and Therapeutic Uses

Alzheimer's Disease (AD) is a progressive neurodegenerative disorder characterized by memory loss, cognitive decline, and behavioral changes. The primary pathological features of AD include amyloid-beta plaques, neurofibrillary tangles, and cholinergic deficits. Pharmacological treatments aim to alleviate symptoms and improve quality of life by targeting these underlying mechanisms. The main classes of drugs used include **cholinesterase inhibitors** and **NMDA receptor antagonists.**

Cholinesterase Inhibitors
Mechanism of Action:

- **Inhibition of Acetylcholinesterase:** Cholinesterase inhibitors block the enzyme **acetylcholinesterase**, which breaks down **acetylcholine** in the synaptic cleft. By inhibiting this enzyme, these drugs increase the concentration of acetylcholine in the brain.
- **Enhanced Cholinergic Transmission:** The increased levels of acetylcholine enhance cholinergic neurotransmission, which is crucial for memory and cognitive function. This helps to partially compensate for the loss of cholinergic neurons seen in AD.

Examples:Donepezil, Rivastigmine, Galantamine.
Therapeutic Uses:

- **Mild to Moderate AD:** Cholinesterase inhibitors are primarily used to treat mild to moderate Alzheimer's disease. They help improve cognitive function, memory, and behavior.
- **Symptom Management:** These drugs can help stabilize symptoms and slow the progression of cognitive decline, although they do not alter the underlying disease process.

NMDA Receptor Antagonists
Mechanism of Action:

- **Inhibition of NMDA Receptors:** NMDA receptor antagonists block the **N-methyl-D-aspartate (NMDA) receptors**, which are involved in glutamatergic neurotransmission. In Alzheimer's disease, overactivation of these receptors by glutamate can lead to excitotoxicity, contributing to neuronal damage.
- **Regulation of Glutamate Activity:** By blocking excessive NMDA receptor activity, these drugs help to regulate glutamate levels, protecting neurons from excitotoxicity and improving synaptic function.

Example:Memantine.
Therapeutic Uses:

- **Moderate to Severe AD:** Memantine is used to treat moderate to severe Alzheimer's disease. It can be used alone or in combination with cholinesterase inhibitors.
- **Cognitive and Behavioral Symptoms:** It helps to improve cognitive function, daily living activities, and behavior, providing symptomatic relief and enhancing quality of life.

10.2 Drugs for Alzheimer's Disease: Mechanisms and Therapeutic Uses

Alzheimer's Disease (AD) is a progressive neurodegenerative disorder characterized by memory loss, cognitive decline, and behavioral changes. The primary treatment strategies involve enhancing cholinergic function and regulating glutamatergic activity to alleviate symptoms and improve quality of life. The main classes of drugs used in the treatment of AD are **cholinesterase inhibitors** and **NMDA receptor antagonists.**

Cholinesterase Inhibitors

Mechanism of Action:

- **Inhibition of Acetylcholinesterase:**
  - **Primary Action:** Cholinesterase inhibitors block the enzyme **acetylcholinesterase**, which is responsible for breaking down **acetylcholine** in the synaptic cleft.
  - **Increased Acetylcholine Levels:** By inhibiting acetylcholinesterase, these drugs increase the concentration of acetylcholine in the brain, particularly in areas involved in memory and cognition.
  - **Enhanced Cholinergic Transmission:** The increased levels of acetylcholine enhance cholinergic neurotransmission, which is crucial for cognitive function and memory. This compensates for the loss of cholinergic neurons and the subsequent decline in acetylcholine seen in AD.

Examples:Donepezil, Rivastigmine, Galantamine.

Therapeutic Uses:

- **Mild to Moderate AD:** Cholinesterase inhibitors are primarily used to treat mild to moderate Alzheimer's disease. They help improve cognitive function, memory, and behavior by enhancing cholinergic activity.
- **Symptom Management:** These drugs can help stabilize symptoms and slow the progression of cognitive decline, although they do not alter the underlying disease process.

Detailed Mechanisms for Key Cholinesterase Inhibitors:

- **Donepezil:** A reversible inhibitor of acetylcholinesterase that increases acetylcholine concentration by preventing its breakdown.
- **Rivastigmine:** Inhibits both acetylcholinesterase and butyrylcholinesterase, providing a broader enhancement of cholinergic activity.
- **Galantamine:** A reversible inhibitor of acetylcholinesterase and also modulates nicotinic receptors to enhance cholinergic function.

NMDA Receptor Antagonists
Mechanism of Action:

- **Inhibition of NMDA Receptors:**
    - **Primary Action:** NMDA receptor antagonists, such as **memantine**, block **N-methyl-D-aspartate (NMDA) receptors**, which are involved in glutamatergic neurotransmission.
    - **Regulation of Glutamate Activity:** In Alzheimer's disease, there is often excessive glutamate activity, leading to overactivation of NMDA receptors. This overactivation can cause excitotoxicity, contributing to neuronal damage and cognitive decline.
    - **Neuroprotection:** By blocking excessive NMDA receptor activity, memantine helps to regulate glutamate levels, protecting neurons from excitotoxicity and improving synaptic function.

Example:Memantine.
Therapeutic Uses:

- **Moderate to Severe AD:** Memantine is used to treat moderate to severe Alzheimer's disease. It can be used alone or in combination with cholinesterase inhibitors to provide a synergistic effect.
- **Cognitive and Behavioral Symptoms:** Memantine helps to improve cognitive function, daily living activities, and behavior, providing symptomatic relief and enhancing quality of life.

Detailed Mechanism of NMDA Receptor Antagonists:

- **Memantine:** A non-competitive NMDA receptor antagonist that binds to the NMDA receptor with moderate affinity. It blocks the excessive activity of glutamate, which is hypothesized to prevent excitotoxicity, a process that can lead to neuronal injury and death.

10.3 CNS Stimulants and Nootropics

Mechanisms and Uses

Central Nervous System (CNS) stimulants are a class of drugs that enhance brain activity, increasing alertness, attention, and energy. **Nootropics**, also known as "smart drugs" or cognitive enhancers, are substances that improve cognitive function, particularly executive functions, memory, creativity, or motivation in healthy individuals. The types and mechanisms of CNS stimulants and nootropics vary, but they generally work by altering the levels and activity of neurotransmitters in the brain.

Types of CNS Stimulants

1. Amphetamines

Mechanism of Action:

- **Release of Neurotransmitters:** Amphetamines stimulate the release of **dopamine** and **norepinephrine** from presynaptic neurons. They increase the levels of these neurotransmitters in the synaptic cleft by promoting their release and inhibiting their reuptake.
- **Inhibition of Monoamine Oxidase (MAO):** Amphetamines also inhibit MAO, the enzyme responsible for the breakdown of monoamines, further increasing the levels of dopamine and norepinephrine.

Examples:Amphetamine, Dextroamphetamine, Methamphetamine.

Therapeutic Uses:

- **Attention-Deficit/Hyperactivity Disorder (ADHD):** Amphetamines are used to improve attention, focus, and self-control in individuals with ADHD.
- **Narcolepsy:** These drugs help manage excessive daytime sleepiness and sudden sleep attacks in narcolepsy.
- **Obesity:** Amphetamines can be used short-term as appetite suppressants for weight loss.

2. Methylphenidate

Mechanism of Action:

- **Inhibition of Reuptake:** Methylphenidate inhibits the reuptake of **dopamine** and **norepinephrine** by blocking their respective transporters, increasing their concentration in the synaptic cleft.

Examples:Ritalin, Concerta, Metadate.

Therapeutic Uses:

- **ADHD:** Methylphenidate is widely used for managing symptoms of ADHD by enhancing attention and reducing impulsivity and hyperactivity.
- **Narcolepsy:** It is also used to treat narcolepsy by promoting wakefulness.

3. Caffeine
Mechanism of Action:

- **Adenosine Receptor Antagonism:** Caffeine blocks **adenosine receptors** in the brain. Adenosine is an inhibitory neurotransmitter that promotes sleep and relaxation. By antagonizing these receptors, caffeine reduces the inhibitory effects of adenosine, leading to increased arousal and wakefulness.
- **Increased Dopamine Release:** Caffeine also promotes the release of dopamine, contributing to its stimulant effects.

Examples: Found in **coffee**, **tea**, **energy drinks**, and **certain medications**.
Therapeutic Uses:

- **Alertness:** Used to reduce fatigue and improve mental alertness.
- **Headache Relief:** Often combined with other medications in the treatment of headaches and migraines.

4. Modafinil and Armodafinil
Mechanism of Action:

- **Dopamine Reuptake Inhibition:** Modafinil and its R-enantiomer armodafinil inhibit the reuptake of **dopamine** by blocking the dopamine transporter, increasing dopamine levels in the brain.
- **Enhanced Histamine Activity:** These drugs also increase histamine levels in the hypothalamus, promoting wakefulness.

Examples:Modafinil (Provigil), **Armodafinil (Nuvigil)**.
Therapeutic Uses:

- **Narcolepsy:** Used to treat excessive daytime sleepiness associated with narcolepsy.

- **Shift Work Sleep Disorder:** Helps individuals who work night shifts stay awake.
- **Obstructive Sleep Apnea:** Used to manage residual sleepiness in patients with obstructive sleep apnea.

Types of Nootropics
1. Racetams
Mechanism of Action:

- **Modulation of Neurotransmitters:** Racetams, such as **piracetam** and **aniracetam**, modulate the levels of neurotransmitters like acetylcholine and glutamate, enhancing synaptic transmission and cognitive function.

Examples:Piracetam, Aniracetam, Oxiracetam.
Therapeutic Uses:

- **Cognitive Enhancement:** Used to improve memory, learning, and overall cognitive function.
- **Neuroprotection:** Potential use in neurodegenerative diseases due to their neuroprotective properties.

2. Cholinergics
Mechanism of Action:

- **Increase Acetylcholine Levels:** Cholinergic nootropics enhance the cholinergic system by increasing acetylcholine levels, either through direct precursors like **choline** or by inhibiting acetylcholine breakdown.

Examples:Alpha-GPC, Citicoline, Huperzine A.
Therapeutic Uses:

- **Memory Enhancement:** Used to improve memory and cognitive function, particularly in conditions involving cholinergic deficits.
- **Alzheimer's Disease:** Some cholinergic nootropics are investigated for potential benefits in Alzheimer's disease.

3. Natural Nootropics
Mechanism of Action:

- **Various Pathways:** Natural nootropics, such as **Ginkgo biloba** and **Panax ginseng**, work through multiple mechanisms, including antioxidant effects, modulation of neurotransmitter levels, and enhancement of blood flow to the brain.

  Examples:Ginkgo biloba, Panax ginseng, Bacopa monnieri.
  Therapeutic Uses:

- **Cognitive Enhancement:** Used to improve cognitive function, memory, and focus.
- **Neuroprotection:** Potential use in protecting against cognitive decline and neurodegenerative diseases.

Table 10.1: **Drugs for Parkinson's Disease**

Drug	Mechanism of Action	Example
Levodopa	Converts to dopamine in the brain	Sinemet
Dopamine Agonists	Stimulate dopamine receptors	Pramipexole, Ropinirole

Table 10.2: **Drugs for Alzheimer's Disease**

Drug	Mechanism of Action	Example
Cholinesterase Inhibitors	Prevent breakdown of acetylcholine	Donepezil, Rivastigmine
NMDA Receptor Antagonists	Block glutamate receptors	Memantine

Table 10.3: **Classes of CNS Stimulants**

Class	Mechanism of Action	Example
Amphetamines	Increase release of norepinephrine and dopamine	Adderall, Ritalin
Nootropics	Enhance cognitive function	Piracetam, Modafinil

CHAPTER XI

Opioid Analgesics and Antagonists

11.1 Types of Opioid Analgesics

Mechanisms and Uses

Opioid analgesics are a class of drugs that are used to manage pain by interacting with opioid receptors in the central and peripheral nervous systems. They can be categorized into **natural**, **semi-synthetic**, and **synthetic opioids**. Each type has distinct mechanisms of action and clinical uses.

Natural Opioids

Mechanism of Action:

- **Binding to Opioid Receptors:** Natural opioids, primarily derived from the opium poppy, bind to **mu (μ)**, **delta (δ)**, and **kappa (κ)** opioid receptors in the brain, spinal cord, and other tissues.
- **Inhibition of Pain Transmission:** By binding to these receptors, they inhibit the release of neurotransmitters involved in pain transmission, such as **substance P** and **glutamate**.
- **Activation of Descending Inhibitory Pathways:** They also enhance the activity of descending inhibitory pathways in the central nervous system, reducing the perception of pain.

Examples:Morphine, Codeine.

Therapeutic Uses:

- **Acute and Chronic Pain:** Used to manage moderate to severe pain, including post-surgical pain and pain from injuries.
- **Cough Suppression:** Codeine is used in lower doses as an antitussive (cough suppressant).

Semi-Synthetic Opioids

Mechanism of Action:

- **Enhanced Affinity and Efficacy:** Semi-synthetic opioids are chemically modified versions of natural opioids. They often have enhanced affinity for opioid receptors and improved efficacy.

- **Similar Mechanisms:** They work similarly to natural opioids by binding to opioid receptors and inhibiting pain transmission.

Examples:Oxycodone, Hydrocodone, Oxymorphone, Hydromorphone.

Therapeutic Uses:

- **Moderate to Severe Pain:** Used for managing moderate to severe pain, often in cases where natural opioids are less effective.
- **Extended-Release Formulations:** Available in extended-release formulations for chronic pain management.

Synthetic Opioids

Mechanism of Action:

- **Targeted Receptor Binding:** Synthetic opioids are entirely man-made and designed to target specific opioid receptors with high affinity.
- **Potency and Duration:** They can be more potent than natural and semi-synthetic opioids, with varying durations of action.

Examples:Fentanyl, Methadone, Tramadol, Buprenorphine.

Therapeutic Uses:

- **Severe Pain:** Fentanyl is used for severe pain, often in cancer patients or post-operative settings.
- **Chronic Pain and Opioid Dependence:** Methadone is used for chronic pain and as a maintenance therapy for opioid dependence.
- **Moderate Pain and Neuropathic Pain:** Tramadol is used for moderate pain and has additional effects on serotonin and norepinephrine reuptake, making it useful for neuropathic pain.
- **Partial Agonist for Opioid Dependence:** Buprenorphine is a partial agonist used in the treatment of opioid dependence and chronic pain.

Summary

Opioid analgesics are classified into **natural**, **semi-synthetic**, and **synthetic** categories, each with distinct mechanisms and therapeutic uses:

- **Natural opioids** like **morphine** and **codeine** bind to opioid receptors to inhibit pain transmission and are used for moderate to severe pain and cough suppression.
- **Semi-synthetic opioids** such as **oxycodone** and **hydrocodone** are modified from natural opioids, providing enhanced efficacy for moderate to severe pain.
- **Synthetic opioids** like **fentanyl**, **methadone**, **tramadol**, and **buprenorphine** are entirely man-made, offering potent pain relief and various specialized uses, including chronic pain management and opioid dependence treatment.

11.2 Opioid Antagonists

Mechanisms and Uses

Opioid antagonists are drugs that bind to opioid receptors but do not activate them, effectively blocking the effects of opioid agonists. They are primarily used to reverse opioid overdose, treat opioid dependence, and mitigate opioid-induced side effects. The main opioid antagonists are **naloxone** and **naltrexone**.

Mechanisms of Action of Naloxone and Naltrexone

Naloxone

Mechanism of Action:

- **Competitive Antagonism:** Naloxone binds competitively to **mu (μ)**, **delta (δ)**, and **kappa (κ)** opioid receptors without activating them. It has the highest affinity for μ-opioid receptors.
- **Reversal of Opioid Effects:** By occupying these receptors, naloxone displaces opioid agonists (e.g., morphine, heroin) from the receptors, thereby reversing their effects, including respiratory depression, sedation, and hypotension.

Naltrexone

Mechanism of Action:

- **Competitive Antagonism:** Like naloxone, naltrexone is a competitive antagonist at opioid receptors, with a high affinity for μ-opioid receptors.
- **Longer Duration:** Naltrexone has a longer duration of action compared to naloxone, making it suitable for use in maintaining abstinence in opioid-dependent individuals.

Clinical Applications
Naloxone
Clinical Applications:

- **Opioid Overdose:** Naloxone is the drug of choice for the emergency treatment of opioid overdose. It rapidly reverses life-threatening respiratory depression and sedation caused by opioids.
  - **Administration:** It can be administered intravenously (IV), intramuscularly (IM), subcutaneously (SC), or intranasally. The onset of action is rapid, typically within minutes.
- **Diagnostic Purposes:** Naloxone can be used diagnostically to determine if a patient's symptoms are due to opioid overdose.
- **Postoperative Opioid Effects:** It is sometimes used to reverse the effects of opioids given during surgery.

Naltrexone
Clinical Applications:

- **Opioid Dependence:** Naltrexone is used as part of a comprehensive treatment program for opioid dependence. It helps prevent relapse by blocking the euphoric and sedative effects of opioids.
  - **Administration:** Available in oral tablets and as a monthly injectable (extended-release formulation). Oral naltrexone is taken daily, while the extended-release injection is given once a month.
- **Alcohol Dependence:** Naltrexone is also approved for the treatment of alcohol dependence. It reduces cravings and helps maintain abstinence by modulating the reward pathways in the brain.
- **Chronic Pain:** In some cases, naltrexone is used off-label in low doses to manage chronic pain conditions such as fibromyalgia and multiple sclerosis. The low-dose naltrexone (LDN) is thought to modulate the immune system and reduce inflammation.

11.3 Drug Addiction, Abuse, and Dependence
Mechanisms and Management

Drug addiction, abuse, and dependence are complex conditions characterized by the compulsive use of substances despite harmful consequences. Understanding the mechanisms of addiction and dependence is crucial for developing effective management and treatment strategies.

Mechanisms of Addiction and Dependence

1. Neurobiological Mechanisms

Reward Pathway Activation:

- **Dopaminergic System:** Drugs of abuse activate the brain's **reward system**, primarily the **mesolimbic dopamine pathway**, which includes the **ventral tegmental area (VTA)** and the **nucleus accumbens**. This pathway is crucial for the sensation of pleasure and reinforcement of behaviors.
- **Increased Dopamine Release:** Substances such as opioids, stimulants, and alcohol increase dopamine levels in the nucleus accumbens, leading to feelings of euphoria and reinforcing drug-taking behavior.

Neuroplasticity and Tolerance:

- **Receptor Downregulation:** Chronic exposure to drugs leads to neuroadaptive changes, such as downregulation of dopamine receptors. This results in **tolerance**, where higher doses of the drug are required to achieve the same effect.
- **Altered Neurotransmitter Systems:** Long-term drug use alters other neurotransmitter systems, including **serotonin**, **glutamate**, and **GABA**, contributing to the persistence of addiction and the difficulty in achieving abstinence.

2. Psychological Mechanisms

Conditioning and Learning:

- **Classical Conditioning:** Environmental cues associated with drug use (e.g., places, people, paraphernalia) can trigger cravings and relapse through conditioned responses.
- **Operant Conditioning:** The reinforcing effects of drug use (e.g., euphoria, relief from withdrawal symptoms) strengthen drug-seeking behavior through positive and negative reinforcement.

3. Social and Environmental Factors
Stress and Peer Influence:

- **Stress:** Chronic stress and adverse life events can increase vulnerability to addiction by promoting drug use as a coping mechanism.
- **Peer Influence:** Social factors, including peer pressure and availability of drugs, play a significant role in initiating and maintaining drug use.

Strategies for Management and Treatment
1. Pharmacological Treatments
Medications for Opioid Dependence:

- **Methadone:** A long-acting opioid agonist used in maintenance therapy to reduce withdrawal symptoms and cravings. It stabilizes patients and allows for gradual tapering.
- **Buprenorphine:** A partial opioid agonist that reduces withdrawal symptoms and cravings with a lower risk of overdose. It is often combined with naloxone to prevent misuse.
- **Naltrexone:** An opioid antagonist that blocks the effects of opioids, used to prevent relapse in detoxified patients.

Medications for Alcohol Dependence:

- **Disulfiram:** Causes unpleasant reactions when alcohol is consumed, acting as a deterrent.
- **Acamprosate:** Modulates glutamatergic neurotransmission to reduce cravings and withdrawal symptoms.
- **Naltrexone:** Reduces cravings and the reinforcing effects of alcohol.

Medications for Stimulant Dependence:

- Currently, no FDA-approved medications specifically for stimulant dependence, but some medications like bupropion and modafinil are being studied for their potential benefits.

2. Behavioral Therapies
Cognitive-Behavioral Therapy (CBT):

- **Skill Development:** Teaches individuals to recognize and cope with triggers, stress, and cravings.
- **Relapse Prevention:** Develops strategies to avoid relapse and manage relapse if it occurs.

Contingency Management:

- **Incentive-Based Approach:** Provides tangible rewards for positive behaviors such as abstinence, adherence to treatment, and attendance at therapy sessions.

Motivational Interviewing:

- **Enhancing Motivation:** Helps individuals resolve ambivalence about quitting drug use and enhances their motivation to change through goal setting and exploring the consequences of drug use.

3. Supportive Interventions
Peer Support Groups:

- **12-Step Programs:** Groups like Alcoholics Anonymous (AA) and Narcotics Anonymous (NA) provide peer support, encouragement, and a structured program for recovery.

Family Therapy:

- **Family Involvement:** Addresses family dynamics that may contribute to addiction and engages family members in the recovery process to provide support.

4. Integrated Treatment Programs
Comprehensive Care:

- **Integrated Approaches:** Combine pharmacological, behavioral, and supportive interventions tailored to the individual's needs.
- **Addressing Co-occurring Disorders:** Treating co-occurring mental health conditions, such as depression or anxiety, which are common in individuals with substance use disorders.

CHAPTER XII

Glossary of Key Pharmacological Terms

1. **Absorption**: The process by which a drug enters the bloodstream from its site of administration.
2. **ACE Inhibitors**: A class of drugs that block the conversion of angiotensin I to angiotensin II, used primarily to treat high blood pressure and heart failure.
3. **Active Metabolite**: A metabolite of a drug that has pharmacological activity of its own.
4. **Active Transport**: The movement of substances across cell membranes against a concentration gradient, requiring energy, often in the form of ATP.
5. **Adjuvant Therapy**: Additional treatment given to enhance the primary treatment's effectiveness, commonly used in cancer therapy.
6. **Agonist**: A substance that binds to a receptor and activates it to produce a biological response.
7. **Aldosterone Antagonists**: Drugs that block the action of aldosterone, often used in treating conditions like heart failure and hypertension.
8. **Allosteric Modulator**: A substance that indirectly influences the effects of a primary ligand by binding to a different site on the receptor.
9. **Analgesic**: A drug that relieves pain without causing loss of consciousness.
10. **Anaphylaxis**: A severe, potentially life-threatening allergic reaction that requires immediate medical attention.
11. **Angiotensin Receptor Blockers (ARBs)**: A class of drugs that block the action of angiotensin II, used to treat high blood pressure and heart failure.
12. **Antagonist**: A substance that binds to a receptor but does not activate it, thereby blocking the action of agonists.
13. **Antibiotic**: A drug used to treat bacterial infections by killing or inhibiting the growth of bacteria.
14. **Anticholinergic**: Drugs that block the action of acetylcholine in the central and the peripheral nervous system, used to treat conditions like asthma, COPD, and overactive bladder.

15. **Anticoagulant**: A drug that helps prevent blood clotting by inhibiting the coagulation pathway.
16. **Anticonvulsant**: A drug used to prevent or control seizures.
17. **Antidepressant**: A drug used to treat depressive disorders by altering neurotransmitter levels in the brain.
18. **Anti-emetic**: A drug used to prevent or treat nausea and vomiting.
19. **Antifungal**: A drug used to treat infections caused by fungi.
20. **Antihistamine**: A drug that blocks histamine receptors, used to treat allergic reactions.
21. **Antihypertensive**: A drug used to lower high blood pressure.
22. **Antineoplastic**: A drug used to treat cancer by inhibiting the growth and spread of malignant cells.
23. **Antiplatelet**: A drug that prevents platelet aggregation and thrombus formation, used to prevent strokes and heart attacks.
24. **Antipsychotic**: A drug used to treat psychiatric conditions like schizophrenia, bipolar disorder, and severe depression.
25. **Antipyretic**: A drug that reduces fever by acting on the hypothalamus.
26. **Antiretroviral**: A drug used to manage and treat infections caused by retroviruses, including HIV.
27. **Antiviral**: A drug used to treat viral infections by inhibiting the development or replication of viruses.
28. **Autoimmune Disease**: A condition in which the immune system mistakenly attacks the body's own cells and tissues.
29. **Bioavailability**: The proportion of a drug that reaches the systemic circulation in an active form after administration.
30. **Biotransformation**: The chemical alteration of a drug by the body, primarily through enzymatic action, usually in the liver.
31. **Blood-Brain Barrier (BBB)**: A selective permeability barrier that protects the brain from harmful substances while allowing essential molecules to pass through.
32. **Bolus**: A single, large dose of a drug administered rapidly, typically intravenously, to achieve a quick therapeutic effect.
33. **Beta-Blockers**: A class of drugs that block the effects of adrenaline on beta receptors, used to manage heart conditions, hypertension, and anxiety.
34. **Bronchodilator**: A drug that relaxes bronchial muscle, expanding the air passages in the lungs and making breathing easier, commonly used in treating asthma and COPD.

35. **Carcinogen:** Any substance that promotes carcinogenesis, the formation of cancer.
36. **Cardioprotective Agents:** Drugs that reduce the risk of damage to the heart, particularly during myocardial infarction or heart surgery.
37. **Cardiotonic:** A drug that increases the force of contraction of the heart muscle, often used in treating heart failure.
38. **Chelating Agent:** A compound that binds to metal ions, forming a stable complex that can be excreted from the body, used in the treatment of heavy metal poisoning.
39. **Chemotherapeutic Agents:** Drugs used to treat cancer by inhibiting the growth and proliferation of cancer cells.
40. **Cholinergic:** Refers to nerve cells that use acetylcholine as a neurotransmitter.
41. **Clearance:** The volume of plasma from which a drug is completely removed per unit time, often used to measure the efficiency of drug elimination from the body.
42. **Clinical Trial:** A research study conducted to evaluate the efficacy and safety of a new drug or treatment in humans.
43. **Contraindication:** A specific situation or condition where a drug should not be used because it may be harmful to the patient.
44. **Cytochrome P450 Enzymes:** A family of enzymes that play a significant role in the metabolism of drugs and the synthesis of cholesterol, steroids, and other lipids.
45. **Depot Injection:** A slow-release, long-acting formulation of a drug administered via injection, often used for antipsychotic medications.
46. **Desensitization:** The process by which a receptor decreases its response to a stimulus over time, often due to continuous exposure to an agonist.
47. **Diuretic:** A drug that increases urine production, used to treat conditions like hypertension, heart failure, and certain kidney disorders.
48. **Dopamine Agonist:** A drug that stimulates dopamine receptors, often used in the treatment of Parkinson's disease and restless legs syndrome.
49. **Dose-Response Curve:** A graph that plots the effect of a drug against its dose, illustrating the relationship between the dose and the magnitude of the drug's effect.
50. **Drug-Drug Interaction:** A modification of the effect of one drug by the prior or concurrent administration of another drug.
51. **Drug Half-Life:** The time it takes for the plasma concentration of a drug to reduce to half its original value, an important factor in determining

dosing intervals.

52. **Drug Tolerance**: A state in which repeated administration of a drug leads to a reduced effect, requiring increased doses to achieve the same effect.
53. **Elimination Half-Life**: The time required for the concentration of a drug in the plasma to decrease by 50% through the processes of metabolism and excretion.
54. **Enzyme Induction**: The process by which a drug increases the production of enzymes, leading to increased metabolism of the drug and potentially decreased efficacy.
55. **Enzyme Inhibition**: The process by which a drug decreases the activity of enzymes, leading to reduced metabolism and potentially increased drug levels and effects.
56. **Excretion**: The process by which drugs and their metabolites are eliminated from the body, primarily through the kidneys in urine, but also through bile, sweat, and exhalation.
57. **First-Pass Metabolism**: The initial metabolism of a drug in the liver after oral administration, reducing the amount of active drug reaching systemic circulation.
58. **Fluoroquinolones**: A class of broad-spectrum antibiotics used to treat various bacterial infections, including respiratory and urinary tract infections.
59. **Gastrointestinal Tract**: The digestive tract, including the stomach and intestines, through which food passes, and where digestion and absorption occur.
60. **Glucocorticoids**: A class of corticosteroids that reduce inflammation and suppress the immune response, often used in the treatment of asthma, allergies, and autoimmune diseases.
61. **Glutamate**: An excitatory neurotransmitter in the brain involved in cognitive functions such as learning and memory.
62. **Hepatotoxicity**: Liver damage caused by chemical substances, including drugs, which can lead to conditions like hepatitis and cirrhosis.
63. **Hyperkalemia**: A condition characterized by an abnormally high concentration of potassium in the blood, which can be life-threatening if not treated.
64. **Hypertensive Crisis**: A severe increase in blood pressure that can lead to stroke, heart attack, or other life-threatening conditions.
65. **Hypersensitivity Reaction**: An exaggerated response by the immune system to a drug or other substance, potentially leading to an allergic

reaction.

66. **Idiosyncratic Reaction**: An unusual or unexpected reaction to a drug that is different from the drug's known pharmacological effects.
67. **Immunosuppressant**: A drug that inhibits or reduces the activity of the immune system, commonly used to prevent organ transplant rejection and to treat autoimmune diseases.
68. **Inotrope**: A drug that affects the force of contraction of the heart muscle, used in the treatment of heart failure and cardiogenic shock.
69. **Intramuscular Injection**: The administration of a drug directly into a muscle, allowing for slow and sustained absorption into the bloodstream.
70. **Intravenous Injection (IV)**: The administration of a drug directly into a vein, allowing for immediate absorption and rapid onset of action.
71. **Isomer**: Compounds with the same molecular formula but different structural arrangements, often leading to different pharmacological properties.
72. **JAK-STAT Pathway**: A signal transduction pathway activated by cytokines, leading to the transcription of specific genes involved in immune responses.
73. **Lipid-Soluble Drugs**: Drugs that dissolve in fats and oils, which can easily pass through cell membranes and are often stored in fatty tissues.
74. **Loop Diuretics**: A class of diuretics that inhibit sodium reabsorption in the loop of Henle in the kidneys, leading to increased urine production and decreased blood volume.
75. **Maintenance Dose**: The dose of a drug that maintains or keeps the drug concentration within the therapeutic window.
76. **Mechanism of Action**: The specific biochemical interaction through which a drug produces its pharmacological effect.
77. **Metabolism**: The chemical processes by which a drug is converted into metabolites, usually in the liver, before being excreted from the body.
78. **Monoamine Oxidase Inhibitors (MAOIs)**: A class of antidepressants that inhibit the activity of monoamine oxidase enzymes, increasing the levels of norepinephrine, serotonin, and dopamine in the brain.
79. **Myelosuppression**: The decreased production of blood cells in the bone marrow, a common side effect of chemotherapy.
80. **Neuroleptic Malignant Syndrome**: A life-threatening reaction to antipsychotic drugs, characterized by fever, muscle rigidity, and autonomic dysfunction.

81. **Neurotransmitter**: Chemicals released by neurons to transmit signals across a synapse to another neuron, muscle, or gland.
82. **NSAIDs (Nonsteroidal Anti-Inflammatory Drugs)**: A class of drugs that provide anti-inflammatory, analgesic, and antipyretic effects, commonly used to treat pain and inflammation.
83. **Opiate Receptor Agonists**: Drugs that bind to opioid receptors in the brain and nervous system, producing pain relief and euphoria.
84. **Oral Bioavailability**: The fraction of an orally administered drug that reaches the systemic circulation in an active form.
85. **P450 Enzymes**: A family of enzymes involved in the metabolism of drugs and the synthesis of cholesterol, steroids, and other lipids.
86. **Parenteral Administration**: The delivery of a drug by injection, bypassing the gastrointestinal tract, which includes intravenous, intramuscular, and subcutaneous routes.
87. **Partial Agonist**: A drug that binds to a receptor and produces a partial effect compared to a full agonist, often used in managing withdrawal symptoms.
88. **Pharmacodynamics**: The study of how drugs affect the body, including the mechanisms of drug action and the relationships between drug concentration and effect.
89. **Pharmacokinetics**: The study of how the body affects a drug, including the processes of absorption, distribution, metabolism, and excretion.
90. **Placebo Effect**: The beneficial effect in a patient following a particular treatment that arises from the patient's expectations concerning the treatment rather than from the treatment itself.
91. **Plasma Protein Binding**: The degree to which drugs attach to proteins within the blood, which affects the drug's distribution, metabolism, and excretion.
92. **Prodrug**: An inactive compound that is metabolized in the body to produce an active drug.
93. **QT Prolongation**: An elongation of the QT interval on an electrocardiogram, which can lead to potentially life-threatening arrhythmias.
94. **Receptor Downregulation**: A decrease in receptor numbers on the surface of target cells, often in response to prolonged exposure to an agonist, leading to decreased sensitivity to the drug.
95. **Renal Clearance**: The volume of plasma that is cleared of a drug by the kidneys per unit time, an important factor in drug excretion.

96. **Serotonin Syndrome**: A potentially life-threatening condition caused by excessive levels of serotonin in the brain, usually as a result of drug interactions.
97. **Sodium Channel Blockers**: A class of drugs that inhibit sodium channels, reducing the ability of neurons to fire, often used as anticonvulsants and antiarrhythmics.
98. **Steady-State Concentration**: The condition in which the overall intake of a drug is in dynamic equilibrium with its elimination, leading to a constant effective concentration in the blood.
99. **Subcutaneous Injection**: The administration of a drug into the layer of skin directly below the dermis and epidermis, allowing for slow absorption.
100. **Sympatholytic Drugs**: Medications that inhibit the effects of the sympathetic nervous system, used to treat conditions such as hypertension.
101. **Sympathomimetic Drugs**: Medications that mimic the effects of the sympathetic nervous system, used to treat conditions such as asthma, heart failure, and shock.
102. **Tachyphylaxis**: A rapid decrease in the response to a drug after repeated administration, often requiring increased doses to achieve the same effect.
103. **Therapeutic Index**: The ratio of the dose that produces toxicity to the dose that produces a clinically desired or effective response in a population.
104. **Toxicokinetics**: The study of how a toxic substance enters, moves through, and exits the body, including absorption, distribution, metabolism, and excretion.
105. **Toxicology**: The branch of science concerned with the nature, effects, and detection of poisons and the treatment of poisoning.
106. **Transdermal Patch**: A medicated adhesive patch placed on the skin to deliver a specific dose of medication through the skin and into the bloodstream over time.
107. **Tricyclic Antidepressants (TCAs)**: A class of antidepressant drugs that work by inhibiting the reuptake of norepinephrine and serotonin, increasing their levels in the brain.
108. **Upregulation**: An increase in the number of receptors on the surface of a target cell, often in response to decreased levels of neurotransmitter or hormone, leading to increased sensitivity to the drug.

109. **Vasodilators**: Drugs that widen blood vessels, increasing blood flow and reducing blood pressure, used in treating hypertension, angina, and heart failure.
110. **Volume of Distribution (Vd)**: A pharmacokinetic measurement that quantifies the extent of drug distribution in the body, calculated as the dose of drug divided by the drug concentration in the plasma.
111. **Withdrawal Syndrome**: A group of symptoms that occur upon the abrupt discontinuation or decrease in the intake of a drug, often characterized by physical and psychological effects.
112. **Zero-Order Kinetics**: A type of drug elimination process where the drug is metabolized at a constant rate regardless of its concentration, typically seen with drugs that saturate metabolic pathways at therapeutic doses.

CHAPTER XIII

Bibliography

1. **Rang, H.P., Dale, M.M., Ritter, J.M., Flower, R.J., & Henderson, G. (2012).***Rang & Dale's Pharmacology* (7th ed.). Elsevier Churchill Livingstone.
2. **Goodman, L.S., Gilman, A., Brunton, L., Lazo, J.S., & Parker, K.L. (2006).***Goodman & Gilman's: The Pharmacological Basis of Therapeutics* (11th ed.). McGraw-Hill.
3. **Katzung, B.G., Masters, S.B., & Trevor, A.J. (2018).***Basic and Clinical Pharmacology* (14th ed.). McGraw-Hill Education.
4. **Neal, M.J. (2015).***Medical Pharmacology at a Glance* (8th ed.). Wiley-Blackwell.
5. **Tripathi, K.D. (2019).***Essentials of Medical Pharmacology* (8th ed.). Jaypee Brothers Medical Publishers.
6. **Mycek, M.J., Harvey, R.A., & Champe, P.C. (2000).***Lippincott's Illustrated Reviews: Pharmacology* (2nd ed.). Lippincott Williams & Wilkins.
7. **Brenner, G.M., & Stevens, C.W. (2018).***Pharmacology* (5th ed.). Saunders Elsevier.
8. **Brunton, L.L., Knollmann, B.C., & Hilal-Dandan, R. (2017).***Goodman & Gilman's Manual of Pharmacology and Therapeutics* (2nd ed.). McGraw-Hill Education.
9. **Lehne, R.A. (2013).***Pharmacology for Nursing Care* (8th ed.). Elsevier Health Sciences.
10. **Finkel, R., Cubeddu, L.X., & Clark, M.A. (2009).***Pharmacology* (4th ed.). Lippincott Williams & Wilkins.
11. **DiPiro, J.T., Talbert, R.L., Yee, G.C., Matzke, G.R., Wells, B.G., & Posey, L.M. (2014).***Pharmacotherapy: A Pathophysiologic Approach* (9th ed.). McGraw-Hill Education.
12. **Brunton, L., Hilal-Dandan, R., & Knollmann, B. (2017).***Goodman and Gilman's The Pharmacological Basis of Therapeutics* (13th ed.). McGraw-Hill Education.
13. **Hoffman, B.B., & Lefkowitz, R.J. (2015).***Catecholamines and Sympathomimetic Drugs.* In: Goodman and Gilman's The

Pharmacological Basis of Therapeutics (12th ed.). McGraw-Hill Education.

14. **Satoskar, R.S., Rege, N.N., & Bhandarkar, S.D. (2015).***Pharmacology and Pharmacotherapeutics* (25th ed.). Elsevier India.
15. **British Pharmacopoeia Commission. (2020).***British Pharmacopoeia*. TSO (The Stationery Office).

www.ingramcontent.com/pod-product-compliance
Ingram Content Group UK Ltd.
Pitfield, Milton Keynes, MK11 3LW, UK
UKHW062310290726
14090UKWH00018B/992